Innovation, Collective Intelligence and Resiliency
in Healthcare Organizations

Health and Innovation Set

coordinated by
Corinne Grenier

Volume 4

Innovation, Collective Intelligence and Resiliency in Healthcare Organizations

Edited by

Aline Courie-Lemeur

WILEY

First published 2023 in Great Britain and the United States by ISTE Ltd and John Wiley & Sons, Inc.

ISTE Ltd
27-37 St George's Road
London SW19 4EU
UK

www.iste.co.uk

John Wiley & Sons, Inc.
111 River Street
Hoboken, NJ 07030
USA

www.wiley.com

Library of Congress Control Number: 2023943293

British Library Cataloguing-in-Publication Data
A CIP record for this book is available from the British Library
ISBN 978-1-78630-844-3

Contents

**Foreword. Building Meta-Resilience
in Healthcare Organizations**.   xi
Annie BARTOLI

Foreword. Resiliency.   xv
Yves CHARPAK

List of Acronyms.   xix

About the Authors.   xxv

Introduction   xxxi
Aline COURIE-LEMEUR

Part 1. Organizational Resilience in the Healthcare Field.   1

Introduction to Part 1.   3
Aline COURIE-LEMEUR

Chapter 1. Resilience in Healthcare Organizations: Bibliometric Analysis   7
Olena Yuriivna CHYGRYN and Liliia Mykolaivna KHOMENKO

    1.1. Context and issues   7
    1.2. Literature review   9
        1.2.1. Methodology   9
        1.2.2. Results   10
    1.3. Lessons learned   21
    1.4. References   23

Chapter 2. Response to Exceptional Health Situations at the Meso-Level: CPTSs in the Covid-19 Crisis   25
Sylvain GAUTIER

    2.1. Context and questions   25
    2.2. Conceptual framework   28
    2.3. Case studies   31
    2.4. Lessons learned   34
    2.5. References   35

Chapter 3. Dynamic Capabilities and Resilience of a Health Organization: The Case of an EHPAD-Medicalized Retirement Home   37
Benoît NAUTRE

    3.1. Background context and questions   37
    3.2. Conceptual framework   38
        3.2.1. Resilience in the field of health organizations   38
        3.2.2. From the concept of resilience to that of dynamic
resilience capacity   40
    3.3. Case studies   42
        3.3.1. The field of study   42
        3.3.2. The research process   44
        3.3.3. Building a dynamic capacity for resilience in a crisis context   48
    3.4. Lessons learned   53
    3.5. References   55

**Chapter 4. The Health Pathway: A Resilient Model for
Transforming the Governance of Health Authorities?**   57
Laëtitia BOREL

4.1. Background context and questions   57
4.2. Conceptual framework   60
4.3. Case studies.   64
4.4. Lessons learned   74
4.5. References   77

**Part 2. Collective Intelligence and the Resilience of
Healthcare Organizations.**   79

Introduction to Part 2.   81
Aline COURIE-LEMEUR

**Chapter 5. Co-creation, Co-production and Collective
Intelligence in Digitized Healthcare Policies.**   83
Jan MATTIJS and Vincent MABILLARD

5.1. Context and issues.   83
5.2. Theoretical and conceptual overview.   85
  5.2.1. Co-creation, collective intelligence and co-production
  of public services.   86
  5.2.2. Digitization in the public sector   88
  5.2.3. Co-creation and digitization in healthcare   90
5.3. Literature review.   91
5.4. Lessons learned   93
  5.4.1. From multi-disciplinarity to interdisciplinarity   94
  5.4.2. Tensions between bright technological prospects and
  governance worries.   94
  5.4.3. Lack of discussion on co-creation in e-health   95
  5.4.4. What is patient involvement?.   95
5.5. Appendix   96
5.6. References   100

Chapter 6. The Patient Educator: A Profession, A Political Mandate or A Social Mandate?   105

Fatima YATIM

6.1. Background context and questions   105
6.2. Conceptual framework   107
    6.2.1. From patient to expert patient.   107
    6.2.2. A health system enhanced by expertise   109
6.3. Illustrations   111
    6.3.1. Methodology   112
    6.3.2. Results   112
6.4. Lessons learned   117
6.5. References   119

Chapter 7. The Emergence of an Innovative and Resilient Organization of Healthcare Actors: The *Alliance Santé de Seine-et-Marne*   121

Béatrice PIPITONE and Hélène MARIE

7.1. Background context and questions   121
7.2. Illustrations   123
    7.2.1. The emergence of a collective organization of healthcare actors in Seine-et-Marne   123
    7.2.2. Concrete results in the fight against the Covid-19 pandemic and beyond   127
    7.2.3. Barriers and mechanisms to the implementation of collaborative, innovative and resilient organizations   132
7.3. Lessons learned   138
7.4. Acknowledgments.   140

Chapter 8. The Alliance Manager: A Key Actor in Healthcare Coordination Systems   141

Laurent CENARD

8.1. Background context and questions   141
8.2. Case studies.   143
    8.2.1. Coordination systems   143
    8.2.2. The strategic alliance, a new partnership vision for DACs.   147
    8.2.3. Which alliances for DACs?   149
    8.2.4. Human resources: the key to a successful strategic alliance   151
    8.2.5. The alliance manager, a key DAC professional?   152

8.3. Lessons learned   154

8.4. References   158

**Part 3. Innovation and Resilience of Healthcare
Organizations**   161

Introduction to Part 3.   163
Aline COURIE-LEMEUR

**Chapter 9. Social Innovation Through Design in Hospitals:
Challenges and Proposals for Conditions of Success.**   165
Jihane SEBAI and Bérangère L. SZOSTAK

9.1. Background context and questions   165

9.2. Conceptual framework   167

9.2.1. Social innovation through design   168

9.2.2. Hospital design in France   169

9.2.3. Social innovation through design in hospitals: a question
of appropriating management tools   170

9.3. Case studies.   172

9.3.1. The appropriation of social innovation through design
by hospital management.   172

9.3.2. Legitimization and defense of social innovation through
design by actors.   174

9.3.3. The need for democratic consultation between actors
and the adaptability of design to the hospital context.   175

9.4. Lessons learned   176

9.5. References   178

**Chapter 10. Article 51: Innovative Experiments to Help
the French Healthcare System?**   181
Cécile DEZEST, Isabelle FRANCHISTEGUY-COULOUME and
Emmanuelle CARGNELLO-CHARLES

10.1. Background context and questions   181

10.2. Conceptual framework   182

10.2.1. Innovation spaces: a concept that brings innovation
to healthcare?   183

10.2.2. From participatory design to living lab   184

10.2.3. Article 51, a space for innovation?   185

10.3. Case studies. 187
    10.3.1. Project context and implementation 187
    10.3.2. Results of the *Ange Gardien* project 191
    10.3.3. Discussion 193
10.4. Lessons learned. 196
10.5. References. 198

**Chapter 11. Innovation and Training for Healthcare Professionals:
Impact on the Structural Resilience of Organizations** 201
Marianne SARAZIN

11.1. Background context and questions 201
11.2. Illustrations 203
    11.2.1. The Pepper robot 203
    11.2.2. Telemedicine. 206
11.3. Lessons learned. 208
11.4. References. 209

**Chapter 12. Analysis of Two Innovative Working Methods
at the Ile-de-France RHA** 211
Sophie BATAILLE, Élise BLÉRY, Charlotte ROUDIER-DAVAL and
Michel MARTY

12.1. Background context and questions 211
12.2. Case Studies. 212
    12.2.1. Article 51 and the mobilization of collective intelligence 212
    12.2.2. Local coordination: a case study on the Chronic Heart
    Failure pathway. 219
12.3. Lessons learned. 225

Appendix: Brief Descriptions of Organizations 227
Aline COURIE-LEMEUR

List of Authors 233

Index 235

Foreword
by Annie Bartoli

Building Meta-Resilience
in Healthcare Organizations

If there is one environment in which the need for resilience seems instantaneously paramount, it is that of health institutions. At first glance, this seems obvious, since the ability of health organizations and professionals to cope with difficulties is implicitly considered to be the keystone and the safety net for the functioning of modern civilizations. Therefore, in order to help individuals to overcome pathologies or painful episodes in their lives, for organizations and their members to be able to overcome sometimes devastating crises or destabilizing changes, for societies to be able to recover after shocks, ruptures or tragedies, the support of resilient health systems, capable of helping people and structures to continue to live and progress, constitutes a necessary and almost unavoidable condition.

Is it not, in essence, a question of meta-resilience, that is to say a capacity placed "alongside", or even at a higher level, in order to contribute to the resilience of others?

This, however, may be a false sense of the obvious, about which too little analysis has been conducted to date. Beyond the political will and the resources allocated, which are certainly necessary but not sufficient, what else can promote the organizational resilience of health systems? How far should we go in the search for this resilience without risking creating perverse effects, excesses or blockages in the modes of operation, which could then become counterproductive? How can we build organizations that are not only resilient but also efficient, that is, capable of enabling societies to overcome crises, while remaining adapted to routine activities?

It is these fundamental questions that the beautiful book, coordinated by Aline Courie-Lemeur, attempts to respond to with as much ambition as it has humility.

The organizational resilience that is at the heart of this book is certainly not, in and of itself, a new concept, but here it has been updated, contextualized and communicated through theoretical and practical interpretations, as a result of analyses carried out in context of health systems.

The concept of organizational resilience was studied in the 1980s by Karl Weick (1987) in relation to the principles of organizational reliability. For him, it was a matter of building a system of organized actions and maintaining that system in the face of difficult situations, with reference to situations of organizational shock that were likely to be destabilizing. In the logic of this researcher, who is also known for his contributions to the management of organizations through meaning, the resilience of systems is not limited to the addition of individual resilience but is based, above all, on organized and sustainable cohesion, in order to be able to survive and progress in the event of a major contingency. In his work with Sutcliffe and Obstfeld (1999), Weick thus analyzes the processes of managing the unexpected, the need for which may arise either in visibly manifest forms or, conversely, in a more subtle manner.

It is true that the unexpected, whether it be a violent crisis or an epiphenomenon with cascading consequences, has become a type of new normal, which paradoxically leads to the need to prepare for it through learning and action processes that are both structured and flexible. The challenges to be faced have been particularly highlighted in the health and medico-social fields in many countries in recent years, especially when organizational resilience was praised, even advocated, by the World Health Organization (WHO), which described resilience as "the ability of a system, community or society exposed to hazards to resist, absorb, accommodate to and recover from the effects of a hazard in a timely and efficient manner, including through the preservation and restoration of its essential basic structures and functions" (WHO 2022).

Such incentives, which aim to ensure the health security of populations while preserving the economic and social systems of countries, can only find their coherence by being applied at different complementary levels: at the "macro" level of nations or supranations, at the "meso" level of territories and organizations and at the "micro" level of communities and individuals. In the field of health, perhaps even more so than elsewhere, these registers interact, thus creating systemic complexity and increased challenges for knowledge as well as for action. Aline Courie-Lemeur and the many contributors to the book help us to understand what the hidden face of this much-needed resilience might be. Their combined work leads to the identification of certain interrelated factors that may well be the keys to its development. Innovation, in the broadest sense of the term, and collective intelligence, as a stimulated approach, are among these factors, which have become crucial in times of crisis.

Now, as we know, crisis is as much a danger as an opportunity. The term continues to be polysemous and ambiguous, recalling its plural origins: on the one hand, there is the Latin meaning of the word "crisis", which can be associated with the serious and paroxysmal moments of pathological situations, while on the other hand, the Greek *krisis* instead indicates a delicate period of transformation with more or less favorable consequences. However, times of crisis stimulate emergency action, creativity and innovation, leading to different and sometimes more united thinking, and can therefore become an opportunity for strengthening. Everything then depends on the strategic capacity to transform the threat into an opportunity (Ansoff 1977), or what Altintas (2020) calls the dynamic resilience capacity of the organization.

The public management literature of the early 21st century tended to focus on the economic or geopolitical dimensions of crisis situations (Bartoli and Blatrix 2012), while today the global pandemic of Covid-19 has brought health crises and the importance of considering "one health" – human, animal and environmental – back to the forefront (Zinsstag et al. 2020). As a result, health seems to have returned to being seen by many as a common or collective good, leading, fortunately, to its professionals and institutions being seen more as socio-organizational resources that need to be respected and preserved.

It is in this troubled and fragile context that the viewpoints exchanged by international researchers and professionals from healthcare institutions, cleverly brought together in this book, are timely. The authors highlight and significantly update certain conditions for success, such as the process of decommissioning, the co-construction of organizational innovations, formal and informal leadership and the coordinated commitment of actors. All of this can lead to collective forms of knowledge and know-how that guarantee better coherence of analysis and action processes and, as this judicious work demonstrates, a better organizational resilience for our health systems, which are very precious and yet remain highly vulnerable.

This book reveals reflective and distanced, as well as pragmatic and operational ways to innovate in this direction and consolidate in a sustainable way the meta-resilience of health organizations, placed at the service of the resilience of others, whatever its form or its scope of action may be.

The collective intelligence of the authors, presented in this work coordinated by Aline Courie-Lemeur, whether they are researchers, practitioners or institutions, can only help us progress in this direction!

Annie BARTOLI
Université Paris-Saclay, UVSQ, Larequoi, Versailles, France
Georgetown University, Washington, DC, USA

References

Altintas, G. (2020). La capacité dynamique de résilience : l'aptitude à faire face aux évènements perturbateurs du macro-environnement. *Management et Avenir*, 115, 113–133.

Ansoff, H.I. (1977). The changing shape of the strategic problem. *Journal of General Management*, 4(4), 42–58.

Bartoli, A. and Blatrix, C. (2012). Des sciences modestes de l'action publique ? Politiques et management publics face à la crise. *Revue politiques et management public*, 29(3), 289–304.

Weick, K.E. (1987). Organizational culture as a source of high reliability. *California Management Review*, 29(2), 112–127.

Weick, K.E., Sutcliffe, K.M., Obstfeld, D. (1999). Organizing for high reliability: Processes of collective mindfulness. *Research in Organizational Behavior*, 21, 81–123.

WHO (2022). Urban planning for resilience and health: Key messages. Summary report on protecting environments and health by building urban resilience. Report, WHO European Centre for Environment and Health [Online]. Available at: https://www.who.int/europe/publications/i/item/WHO-10665-355760 [Accessed April 15, 2022].

Zinsstag, J., Schelling, E., Waltner-Toews, D., Whittaker, M.A., Tanner, M. (2020). *One Health, une seule santé : théorie et pratique des approches intégrées de la Santé*. Éditions Quae, Versailles.

Foreword
by Yves Charpak

Resiliency

When I was asked to write the foreword to this book, I accepted without really imagining where it would take me.

I was flattered by the offer, which referred to my varied career path, which started out first as a junior general practitioner, then as a researcher in clinical epidemiology and evaluator of healthcare technologies and practices, then as a consultant and owner of a private evaluation consultancy firm, while keeping the "spirit of science" in my work with nearly all possible actors in the healthcare field. Particularly since the late 1980s, I have been working on "care networks", from perinatal care to addiction, via public–private collaboration projects, linking city and hospital, general practitioners and specialists, and so on.

My various past activities in academic and professional societies, in public health, epidemiology, and in expert bodies (*Haut Conseil de la santé publique, Haut Conseil pour l'avenir de l'assurance maladie*, etc.), made reading the contributions in this book a pleasure and a lesson, showing strong commitments to bringing organizations to life, finding solutions to external difficulties (Covid-19 among others), common to healthcare operators as well as to administrative bodies. In addition, these contributions naturally led to a better understanding of the concept of resiliency of which I have never been a specialist and which revealed itself to be a framework that has accompanied me throughout my career.

To ask someone who is not an expert on the subject to write a foreword is to ask them to immerse themselves in what is to be found in the book, and to discover the authors' expertise in the visible and less visible dynamics of the ongoing transformation of healthcare organizations in response to the unavoidable changes in healthcare problems and the responses to be provided.

This book offers a tremendous variety of insights, experiences and proposals for making organizations as resilient as possible; in particular, by being able to respond to the unexpected and to crises in an effective way, particularly by drawing on what happened during the Covid-19 crisis, and also by suggesting numerous ways in which the same organizations can be better prepared to face future difficulties and crises in order to mitigate their impact. We learn about the need for professionals to develop resiliency skillsets and about the need to organize the management of institutions to facilitate collective resiliency, to set up organizational collaborations between actors, and to build alliances, particularly at the local level.

I suppose it is implicit that the institutional resilience capacity is only beneficial if it leads to a better collective handling of problems, and not just to "surviving". This is because the "common good" is often at odds with individual or institutional logics. The possible opposition between the resilience of a business unit and a political strategy for the common good made me recall the response of a friend, in charge of communications in a large foreign chemical group, to whom I asked how they managed their crises. He replied: "We haven't had any crises since internal management and communication processes were put in place so that everyone 'knows what to do' when there's a problem". He meant that the organization was 100% resilient in protecting itself, but not exactly that it was resilient in preventing mishaps. However, I believe that the resiliency desired by society is that which enables us to better deal with problems, including through changes that may impact organizations and individuals when necessary.

But once I had been invited to delve into the book, there was also the risk that the second part of my career and my expertise, focused on health and not just on care, might lead me to wander onto other paths. My experiences at the WHO, in international affairs at the *Institut Pasteur*, at the prospective blood transfusion organization (EFS), in professional public health societies in France and Europe, and now my status of elected municipal official, make me read the book slightly outside the box, with the subtle nuance that it describes essential experiences in the organization of care rather than "health". And the nuance is not just semantic.

To put it plainly, how can we enter into direct interaction, particularly at the local level, with all the actors who contribute to people's health – and not just to healthcare – in order to ensure good health, clear policies to protect health upstream of disease, prevent chronic illnesses and the consequences of today's unavoidable threats to health: the environment, social inequalities, diet, lifestyles, urban planning and housing, mobility, etc.?

The actors involved in healthcare issues, particularly at the local level, are not just those involved in providing care.

Should the examples of coordination still being used experimentally in the healthcare sector not be extended as far as possible to other health providers and operators? Could these alliances be extended beyond care? For a future book, perhaps?

Yves CHARPAK
Public health physician, epidemiologist, evaluator,
President of the Charpak Foundation:
l'esprit des sciences (the Spirit of Sciences), and local elected official

List of Acronyms

ANAP: *Agence nationale de l'appui à la performance* is the French national agency for supporting the performance of health and medico-social establishments.

APRN: advanced practice registered nurse is commonly referred to as an IPA or *Infirmier en pratiques avancées* in French.

ARM: see MRA.

ARS: see RHA.

ATIH: *Agence technique de l'information sur l'hospitalisation* is the French technical agency responsible for handling data and information regarding hospitalizations.

CAQES: *Contrat d'amélioration de la qualité et de l'efficience des soins* is a contract defining the quality of care and commitments to improving efficiency in France.

CECICS: *Cellule d'expertise et de coordination des patients insuffisants cardiaques sévères* is the expertise and coordination unit for patients with severe heart failure in France.

CHF: congestive heart failure is commonly known as ICC (*Insuffisance cardiaque chronique*) in French.

CLIC: *Centre local d'information et de coordination* is a local data and coordination center for health and social issues in France.

CME: *Commission médicale d'établissement* is the medical committee of a healthcare institution in France.

CPAM: *Caisse primaire d'assurance maladie* is France's primary health insurance fund.

CPOM: *Contrat pluriannuel d'objectifs et de moyens* is a French multi-year contract outlining the objectives and resources allocated.

CPTS: *Communauté professionnelle territoriale de santé* is a territorial health professional community in France.

CRS: the Comprehensive Rehabilitation Services program serves people who have experienced traumatic injuries. These are commonly referred to by their acronym SSR (*Soins de suite et de réadaptation*) in French.

CTA: *Coordination territoriale d'appui* is a local coordination support system in France.

DAC: *Dispositif d'appui à la coordination* is a coordination support organization in France.

DCGDR: *Direction de la coordination et de la gestion du risque (structure régionale de l'assurance maladie)* is the department for risk management and coordination in France (whose mandate is the regional structure of health insurance).

DD: *Délégations départementales – échelons départementaux de l'AR délégations départementales* are departmental delegations/branches of the RHA (ARS) in France.

DDASS: *Direction départementale des affaires sanitaires et sociales* is the French departmental directorate for health and social affairs.

DLU: *Dossier de liaison d'urgence* is a French emergency liaison record.

DREES: *Direction de la recherche, des études, de l'évaluation et des statistiques* is the French directorate for research, studies, evaluations and statistics.

EHPAD: *Établissement d'hébergement pour personnes âgées dépendantes* is the French abbreviation for an accommodation facility for dependent elderly people.

EMS: emergency medical services in France is commonly referred to by its abbreviation SAMU (*Service d'aide médicale urgente*).

ES: see HCF.

ETP: see TPE.

FIQCS: *Fonds d'intervention pour la qualité et la coordination des soins* is an intervention fund for the quality and coordination of care in France.

GHT: *Groupement hospitalier territorial ou de territoire* is a local (territorial) hospital group in France.

GHU: *Groupement hospitalo-universitaire* is a university hospital group in France.

HAD: see HaH.

HaH: Hospitalization at Home, in French known as HAD (*Hospitalisation à domicile*).

HAS: *Haute Autorité de santé* is the French National Authority for Health.

HCAAM: *Haut Conseil pour l'avenir de l'assurance maladie* is the French High Council for the Future of Health Insurance.

HCF: a healthcare facility is commonly known as an ES (*Établissement de santé*) in French.

HPST: *Loi du 21 juillet 2009 portant réforme de l'Hôpital et relative aux patients, à la santé et aux territoires* is the Law of July 21, 2009 reforming the hospital as it relates to patients, health and territories.

HR: human resources is commonly known in French as RH (*Ressources humaines*).

HSTS: health system transformation strategies are commonly referred to by their acronym STSS (*Stratégie de transformation du système de santé*) in French.

ICC: see CHF.

IDE: see SRN.

IDF: Ile-de-France is the region in north-central France surrounding the nation's capital, Paris.

IPA: see APRN.

LFFS: *Loi de financement de la Sécurité sociale* is the French Social Security Financing Act.

MAIA: method of action for the integration of healthcare and support services in the field of Autonomy.

MRA: is a "medical regulatory assistant". These are commonly referred to as ARM (*Assistant de régulation médicale*) in French.

OSNP: see UCP.

PAERPA: *Parcours de santé des personnes âgées en risque de perte d'autonomie* is a scheme in France whose mandate is to assist "elderly people at risk of loss of autonomy".

PME: see SME.

PRADO: *Programme de retour à domicile* is a return home program in France.

PRS: see RHP.

PTA: *Plateforme territoriale d'appui* is a local support platform in France.

RH: see HR.

RHA: Regional Health Agency, or *Agence régionale de santé* (ARS) in France, an autonomous, regional public institution placed under the supervision of the Ministry of Health.

RHP: Regional Health Project, in French these are commonly referred to as PRS (*Projet régional de santé*).

SAMU: see EMS.

SAS: *Service d'accès aux soins* is France's access to care service.

SME: small and medium-sized enterprises are commonly referred to as PME (*Petite moyenne entreprise*) in French.

SNDS: *Système national des données de santé* is France's national health data system.

SRN: state-registered nurse is commonly known as an IDE (*Infirmier diplômé d'État*) in French.

STSS: see HSTS.

TMHP: territorial mental health projects.

TPE: see VSE.

TPE: therapeutic patient education is commonly known as *Éducation thérapeutique du patient* (ETP) in French.

UCP: unscheduled or urgent care practitioner is commonly referred to as an OSNP (*Opérateur de soin non programmé*) in French.

UNCAM: *Union nationale des caisses d'assurance maladie* is France's national union of health insurance funds.

URPS: *Union régionale des professionnels de santé* is France's regional union of health professionals.

VSE: very small enterprises are commonly referred to in French by their acronym TPE (*Toute petite entreprise*).

About the Authors

Annie BARTOLI is a professor of management sciences at the ISM-IAE of the UVSQ, Université Paris-Saclay, and director of the Larequoi Management Research Laboratory. She is also a research professor at Georgetown University, Washington, USA, where she co-directs teaching and research programs in international and intercultural management. One of her major fields of expertise is public and non-market management, with works on local governments and the health sector. Among her numerous national and international publications, *Le grand livre du management public*, published for its 5th edition in 2022 (with C. Blatrix), is a notable reference in the public management field. In addition, she is also editor-in-chief of the scientific journal *Gestion et Management Public* (GMP).

Sophie BATAILLE is an emergency physician, coordinator of the Cardiology Health Data Warehouse of the Ile-de-France Regional Health Agency (RHA) since 2000, and cardiology referent at the Ile-de-France RHA since 2015.

Élise BLÉRY is a general practitioner, as well as a medical adviser for health insurance. Since 2010, she has been in charge of supporting hospital structures in their efforts to improve performance and the relevance of care, and promoting innovations in healthcare.

Laëtitia BOREL is a doctoral student in management sciences at the Larequoi Laboratory, attached to the University of Versailles Saint-Quentin-en-Yvelines. Her research focuses more specifically on the management of healthcare organizations, in line with her professional background. For the past 10 years, she has been involved in several health coordination organizations in the Ile-de-France region. She is currently a project manager for a national public health agency.

Emmanuelle CARGNELLO-CHARLES is a senior lecturer at the University of Pau and Pays de l'Adour (LiREM laboratory). Her research interests are in the field of health management, more specifically in management control and finance.

Laurent CENARD has a state diploma in nursing with an AED in Public Health and a DESS-MBA in Business Management from the IAE Paris. He has held numerous management positions in non-profit organizations in the healthcare field. These roles have made him a privileged observer of organizational innovations, particularly coordination mechanisms between the city and the hospital. He is currently working at the *Fondation Santé Service* ("Health Service Foundation"), as director of the home hospitalization unit. He is also an associate member of Larequoi, the Management Research Laboratory of the University of Versailles Saint-Quentin-en-Yvelines.

Yves CHARPAK is a doctor specialized in public health and in clinical epidemiology and evaluation. He is President of the Charpak Foundation, *l'esprit des sciences* ("the spirit of science") and also a local elected official in Larchant. He is a member of the board of the association *Élus Santé publique et territoires* (ESPT, "Elected public health and territories") and a member of the board of the *Société française de santé publique*, SFSP ("French Public Health Society"). He worked as a researcher in an Inserm team, then in the evaluation company EVAL, at the WHO regional office for Europe, at the Pasteur Institute and then at the *Établissement français du sang*, EFS ("French Blood Establishment"). He was a member of the *Haut Conseil de la santé publique*, HSCP ("High Council for Public Health") and the *Haut Conseil pour l'avenir de l'assurance maladie*, HCAAM ("High Council for the Future of Health Insurance").

Olena Yuriivna CHYGRYN has a PhD in economics and is associate professor in the Department of Marketing, Sumy State University, Ukraine. Her research interests include green marketing, green competitiveness, corporate governance and alternative energy economics[1]. She is author of more than 100 scientific articles (including two monographs, 10 sections of collective monographs and more than 40 articles in scientific journals – 14 are indexed by Scopus, seven by Thompson Reuters) and more than 50 publications in the abstract collections of international scientific conferences.

Aline COURIE-LEMEUR is a senior lecturer qualified to lead research in management sciences at the Larequoi Laboratory and at the ISM-IAE of the University of Versailles Saint-Quentin-en-Yvelines. Her research focuses on the strategic management of inter-organizational collaborations in the healthcare field

---

1 ORCID: https://orcid.org/0000-0002-4007-3728.

and, more specifically, on the issues of consensus and leadership. She is a specialist in organizational innovation.

Cécile DEZEST is a doctoral student of management science at the University of Pau and Pays de l'Adour (LiREM laboratory). She works on the theme of health management and on the management of projects under Article 51 of the French Social Security Financing Act 2018.

Isabelle FRANCHISTEGUY-COULOUME is a senior lecturer in management sciences, authorized to direct research at the IUT of Bayonne and the Basque Country, Université de Pau and Pays de l'Adour (LiREM laboratory). Her research is in the field of health management, with a focus on strategic management and human resources management.

Sylvain GAUTIER is a public health physician at the University of Versailles Saint-Quentin-en-Yvelines. He has a degree in law and health policy from the University of Paris Descartes and Sciences-Po. He is a doctoral student in epidemiology in the "primary care and prevention" research team of UMR 1018, Inserm. His thesis focuses on the localized structuring of primary healthcare, in particular within the framework of CPTS *(Communautés professionnelles territoriales de santé)* local professional health communities.

Liliia Mykolaivna KHOMENKO is a doctoral student in the Department of Marketing at Sumy State University in Ukraine[2].

Vincent MABILLARD is an assistant professor at the Solvay Brussels School of Economics and Management, Université libre de Bruxelles, where he teaches the management and communication of public organizations. His research focuses on the dynamics of transparency and accountability, as well as on localized marketing and communication of public organizations. He is active in an international project on the digitization of processes and services in the healthcare sector.

Hélène MARIE is director of the Seine-et-Marne Departmental Delegation of the Ile-de-France Regional Health Agency (RHA). Trained at the *École des hautes études en santé publique*, EHESP ("School of Advanced Studies in Public Health"), she has held several positions in the design, implementation and evaluation of public policies. At the CNSA and in ministerial offices, she contributed to the development of planning tools and strategies for strengthening the pathway approach in the medico-social field. A stint in the associative sector allowed her to support the operational implementation of projects to support people. As an agent working in the deconcentrated services of the State and then in the RHA, she implemented

---

2 ORCID: https://orcid.org/0000-0001-5690-1105.

public health policies by developing strong partnership logics with the interlocutors of the territories. She has held the position of director of the Seine-et-Marne Delegation of the Ile-de-France RHA since 2016 and has developed several work groups with her team.

Michel MARTY is a doctor at the Ile-de-France regional medical service department (general health insurance scheme) in charge of establishments (health and medico-social) and healthcare pathways.

Jan MATTIJS is a professor at the Solvay Brussels School of Economics and Management, Université libre de Bruxelles, where he teaches organizational change and the conduct of business intervention projects. His research interests include organizational theory, administrative reform and public performance in sectors such as justice, social security and non-market organizations. Socio-material devices and the effects of technology on work and organization are emerging as new topics. He is also interested in the corporeal roots of management in order to articulate personal and social development in the face of the challenges of our time.

Benoît NAUTRE has a doctorate in management science from the IAE in Nantes, a DEA in information systems and strategy from the IAE in Nantes, is a research professor at the MCA-IAE at the University of Clermont Auvergne and is a hospital director.

Béatrice PIPITONE is in charge of the *Dispositifs d'appui à la coordination*, DAC ("Coordination Support Systems") mission in the Innovation Department of the Ile-de-France Regional Health Agency (RHA) and deputy head of the *Parcours et offre de soins* ("Care Pathways and Services") at the Seine-et-Marne Departmental Delegation. Through her experience as a consultant in public action on health issues at the European level, and then in supporting organizational change in the health and medico-social sector in France, she has supported the deployment of numerous innovative public health measures and approaches aimed at improving the healthcare pathways of vulnerable, disabled, chronically ill, deprived and/or elderly people, in particular for the Ministry of Health and Social Cohesion, the CNSA, and several RHA and MDPH. She has been working for 4 years at the Ile-de-France RHA headquarters on the DAC deployment mission and joined the Seine-et-Marne Departmental Delegation part-time in April 2021.

Charlotte ROUDIER-DAVAL is a health geographer. She is currently a project manager in the innovation department on Article 51 and the improvement of pathways at Ile-de-France RHA.

Marianne SARAZIN is a doctor specializing in public health, with a degree in research on "prevention to optimize care", and a doctorate in life sciences from the Engineering and Health Center of the *École nationale supérieure des mines de Saint-Étienne*, on the modeling of predictive scores for aging. She is currently in charge of the *département d'information médicale* ("hospital databases management") for the *Groupe mutualiste de Saint-Étienne* after having worked for 12 years in the Firminy hospital media information department. As of 2013, she has also been an associate in the I4S Department of the Engineering and Health Center, specializing in the optimization of healthcare organization and, since 2006, she has been the regional manager of the *Sentinelles* network, UMRS 1136 Inserm, specializing in the modeling of epidemics.

Jihane SEBAI is a senior lecturer at the ISM-IAE of the University of Versailles Saint-Quentin-en-Yvelines, Université Paris-Saclay. She is a researcher in the Larequoi Management Laboratory. Her research focuses on public management, strategic management, health management, health democracy, coordination structures, integration of care, mental health and more. His publications are available on Cairn and various academic databases.

Bérangère L. SZOSTAK is a university professor at the ISM-IAE of the University of Versailles Saint-Quentin-en-Yvelines, Université Paris-Saclay. She is a full researcher at the Larequoi Laboratory. Her specialty is the strategic management of innovation and organizational creativity in various organizations (SMEs, cultural and creative industries, social economy organizations, hospitals, etc.). His contributions concern the development of creativity, particularly through design thinking. Her work has been published in journals such as *M@n@gement*, *Revue française de gestion*, *Revue internationale de la PME*, *Revue d'Économie Industrielle*, *Journal of Innovation Economics & Management* and *European Journal of Innovation Management*. She is the author of *Innovation and Creativity in SMEs: Challenges, Evolutions and Prospects* (ISTE-Wiley, 2019) in collaboration with C. Gay.

Fatima YATIM is a senior lecturer specializing in the management of healthcare organizations. She is a member of the *Équipe pédagogique nationale santé-solidarité au Laboratoire interdisciplinaire de recherches en sciences de l'action* ("National Health and Solidarity Teaching Team at the Interdisciplinary Research Laboratory in Action Sciences") at CNAM in Paris. Her work focuses on three main themes: health technologies, health democracy and patient engagement, and coordination and care pathways.

Introduction

This book attempts to explore, with humility, the complex issue of resilience in healthcare organizations and to draw lessons from the recent health crisis. As with all "boundary objects" (Trompette and Vinck 2009) located at the intersection of several fields, which encompass various dimensions and are multiple and multifaceted in nature, analyzing them through a single lens is far from judicious and, even worse, may result in a loss of meaning and lead to misinterpretations.

To guard against this, we seek to avoid simplicism that is incompatible with the problem of resilience in the field of health and instead try to approach it in a simplistic approach (Berthoz 2009). This work is complementary to all the approaches challenging the duality between "everything regulated by policies" and "let us do the groundwork" (Grenier 2014), pleading for the adoption of a co-construction approach involving all stakeholders, imperative to building structurally resilient health organizations.

In order to achieve this, we set ourselves goals and took certain precautions. In terms of objectives, this book aims to explore how collective intelligence can promote the structural resilience of healthcare organizations and how innovation can contribute to it. To avoid the bias of a single and mono-dimensional interpretation, we include in health organizations all the structures and devices involved in the care of patients (hospital structures, coordination support structures and devices, medical, social and medico-social structures, health authorities, etc.). We consider "health professionals" to be all caregivers with medical, social or medico-social expertise, institutions, administration and organization professionals, as well as all the actors involved in the care of patients and the management of health organizations.

Introduction written by Aline COURIE-LEMEUR.

The diversity in profiles of the contributors to this work also reflects this position, drawing on French and international university researchers, institutional actors from health authorities, medical practitioners within hospital structures or in health coordination, leaders of health structures and devices.

We also consolidate this position through the forms of the contributions, alternating between theoretical readings and illustrative case studies.

This book is divided into three parts, each comprising four chapters.

The first part focuses on the notion of organizational resilience in the healthcare field and seeks to identify its contours and specificities. It is based on intersecting contributions from two international researchers, a hospital researcher-practitioner, a hospital researcher-manager, and a researcher working in a French national public health agency.

The second part focuses on the interaction between collective intelligence and resilience in health organizations. It works to show the dynamic relationship between them by combining two theoretical readings, one by two international university researchers and the other by a French university researcher, as well as two case studies, one by institutional leaders of the health authority and the other by a leader in a regional health structure.

The third part addresses the relationship between innovation and the resilience of health organizations. It seeks to explore their virtuous interactions based on two theoretical analyses by university researchers who specialize in health management, as well as two case studies, the first laid out by institutional leaders working as a health authority in health insurance, and the other by a hospital researcher and practitioner.

In addition to a standardized structuring of all the contributions, to ensure overall coherence throughout the book and better readability, we have ensured that each contribution illustrates a lesson learnt.

We would like to thank Mrs. Annie Bartoli and Mr. Yves Charpak for their salient forewords and the honor they have bestowed upon this book. Their perception, sharpened by their distinguished careers, transcends this book.

This book humbly aspires to contribute to strengthening organizational resilience in the field of health, in particular through multiple innovations and with thanks to the anchoring of collective intelligence in institutional routines and health organizations, in a context where crises, alas, are no longer the exception.

References

Berthoz, A. (2009). *La simplexité*. Odile Jacob, Paris.

Grenier, C. (2014). Proposition d'un modèle d'espaces favorables aux habiletés stratégiques. *Journal de gestion et d'économie médicales*, 32(1), 3–10.

Trompette, P. and Vinck, D. (2009). Retour sur la notion d'objet-frontière. *Revue d'anthropologie des connaissances*, 3(1), 5–27.

PART 1

Organizational Resilience in the Healthcare Field

Introduction to Part 1

This section explores the notion of organizational resilience in the healthcare field, approached as a problem common to all health organizations. On the one hand, it concerns the position of health authorities and the way they relate to the health workers, and on the other hand, the local structuring of care, perceived as an ecosystem. Therefore, the way in which healthcare organizations use internal resources during a crisis is a major issue for them. The authors have profiles either as foreign researchers, or as researchers and practitioners within French healthcare organizations, resulting in complementary approaches and analyses that transcend one another.

In Chapter 1, Olena Yuriivna Chygryn and Liliia Mykolaivna Khomenko conduct a bibliometric analysis of the international scientific literature on resilience in organizations and, in particular, on what can be implemented in health organizations. This research also includes publications on the themes of collective intelligence, innovation, collaboration and the participatory approach in the healthcare field. The main objective of this study is to obtain an overview of existing scientific research on resilience in healthcare organizations, identify modern research topics and anticipate future research topics. For example, it highlights researchers' findings on multiple outcomes: first, that a transformational leadership style has a statistically significant positive impact on perceived organizational stability; second, that elected officials are more likely to build organizational resilience than designated officials; furthermore, that resilience through mediation may function as a psychological shield that would mitigate burnout; and that the organizational characteristics that indicate resiliency within healthcare organizations are obligation-driven: ability to improvise, reciprocity within the community, leadership of actors during transformations, hope and optimism, and financial

Introduction written by Aline Courie-Lemeur.

transparency. The main areas of modern and future research emphasize the themes of social capital, coaching and communication in health organizations.

In Chapter 2, Sylvain Gautier focuses on the positioning of CPTS (*Communautés professionnelles territoriales de santé*) local professional health communities[1] at the meso-level between clinical integration and systemic integration. He focuses his attention on the organizational and professional dimensions accompanying this positioning in order to better specify the challenges of a local structuring of care with resilient contours. By structuring primary care in a local manner, and by entrusting the actors within this care with local public health missions through the CPTS, the resilience of the health system as a whole is strengthened. It concludes with the fundamental issues and principles of action that underpin structurally resilient community organizations. The obligations of the CPTS must be expanded to first respond more effectively to serious health crises such as Covid-19. And second, to ensure that primary care professionals are genuinely involved in these new public health services, which are far removed from their existing skills. To do this, they need to be trained in crisis management during their studies. Finally, to preserve the flexibility of CPTSs and guarantee the autonomy and empowerment of the healthcare professionals working within them.

In Chapter 3, Benoît Nautre looks at the ways in which a healthcare organization such as an *Établissement d'hébergement pour personnes âgées dépendantes*, EHPAD ("Residential facility for dependent elderly people") will, in the face of a crisis situation such as that of Covid-19, mobilize previously untapped internal resources to initially absorb and improvise in the face of turbulence, and then rapidly engage in a structured organizational learning process. He distinguishes between resilience and dynamic resilience capacities: he associates the former with improvisational actions facing a crisis situation, and the latter with post-crisis learning that goes beyond a return to the initial state. He identifies two indispensable conditions for the development of dynamic resilience capabilities: the first is linked to the presence of internal leaders capable of imposing themselves through innovation, while the second depends on the intensity of the external turbulence to encourage the transformation of existing routines.

In Chapter 4, Laëtitia Borel focuses on the health pathway paradigm, which consists of implementing a resilient, decompartmentalized health organization that promotes cooperation between health actors within the framework of a localized approach, derived from the innovative model of local self-organization. It focuses mainly on its impact on the renewal of the role of health authorities, and in particular the Regional Health Agencies (RHAs), located at the interface of national health

---

1 Acronyms are expanded upon in further detail at the end of the book in the Appendix and/or the List of Acronyms.

policies and the territories. From a position of regulator, the RHA must evolve toward a position of partner guardianship. She uses the DAC (*Dispositif d'appui à la coordination*) coordination support system as a case study to highlight the importance of the RHA establishing a close relationship with local healthcare actors, as well as to give a detailed knowledge of the local ecosystem, in order to be able to occupy this border post. She concludes that it is necessary to question the representations of each person, through the construction of a common cultural meeting zone, on the basis of the collective organizational learning necessary for the construction of a sustainable, resilient health system.

Resilience in Healthcare Organizations: Bibliometric Analysis

The main direction of this chapter is a bibliometric analysis of the scientific literature on resilience in organizations and, particularly, what can be implemented in healthcare organizations. The main purpose of this chapter is to gain a comprehensive view of relevant research on resilience in healthcare organizations, identify modern research and predict future research. Achieving this goal involves the following tasks: analysis of publication trends, fields of application, countries engaged in the most research on resilience in organizations and organizations that fund such research; analysis of the influence of publications, authors, and articles; analysis of directions (clusters) of modern research on resilience in organizations; and forecasting future research directions. In addition, in this chapter the place of publications on collective intelligence, innovation, collaboration and the participatory approach in healthcare, based on the existing database of publications, was determined.

1.1. Context and issues

Interest in resilience in organizations in general and healthcare organizations in particular increases annually. There is a lot of research on resilience in organizations in business economics, engineering, psychology, environmental sciences ecology, public administration, public environmental occupational health, computer science, science technology, and others.

Chapter written by Olena Yuriivna CHYGRYN and Liliia Mykolaivna KHOMENKO.

For a color version of all the figures in this chapter, see www.iste.co.uk/courielemeur/innovation. zip.

Resilience in organizations has been studied by researchers worldwide, particularly Chaskalson (2019), Malinen, Prayag and others. Each of them has more than three research studies on this topic. More works on resilience in organizations focus on management, organizational resilience, performance, impact and models.

Review articles about resilience in organizations focus on cyber resilience, elements of supply chain resilience, group resilience in organizations and diverse perspectives about resilience enhancement. In addition, interventions implemented by highly resilient organization, organizational and team factors that can strengthen team resilience, the concept of organizational resilience and indicators for the evaluation of community resilience.

However, the issue of resilient organizational structures in healthcare is insufficiently represented in the scientific literature. Aspects of collective intelligence in the health system are also insufficiently covered in the research. There is a small amount of research on some aspects of resilient organizational structures in healthcare, including innovation, collaboration and the participatory approach.

There are several studies on innovation in healthcare organizations. Researchers have studied micro-level processes in organizational innovation; the processes of creating working conditions in hospitals with the use of innovative technologies and methods; critical practices in decision-making to improve managerial innovation; the relationship between innovation and efficiency in healthcare facilities; the relationship between the organizational climate, the organization's openness to innovation and innovative behavior at work. There is also research on how knowledge-based activities are designed to foster innovation and create value, and how learning is related to innovation.

Fewer studies on collaboration in healthcare organizations have been found. These studies focus on assessing interprofessional and inter-organizational cooperation, elements of organizational culture as resources that help them cooperate with health professionals. In addition, they studied the role of collaboration in the rapid spread and successful implementation of transformational redevelopment, return to work programs and the partnership challenges IT leaders in healthcare face.

The only publication on the participatory approach in healthcare organizations relates to patient education implementation to become patient partners in care.

The main direction of this chapter is a bibliometric analysis of the scientific literature on resilience in organizations and, particularly, what can be implemented in healthcare organizations. It helps to get a holistic view of relevant research on selected topics; explore trends, areas of application, countries and funding organizations; determine the most influential journals, articles and authors; and analyze the direction of previous and projected future research. This study explores the influence of journals, authors and articles; text analysis; and literature visualization.

The main purpose of this chapter is to gain a comprehensive view of relevant research on resilience in healthcare organizations, identify modern research and predict future research.

Achieving this goal involves the following tasks:

– analysis of publications trends, fields of application, countries engaged in the most research on resilience in organizations and organizations that fund such research;

– analysis of the publications, authors and articles influence;

– analysis of directions (clusters) of modern research on resilience in organizations;

– forecast of future research directions.

In addition, in this study, it is advisable to determine the place of publications on collective intelligence, innovation, collaboration and participatory approach in healthcare based on the existing database of publications.

1.2. Literature review

1.2.1. *Methodology*

Web of Science data were used to analyze trends and citations from existing publications on resilience in organizations. This choice has been associated with the widespread use of this database in modern research.

The literature on resilience in organizations was selected and identified by keywords. In particular, the search was carried out on request: resilience AND organizations. The selection was made only in the titles of publications. This made it possible to obtain the most relevant publications on the selected topic.

Based on Web of Science data, 232 publications were found on resilience in organizations. Article titles, authors, journal titles, year of publication, number of citations and keywords were used for further analysis.

The dynamics of publications by year was studied. Key areas of research on resilience in organizations were identified: the organizations most engaged in research on resilience in organizations, and the authors of countries most involved in research on resilience in organizations.

The dynamics of citations by year of selected publications were analyzed. Based on the number of citations, the most influential publications, journals, authors and their countries of affiliation were identified in terms of resilience in organizations.

Based on keywords, the hierarchical cluster analysis was performed. Visualization of scientific literature topics was carried out with the VOSviewer program. Based on the keywords (more than four repetitions), clusters on resilience in organizations were identified.

Based on the keywords, the research evolution on resilience in organizations was analyzed, and the current and future research topics were identified.

1.2.2. Results

Based on Web of Science data, 232 publications on resilience in organizations were found. More than 50% of these works were published during 2016–2019, indicating a rapidly growing interest in this topic (Figure 1.1).

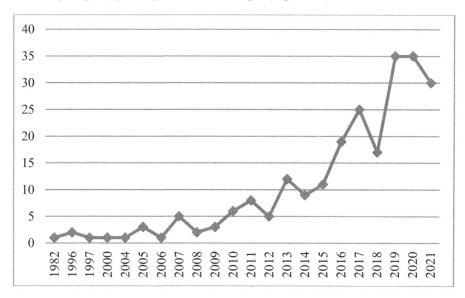

Figure 1.1. *Number of publications by year (developed by authors)*

As can be seen from Figure 1.1, 61% of the works were published during 2018–2021. These works relate to 63 areas of research. The top 10 areas of research are presented in Figure 1.2.

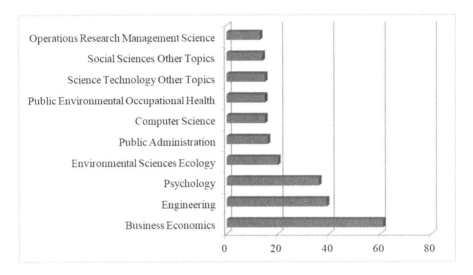

Figure 1.2. *Top 10 areas of publications on resilience in organizations (developed by the authors)*

More works were related to business economics (26.3%), engineering (16.8%), psychology (15.5%), environmental sciences ecology (8.6%) and public administration (6.9%). Less than 6.5% of works were related to environmental and occupational public health and other healthcare directions.

More than 400 organizations conduct research on resilience in organizations. The 10 organizations that conduct the most research on this topic are presented in Figure 1.3.

Most research was conducted by the State University System of Florida (USA), the University of Canterbury (New Zealand), the University of London (England), the University of Birmingham (England), University of California System (USA) and the University of Florida (USA).

Together, they conducted 34 studies on resilience.

Seventy-four organizations fund research on resilience. At the same time, the National Science Foundation and the European Commission only funded three studies. Another six organizations funded two studies, and others funded only one study.

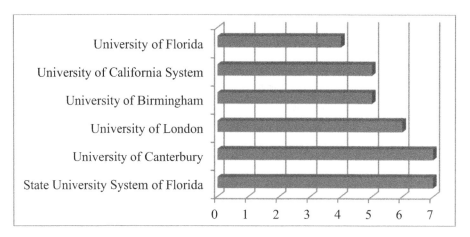

Figure 1.3. *Top six organizations engaged in research on resilience in organizations by number of publications (developed by the authors)*

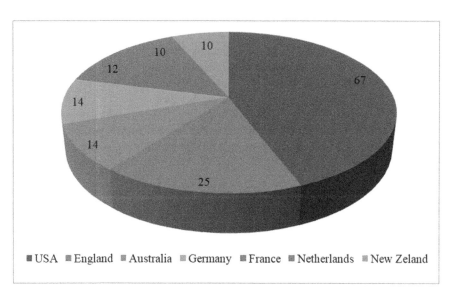

Figure 1.4. *Top seven countries of authors by number of publications (developed by the authors)*

Authors from 55 countries are involved in research on resilience in organizations. Figure 1.4 presents the authors of seven countries who have published 10 or more works.

Five percent of works have been published by authors from the United States, UK, Australia, Germany and France.

To understand the most influential authors, publications and works, we will analyze citations. An analysis of citations showed that all 232 publications on resilience in healthcare organizations had 2,283 citations, their H-Index is 23 and all publications were cited 9.8 times on average.

The number of publications and citations is shown in Figure 1.5.

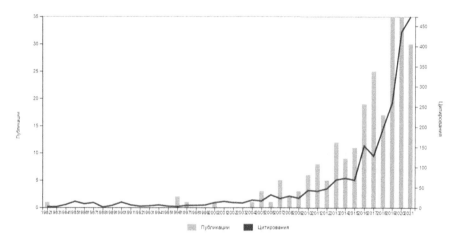

Figure 1.5. *Dynamics of the number of publications and citations by years (developed by the authors)*

As can be seen from Figure 1.5, 45% of citations fall in years 2016–2021 (128–473 citations per year), which may indicate the relevance of this topic.

In this study, 232 papers on resilience in organizations were found. Table 1.1 presents information on the 10 most cited publications.

As can be seen from Table 1.1, half of the most cited works were published during 2010–2013. The articles published in 1997 have the largest number of citations (277). More than half of the works are published in editions belonging to the first or second quartile. Two articles published in 2013 and 2016 have the highest average citation rate, which indicates their relevance and influence in this area.

Author	Publication	Category quartile	Year of publication	Total number of citations	Average citation rate
Cicchetti, D. & Rogosch, F.	*Development and Psychopathology*	Q1	1997	277	11.08
Grossman, G.	*American Naturalist*	Q1/Q2	1982	162	4.05
Lee, A., Vargo, J. & Seville, E.	*Natural Hazards Review*	Q2/Q3	2013	159	17.67
Boin, A. & Van Eeten, M.	*Public Management Review*	Q1/Q2	2013	97	10.78
Kefi, S. et al.	*PLOS Biology*	Q1	2016	90	15
Salanova, M. et al.	*Group & Organization Management*	Q2/Q3	2012	76	7.6
Peterson, G.D.	*Climatic Change*	Q1/Q2	2000	67	3.05
Gordon, T. et al.	*Canadian Journal of Physiology and Pharmacology*	Q3/Q4	2004	58	3.22
Chaskalson, M.	*Mindful Workplace: Developing Resilient Individuals and Resonant Organizations with MBSR*	-	2011	57	5.18
Bowles, S. & Bates, M.	*Military Medicine*	Q3	2010	52	4.33

Table 1.1. *The most cited articles (developed by the authors)*

Publication	Number of publications	Total number of citations
Development and Psychopathology	1	277
American Naturalist	1	162
Natural Hazards Review	1	159
Public Management Review	1	97
PLOS Biology	1	90
Group & Organization Management	2	76
Climatic Change	1	67
International Journal of Human Resource Management	2	61
Safety Science	6	58
Mindful Workplace: Developing Resilience Individuals and Resonant With MBSR	3	57

Table 1.2. *The most cited journals (developed by the authors)*

In total, 227 publications have been published on resilience in organizations. Table 1.2 presents the 10 publications that have the most citations on the selected topics.

As can be seen from Table 1.2, the most influential journals are *Development and Psychopathology*, *American Naturalist* and *Natural Hazards Review*. They have only one publication, but each of these publications has more than 150 citations. In addition, influential publications are *Safety Science* and *Mindful Workplace: Developing Resilient Individuals and Resonant Organizations with MBSR*. They have three to six works on resilience in organizations.

Also worth noting is the publication *Applied Psychology: An International Review*, which published four papers, cited 27 times. This indicates the influence of these publications in the industry.

More than 10,000 authors have published their research on resilience in healthcare organizations. Table 1.3 presents 10 authors with the largest number of citations (and at least two works on selected topics).

As can be seen from Table 1.3, the most influential authors are Seville, Ilorans, Martines and Salanova. They have more than two works and 100 citations. Malinen and Prayag have three publications, cited 45–77 times. This indicates the influence of these authors on the selected topic.

Authors	Number of documents	Number of citations
E. Seville	2	162
S. Ilorans	2	108
I.M. Martines	2	108
M. Salanova	2	108
S. Malinen	3	77
G. Prayag	3	45
M. Chowdhury	2	42
A. Azadeh	2	20
D. Furniss	2	19
S.M. Asadzadeh	2	15

Table 1.3. *The most cited authors (developed by the authors)*

By country to which the authors belong, the most cited works are those of the authors from the USA, UK, New Zealand, France, the Netherlands, Spain and Canada (Table 1.4). This is most likely due to the greater number of works published by authors in these countries.

Country	Number of documents	Number of citations
USA	67	1,111
UK	25	336
New Zeland	10	286
France	13	236
Netherlands	10	149
Spain	8	142
Canada	9	109
Chile	2	95
Australia	14	90
China	5	87

Table 1.4. *The most cited researchers by countries (developed by the authors)*

If we compare the data in Table 1.4 and Figure 1.4, we can see that the USA, UK, New Zealand, France, the Netherlands and Australia are in both lists. Although 14 works have been published by authors from Germany, there are more citations from authors from Canada, Chile and China, which also indicates their influence on the chosen topic.

One of the tasks of the research is to analyze the directions (clusters) of modern research on resilience in organizations. Keywords for publications that are repeated at least four times were analyzed (Figure 1.6).

Hierarchical cluster analysis was used to better understand clusters of resilience in organizations.

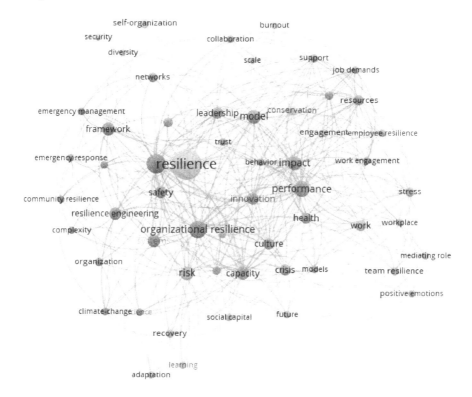

Figure 1.6. *Clusters of resilience in organizations (developed by the authors)*

As a result of hierarchical cluster analysis using VOSviewer, six clusters were identified.

Based on Figure 1.6, we can distinguish the following main areas of modern research: management (community resilience, emergency management, emergency response, networks, organizational resilience, resilience engineering, systems); performance (collaboration, employee resilience, health, impact, innovation, job demands, resources, work engagement); models (capacity, crisis, culture, leadership, safety, sustainability); resilience (engagement, security, self-organization); work (mediating role, positive emotions, stress, team resilience, workplace); risk (adaptation, building resilience, recovery, social capital) and others.

Characteristics of clusters for the most used keywords within each type are shown in Table 1.5.

Clusters	Items in cluster	Links	Total link strengths	Occurences
Cluster 1. Management (red)	14	38	69	24
Cluster 2. Performance (green)	13	37	78	17
Cluster 3. Models (blue)	9	28	41	12
Cluster 4. Resilience (yellow)	8	43	83	58
Cluster 5. Work (violet)	7	23	27	8
Cluster 6. Risk (light blue)	6	23	31	13

Table 1.5. *Clusters obtained from the analysis of keyword sharing (developed by the authors)*

Only one cluster is related to healthcare organizations (green). Most publications from these clusters are related to behavior, collaboration, employee resilience, health, impact, innovation, job demands, perceptions, performance, resources, support, trust and work engagement. In addition, these publications have links with other clusters by keywords, such as risk, social capital, stress, work, workplace, conversation and engagement (Figure 1.7).

Publications on innovation are also only in Cluster 2 (green). These publications are related to collaboration, support, job demands, resources, employee resilience, work engagement, impact, performance, models, culture, capacity, social capital, learning, recovery and framework, as shown in Figure 1.8.

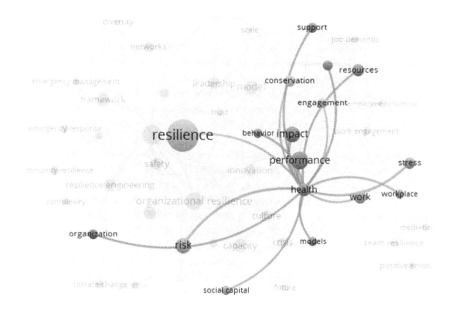

Figure 1.7. *Resilience in healthcare organizations (developed by the authors)*

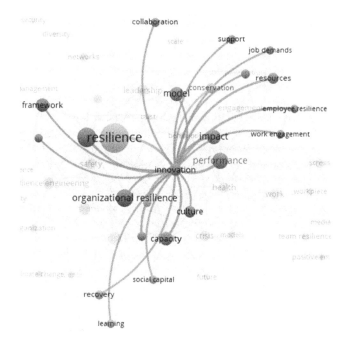

Figure 1.8. *Innovations in resilient organizations (developed by the authors)*

The most rapid changes in research topics took place in 2016–2019. Changes in research requests over this period are illustrated in Figure 1.9.

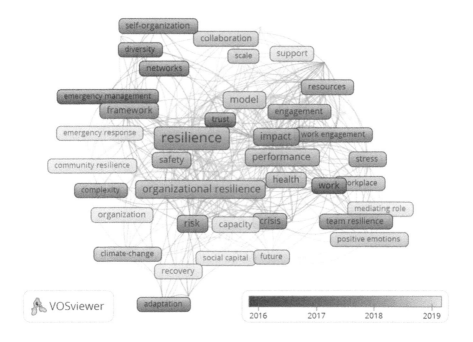

Figure 1.9. *Evolution in resilience in organizations (developed by the authors)*

Most of the articles have been published in the last few years. They reflect the directions of modern research. Based on publications from 2016–2019, we can determine the following main areas of modern and future research: social capital, support, recovery, community resilience and emergency response in health organizations.

Annotations to the most cited publications directly related to the health sector were also analyzed.

Researchers have found that the transformational leadership style has a positive and statistically significant impact on perceived organizational stability. Elected officials are more likely to strengthen organizational resilience than appointed officials in nonprofit health organizations.

Organizational characteristics that indicate the resilience of nonprofit behavioral health organizations included mission commitment, improvisation, community reciprocity, the leadership of employees during transformations, hope and optimism and financial transparency.

Another study examines whether resilience and other personal resources can function as a psychological shield through mediation and/or moderation that mitigates burnout.

There are studies on the development of a computerized system for monitoring human activities to obtain indicators of the stability of the access system.

Other researchers have explored the potential of health ministries to become educational organizations that help develop sustainability.

It has been established that transparent reporting of successes and failures contributes to forming strong organizational structures.

Another study examined the initiatives of working organizations to increase resilience using the resistance–resilience–recovery model of John Hopkins. It is established that such initiatives increase organizational stability and contribute to employee stability.

The authors of one study also provided recommendations for future programs designed to create a sustainable workforce that can sustainably provide high-quality care.

1.3. Lessons learned

The aim of this study was to gain a comprehensive view of relevant research on resilience in healthcare organizations, identify modern research and predict future research.

In this study, four tasks were set.

Based on Web of Science data, 232 publications on resilience in organizations were found. More than 50% of these works were published during 2016–2019, indicating a rapidly growing interest in this topic. More works were related to business economics (26.3%), engineering (16.8%), psychology (15.5%), environmental sciences ecology (8.6%) and public administration (6.9%). Only 6.5% were related to environmental and occupational public health and other healthcare directions. More works have been published by authors from the USA, UK, Australia and Germany. Most research is conducted by the State University System of Florida (USA), University of Canterbury (New Zealand), University of London (UK), University of Birmingham (UK), and University of California System

(USA). The European Commission and National Science Foundation funded a small number of studies on this topic.

An analysis of citations showed that all 232 publications on resilience in healthcare organizations had 2,283 citations, their H-Index is 24 and all publications were cited 9.8 times on average. More than half of the most cited works were published during 2010–2013. The article published in 1997 has the biggest number of citations (277). Two articles published in 2013 and 2016 have the highest average citation rate. The most influential journals are *Development and Psychopathology*, *American Naturalist* and *Natural Hazards Review*. In addition, influential publications are *Safety Science*, *Applied Psychology: An International Review* and *Mindful Workplace: Developing Resilient Individuals and Resonant Organizations with MBSR*. They have three to six works on resilience in organizations. The most influential authors are Seville, Ilorans, Martines and Salanova. They have more than two works and 100 citations.

As a result of hierarchical cluster analysis using VOSviewer, six clusters were identified. The following main areas of modern research have been identified: management (community resilience, emergency management, emergency response, networks, organizational resilience, resilience engineering, systems); performance (collaboration, employee resilience, health, impact, innovation, job demands, resources, work engagement); models (capacity, crisis, culture, leadership, safety, sustainability); resilience (engagement, security, self-organization); work (mediating role, positive emotions, stress, team resilience, workplace); risk (adaptation, building resilience, recovery, social capital) and others. Only one cluster is related to healthcare organizations (green). Most publications were related to behavior, collaboration, employee resilience, health, impact, innovation, job demands, perceptions, performance, resources, support, trust and work engagement.

Based on publications from 2016–2019, we can determine the following main areas of modern and future research: social capital, support and communication in health organizations.

Unfortunately, only Web of Science publications were considered in this study, and Scopus and Google Scholar publications were not included. This is due to technical limitations on VosViewer applications. This could be a topic for future research.

The results of this study could be helpful for healthcare organization owners to make decisions about innovations and their implementation in their activities and for researchers to find sources of funding and future cooperation.

1.4. References

Boin, A. and van Eeten, M.J.G. (2013). The resilient organization: A critical appraisal. *Public Management Review*, 15(3), 429–445.

Bowles, S.V. and Bates, M.J. (2010). Military organizations and programs contributing to resilience building. *Military Medicine*, 175(6), 382–385.

Chaskalson, M. (2011). *Mindful Workplace: Developing Resilient Individuals and Resonant Organizations with MBSR*. John Wiley & Sons, New York.

Chigrin, O. and Pimonenko, T. (2014). The ways of corporate sector firms financing for sustainability of performance. *International Journal of Ecology and Development*, 3(29), 1–13.

Cicchetti, D. and Rogosch, F.A. (1997). The role of self-organization in the promotion of resilience in maltreated children. *Development and Psychopathology*, 9(4), 797–815.

Gordon, T., Thomas, C.K., Munson, J.B., Stein, R.B. (2004). The resilience of the size principle in the organization of motor unit properties in normal and reinnervated adult skeletal muscles. *Canadian Journal of Physiology and Pharmacology*, 82(8/9), 645–661.

Grossman, G.D. (1982). Dynamics and organization of a rocky inter-tidal fish assemblage – The persistence and resilience of taxocene structure. *American Naturalist*, 119(5), 611–637.

Kefi, S., Miele, V., Wieters, E.A., Navarrete, S.A., Berlow, E.L. (2016). How structured is the entangled bank? The surprisingly simple organization of multiplex ecological networks leads to increased persistence and resilience. *PLoS Biology*, 14(8), e1002527.

Lee, A.V., Vargo, J., Seville, E. (2013). Developing a tool to measure and compare organizations' resilience. *Natural Hazards Review*, 14(1), 29–41.

Lyeonov, S., Pimonenko, T., Bilan, Y., Štreimikienė, D., Mentel, G. (2019). Assessment of green investments' impact on sustainable development: Linking gross domestic product per capita, greenhouse gas emissions and renewable energy. *Energies*, 12(20), 3891.

Peterson, G.D. (2000). Scaling ecological dynamics: Self-organization, hierarchical structure, and ecological resilience. *Climatic Change*, 44(3), 291–309.

Rosokhata, A., Minchenko, M., Khomenko, L., Chygryn, O. (2021). Renewable energy: A bibliometric analysis. *E3S Web of Conferences*, 250, 03002.

Salanova, M., Llorens, S., Cifre, E., Martinez, I.M. (2012). We need a hero! Toward a validation of the healthy and resilient organization (HERO) model. *Group & Organization Management*, 37(6), 785–822.

Tielietov, O.S., Nahornyi, Y.I., Letunovska, N.Y., Shevliuha, O.H. (2017). Competitive and sustainable technological development: Focus on business enterprises. *Journal of Security and Sustainability Issues*, 3(6), 491–500.

2

Response to Exceptional Health Situations at the Meso-Level: CPTSs in the Covid-19 Crisis

Born from the 2016 law on the modernization of the French healthcare system in 2016, *Communautés professionnelles territoriales de santé* (CPTSs) ("territorial health professional communities") are tools for structuring the provision of primary care. They are deployed to promote the coordination of territorial actors at the meso-level (i.e. broader than care homes and health centers) in order to better address the health needs of the population in these territories. These complex organizations in which professionals collectively participate in carrying out territorial public health missions are likely to facilitate the development of coordinated and responsive answers to exceptional health situations, as was observed during the health crisis related to the Covid-19 pandemic. After presenting the CPTS concept, this chapter will explore the possibilities of structural resilience of this meso-level structuring tool and the testing of these territorial organizations in the context of the coronavirus epidemic. This will help clarify the stakes of a more resilient territorial structuring of primary care.

2.1. Context and questions

Faced with the challenges posed by demographic and epidemiological transitions, the structuring of the primary care sector, which includes all the actors involved in outpatient care, both curative and preventive, is seen as a major concern. The primary care system in France is based on a non-hierarchical professional model

Chapter written by Sylvain GAUTIER.

that gives significant importance to individual private practice, typically operated solo, and relies predominantly on fee-for-service remuneration for professionals (Bourgueil 2010). Over the past two decades, there has been a movement toward diversifying remuneration methods and promoting more collaborative and coordinated practices, particularly in multi-professional care homes, which have been encouraged for development by public authorities[1].

This movement, in its most recent developments, has been further enhanced by a greater emphasis on population issues, promoting multi-professional care homes to move beyond local clinical coordination and shift their focus from the patient toward the population at a territorial level. The introduction of health centers into the public health code, following the HPST law of 2009, paved the way for early validation of this professional grouping within a territorial framework, extending beyond the boundaries of care homes or health centers. These territorial dynamics, led by professional leaders often from the field of general medicine, have gradually gained prominence in a few metropolitan areas with a long history of structural development.

Established by the Law on the Modernization of our Health System in 2016, CPTSs were initially designed to rely on these "beyond the walls" multi-professional care homes and to support public authorities in accelerating the territorial structuring of primary care by implementing successful models from specific territories. According to the law, CPTSs are initiated by healthcare professionals, who organize themselves into multi-professional teams as part of a population-based approach for a territorial health project. The primary goal is not only to improve the response to individual patient care requests from each professional involved but also to organize a collective response to the health needs of the territorial population. In this context, the CPTS embodies the concept of "population-based responsibility" among primary care actors, which stems from a legacy of a "territorial public health service" that was initially rejected by liberal professionals[2].

Since the enactment of the *Ma santé 2022* ("My Health 2022") law in July 2019, CPTSs have emerged as the preferred tools for territorial structuring of primary care, enabling professionals to undertake territorial public health missions defined in the law as public service obligations. CPTSs are designed to enhance healthcare access, improve patient care coordination in the territory by fostering collaboration and

---

1 *Maisons de santé* (multi-professional care homes) were introduced into the public health code in 2007 by the social security financing law of 19 December 2007.

2 See on this point the March 2014 report by Bernadette Devictor entitled "*Le service public territorial de santé*" (SPTS) on the development of the territorial and population-based approach to healthcare provision.

coordination among health professionals, implement territorial preventive measures, enhance the quality and relevance of care and provide support to healthcare professionals in their respective territories (such as continuous professional development and helping young professionals become established). These diverse missions were defined and clarified early on through interprofessional negotiations between *Assurance maladie*, France's national health insurance scheme, and organizations representing healthcare professionals. An ACI (*Accord conventionnel interprofessionnel*), an interprofessional conventional agreement, was signed in June 2019. The interprofessional nature of this agreement underlines[3] the significant value the system places on initiating collaborations among numerous actors in the territory and formalizing sustainable multi-professional groups that contribute to the quality of patient care.

In concrete terms, the ACI interprofessional conventional agreement outlines the financing of CPTSs through an annual flat rate determined by the size of the population covered by the community (four different sizes of territory are considered). In addition to this flat rate, there are specific flat rates assigned for each mission, which vary depending on the size of the CPTS. Some missions are optional, while others are considered "essential" as they are mandatory for CPTSs to receive financing based on the ACI interprofessional conventional agreement. These essential missions include improving access to care (such as access to a general practitioner and unscheduled care), organizing multi-professional pathways centered around the patient and developing territorial prevention actions. CPTSs that commit to implementing these various public health missions enter into a tripartite contract with the primary health insurance fund in their territory and the Regional Health Agency (RHA[4]) with regional jurisdiction.

Therefore, the missions of CPTSs aim to the improve the quality and accessibility of health services, and they are intended for the entire population of a territory rather than solely for individuals who are ill. To achieve this, the CPTS operates at an intermediate level of integration, bridging the gap between local clinical coordination (micro) focused on individual patient care and systemic integration (macro) that typically encompasses territorial social and health policies. The meso-level where the CPTS emerges can be considered a virtual space that combines organizational and professional approaches (Valentijn 2013). The meso-level serves as an interface between the functions of primary care and those of public health.

---

3 This likely reflects a persistent shift in the strategy of the health insurance funder, which prioritizes multi-professional negotiations over a segmented, single-professional approach. This shift may be aimed at mitigating the predominant influence of the medical profession within the ambulatory care sector.

4 *Agence regional de santé* (ARS), hereafter referred to as the RHA.

For health professionals involved in CPTSs, this represents a significant shift in scale and perspective: moving from a care approach focused on individual patients to one that encompasses the health of the entire population. This paradigm shift is not self-evident, and it is crucial to provide support to ensure that CPTSs do not become limited to pursuing mutual knowledge, defending categorical interests and reinforcing liberal ideologies at the expense of public health issues (Gautier 2019). This is especially important because these territorial organizations, when implemented[5], often remain fragile and rely on a few individuals who have limited time and resources. Many are still in the early phase of their development. Existing CPTSs typically exhibit hybrid configurations with *adhocratic* functioning, representing transitional forms between communities and organizations. They rely on coordination modes based on mutual adjustment (Gautier 2019). Moreover, their organizational characteristics can vary significantly depending on the profiles of the territories where they are being developed. This variability is intentionally embraced by the RHA, which advocates for the adaptability of the CPTS tool and a low level of bureaucratic organization to encourage professionals to engage in the process. Within this context, the robustness of these organizations needs to be examined, particularly regarding their structural capacities for organizational resilience.

2.2. Conceptual framework

In 2018, Barasa et al. (2018) proposed a definition of organizational resilience applied to the healthcare system. They define it as "the maintenance of positive adjustment under challenging conditions such that the organization emerges from those conditions strengthened". Through an analysis of nearly 34 original studies, the authors identified nine factors that can influence organizational resilience, which need to be considered when describing, planning, guiding and enhancing resilience. These nine factors align with some of the specific characteristics of CPTSs that have been highlighted in previous exploratory work (Gautier 2019). These characteristics, when viewed in the context of the conceptual framework proposed by Barasa et al., contribute to the development of a structurally resilient CPTS.

The first crucial factor in organizational resilience is the availability of material resources, including financial and technological resources that can provide significant flexibility during a crisis. Within the territories, CPTSs serve as collaborative spaces that facilitate the pooling of these resources. By acquiring equipment or digital solutions for all stakeholders within a single CPTS, economies of scale can be achieved, enabling easier sharing at the territorial level. This

---

5 The ambition to have 1,000 CPTSs by 2022 seems difficult to achieve. In January 2021, France had 123 CPTSs in operation and some 328 in the pipeline (source: *Fédération nationale des CPTS*).

reevaluation of material resources is accompanied by a focus on logistical considerations such as equipment storage and maintenance, transportation and distribution within the territory, all of which require careful planning and anticipation by the organizations.

Indeed, preparedness and planning, the second factor, play a paramount role in an organization's ability to adapt to a crisis situation. For CPTSs, the regional health project serves as the foundation for this preparation. Validated by the RHA, which ensures its alignment with the regional health project, it allows for the specification of procedures and concrete actions to be undertaken by each party involved in the CPTS, both during normal times and in a crisis situation. It also provides guidance on the continuity of missions, including considerations for degraded operations. From an operational perspective, the responsibilities of each CPTS actor can be defined and, if applicable, multi-professional protocols can outline the areas of intervention for different members of the care teams.

The multi-professional protocol within the CPTS also enables the consideration of substituting certain professionals when needed, provided that this is planned in advance. Barasa et al. (2018) emphasize the significance of alternative strategies and redundancy (the third factor) in order to address occasional shortages and ensure the continuity of organizational functions. In the context of CPTSs, the development of advanced practices holds great significance and can offer alternative clinical pathways during a crisis. This is particularly evident in cases where certain professionals are granted prescription authorization.

Organizational resilience is also contingent upon effective information management (the fourth factor), particularly in a context of uncertainty where the quality of communicated messages is crucial. In this regard, CPTSs serve as a significant asset as they facilitate the structuring of a professional network that can be leveraged during times of crisis for information dissemination. These organizations, built on inter-knowledge of the actors, utilize communication tools from the outset. CPTSs typically have shared information systems that enable them to function on a regular basis and also facilitate informal exchanges among the participating professionals within the system.

When an exceptional health situation arises, organizations must be able to rely on their human capital (the fifth factor). While certain territories may experience a shortage of healthcare professionals, especially in terms of medical resources, the collaborative nature of CPTSs allows for the involvement of a significant number of members, including healthcare providers, social actors and local healthcare institutions. Although a professional hierarchy may exist within CPTSs, as is the case in the primary care sector as a whole, where doctors often assume leadership roles, it is not uncommon to observe strong engagement from professionals in other fields such as pharmacy, midwifery, massage therapy or nursing.

All of these professionals are required to participate in the decision-making processes of the CPTS. In times of crisis, leadership and management practices become crucial, constituting the sixth factor. It is essential to ensure that participation of all actors in decision-making is guaranteed so that everyone feels fully involved in managing the situation. In the case of CPTSs, they are established as associations under the 1901 law, which allows for such participation. CPTS actors are expected to be members of the association, granting them a voice in its governance (the seventh factor). During times of crisis, it is recommended to adopt a horizontal approach to governance, following a bottom-up logic rather than top-down approach. This fosters trust and support among the actors. The flexible and *adhocratic* organizational structure of the CPTS described above facilitates this governance model, which contributes to organizational resilience.

How an organization perceives the challenges it faces is influenced by its organizational culture (the eight factor). Structurally resilient organizations view these challenges as opportunities to enhance internal coherence and cohesion and develop new skills. While it may be challenging to define a specific organizational culture for the CPTS, it is true that they are encouraged to maintain a certain level of reflexivity in their actions. The logic of contractualization in which they are engaged implies a certain level of reciprocity, *quid pro quos*, and the need to periodically engage with their contractual partners, namely health insurance and the RHA. Adopting indicator-based management practices contributes to establishing an organizational culture that fosters creativity and innovation, both of which are essential for adaptation during crisis situations.

Finally, because of the CPTS, primary care professionals can unite on a territorial scale and achieve a critical mass, allowing them to engage in dialogue with other institutions in the territory, such as hospitals, the RHA and elected representatives This external recognition of primary care actors as a unified territorial entity enables CPTSs to easily establish partnerships and foster a network-oriented approach (the ninth factor), which is beneficial for their organizational resilience in times of crisis.

Therefore, CPTSs possess the foundational elements of a structurally resilient meso-level territorial organization. As an example, the solicitation of primary care during the Covid-19 health crisis served as an unprecedented test of this resilience.

2.3. Case studies

For the recently established CPTS, the health crisis resulting from the Covid-19 pandemic in France in the early months of 2020 presented a dual challenge. On the one hand, there was a need to further strengthen these systems to ensure their resilience against the anticipated disruptions. On the other hand, it was essential to ensure their continued operation by promptly responding to and addressing the challenges and difficulties posed by the crisis. From a broader systemic perspective, the objective was also to preserve and even enhance the territorial dynamics that had been set in motion.

Numerous quantitative and qualitative studies have documented the factors contributing to the resilience of primary care actors, CPTSs and the meso-level during this period. In this context, the Accord[6] research network, comprising practitioners and researchers, conducted a series of surveys among primary care providers (general practitioners and private midwives) and healthcare structures (health centers) to gain a better understanding of the adaptations made at the beginning and end of the March–April 2020 lockdown. These surveys highlighted the early and diverse nature of these adaptations, particularly in multi-professional structures or teams (Ray 2020; Saint-Lary 2020; Baumann 2021). The increased mobilization of professionals practicing in groups, especially multi-professional groups, was also evident in a survey conducted by the DREES (*Direction de la recherche, des études, de l'évaluation et des statistiques*), the "directorate of research, studies, evaluation and statistics", of the French ministry for Solidarity and Health, which examined a representative panel of general practitioners (Monziols 2020). All of these studies demonstrated that primary care professionals established dedicated consultations and channels for managing patients with Covid-19 and that they made significant efforts to maintain their activities and continuity of care by adapting home consultations and extensively utilizing teleconsultation. Some primary care organizations, including CPTSs, even established dedicated "Covid centers" aimed at limiting the spread of the virus by specifically receiving patients

---

6 The Accord (Assemble, Coordinate, Understand, Research, Debate in Primary Care) network aims to build an ecosystem of research in primary care. Funded by the *Institut de recherche en santé publique* (IRESP) for its creation in 2020, the Accord network has two ambitions: to create a network of research investigators and to help develop research projects focused on primary care issues. The founding partners are professional networks (AVECsanté, the Asalée association), research networks (CNGE – *Collège national des généralistes enseignants*, IJFR – *Institut Jean-François Rey*), as well as university and academic teams (RETInES team – Risks, Epidemiology, territory, information, education, health, the university department of maieutics of the Simone Veil-Health UFR of the University of Versailles Saint-Quentin-en-Yvelines, the RESPIRE mission – Research in innovative and renewed primary care, of the *École des hautes études en santé publique*).

with symptoms and assigning dedicated medical and paramedical staff to manage these centers.

During an online seminar held in November 2020, the Accord network conducted a comprehensive synthesis of all the surveys it had carried out, complemented by valuable feedback (Gautier 2021). This collective work, which made it possible to intersect points of view and compare experiences, made it possible to better understand and describe adaptations at the meso-level, which are inherently more complex to understand. Consequently, crisis management at the territorial level was organized through collaborative stock management of personal protective equipment (such as masks, goggles and overcoats) and information sharing. Platforms for reporting difficulties encountered or solutions adopted to deal with them have thus been set up, based in particular on existing tools used by local operators (secure messaging systems, professional social networks, websites, etc.).

The capitalization work conducted during this Accord network seminar also revealed the widespread establishment of territorial crisis units to manage the exceptional health situation on a daily basis and facilitate collaboration with other institutions in the area and local elected officials. The involvement of elected officials in crisis management was frequently mentioned, especially in areas where a strong organizational structure was in place, allowing for easy identification of key individuals to contact (such as professional leaders, elected health officials and association representatives). Certain professions, including ASALEE (*Action de santé libérale en équipe*)[7] nurses and public health nurses, played a vital role in ensuring the continued care of chronic patients, who may have faced difficulties accessing healthcare during lockdowns and stay-at-home orders. Patients who needed medication refills benefited from the authorization granted to pharmacists to renew prescriptions directly. Additionally, multi-professional protocols related to Covid-19, addressing the management of patients with the virus or care delivery during the epidemic, were developed by the healthcare teams.

The impact of the health crisis on territorial dynamics has been explored in more detail through qualitative sociological studies conducted in metropolitan areas with well-established histories and contexts (Fournier 2021; Fournier and Clerc 2021). The findings of these studies demonstrate that the health crisis either suspended, activated or amplified pre-existing multi-professional cooperation and inter-sectoral coordination. It often did not lead to the creation of new dynamics but rather contributed to the reinforcement or weakening of previous territorial dynamics. While the link between the ambulatory sector and the hospital may have been affected by the health crisis, possibly due to an excessive focus on the hospital

---

7 A French cooperation protocol between general practitioners and nurses, aiming to improve the quality of care.

sector, the territorial approach and CPTS initiatives have been strengthened. Consequently, the epidemic served to legitimize the projects of certain CPTSs and to expand the existing groups to include other professionals in the territory, who perceived in the CPTS and the crisis response actions a dynamic in which they wanted to participate.

Other sociological studies conducted directly with the CPTS have provided insights into the nature of the actions carried out by the professionals who have grouped together in these structures (Falcoff 2021). CPTSs, for instance, have been involved in collecting, manufacturing and distributing personal protective equipment. They have also established mutual aid groups among independent professionals. Moreover, their in-depth knowledge of the territory has facilitated targeted interventions for vulnerable individuals and groups. These interventions have included providing night and weekend services in institutions serving the elderly, offering emergency care, conducting screenings and health education in social residences and reaching out to populations who are typically marginalized from the healthcare system, such as migrants and homeless individuals.

More recently, the territorial initiatives of the CPTS have focused on the rollout of vaccination programs. They have facilitated the establishment of dedicated vaccination centers, often in collaboration with local municipalities, building upon the screening centers that were previously set up with the assistance of primary care teams. To ensure the smooth operation of these centers and the administration of vaccines, efforts have been made to equip them with the necessary medical and paramedical professionals. In order to reach the most vulnerable individuals, particularly those who are isolated or unable to travel, certain CPTSs have also deployed mobile vaccination teams. These targeted actions aim to ensure that vaccinations are accessible to all segments of the population.

In summary, the documented adaptations, both in terms of quantity and quality, demonstrate the organizational resilience of the CPTS during the Covid-19 pandemic. These adaptations have been driven by various actors at the meso-level and have collectively contributed to enhancing the resilience of the entire territory. However, it should be noted that these adaptations have been diverse and varied across different territories, lacking a systematic approach. Some teams or meso-organizations have demonstrated a higher level of resilience compared to others. This observation emphasizes the significance of ongoing territorial structuring efforts, aiming to enhance resilience at the territorial level and ensure a more cohesive and coordinated response to future challenges.

2.4. Lessons learned

The Covid-19 health crisis raises questions regarding the expectations associated with territorial structuring, which, while well established in certain areas, remains in its early stages in others. Some may interpret the incomplete nature of this structuring and the limitations it may have encountered during the crisis as evidence of the anticipated failure of the CPTS (Dépinoy 2021), leading them to advocate for dismantling the system. Conversely, others emphasize the importance of continuing territorial structuring efforts, while calling for increased support from public authorities (Bontemps 2020). In this context, several key considerations emerge as crucial in ensuring the development of a structurally resilient territorial structuring.

The first issue is undoubtedly the expansion of CPTS missions to ensure a more effective response to severe health crises. As of December 2021, an amendment[8] to the CPTS ICA has been signed by the contracting partners to introduce a new "core" mission focused on this matter. The CPTS will be required to develop and implement an action plan that outlines response strategies for exceptional health situations, following a national framework. The plan should encompass at least five main types of health crisis: care for somatic or psychological injuries (such as attacks, fires, explosions and riots); care for patients affected by an infectious, climatic or environmental episode (such as seasonal epidemics, heatwaves, extreme cold and pollution); care for patients with chronic illnesses (e.g. cancer, heart disease and stroke); care for patients impacted by emerging infectious agents; care for patients affected by nuclear, radiological or chemical accidents or attacks; and lastly, events affecting the supply of care (such as drug shortages and floods). These plans will be developed within each CPTS territory and coordinated with various health crisis management plans, whether hospital-based or from the medico-social sector. They could potentially serve as the equivalent of "city white plans", drawing an analogy to the existing "hospital white plan".

A second crucial challenge is to ensure the involvement of primary care professionals in these public health missions, which may deviate significantly from their initial culture and training. The task in this regard is immense and will undoubtedly necessitate the development of crisis management training for all healthcare professionals right from the early stages of their education. This also involves the possibility recently granted to the CPTS to be able to compensate professionals who participate in one or more collective actions organized by the community. As of May 2021, the legal structure of the CPTS as an association under

---

8 Amendment 2 to the interprofessional agreement in favor of the development of coordinated practice and the deployment of regional professional health communities.

the 1901 Law no longer impedes the remuneration of its members[9]. This provision is likely to encourage the collective engagement of healthcare professionals.

Alongside the involvement of professional actors, there remains a challenge in developing health administration in primary care and ensuring its professionalization. While the CPTS can support the development of this administration, it is crucial to maintain a certain level of efficiency and, consequently, preserve the flexibility that currently characterizes the CPTS. Excessive bureaucracy must be avoided as it could undermine the agency of the actors. Guaranteeing the autonomy and empowerment of health professionals within the CPTS thus becomes a guiding principle for action, forming the foundation of structurally resilient community organizations. Through a well-established territorial network of CPTSs with resilient frameworks, the primary care system can demonstrate its enduring capacity for resilience in the face of exceptional health situations.

2.5. References

Barasa, E., Mbau, R., Gilson, L. (2018). What is resilience and how can it be nurtured? A systematic review of empirical literature on organizational resilience. *International Journal of Health Policy and Management*, 6, 491–503.

Baumann, S., Gaucher, L., Bourgueil, Y., Saint-Lary, O., Gautier, S., Rousseau, A. (2020). Adaptation of independent midwives to the COVID-19 pandemic: A national descriptive survey. *Midwifery*, 94, 102–918.

Bontemps, A. (2020). Accompagner la structuration des soins primaires après la COVID-19 : un nécessaire renversement du fonctionnement des institutions publiques de la santé. *Regards*, EN3S, 225–241.

Bourgueil, Y. (2010). Systèmes de soins primaires : contenus et enjeux. *Revue française des affaires sociales*, 3, 11–20.

Dépinoy, D. (2021). Les CPTS peuvent-elles sauver les soins primaires ? *Coopération santé*, 26, 1.

Falcoff, H., Gasse, A-L., Berraho-Bundhoo, Y., Dubois, S. (2021). Les Communautés professionnelles territoriales de santé (CPTS) face à la crise Covid. L'exemple des 13e et 14e arrondissements de Paris. In *Crise Covid et organisation du système de santé. Témoignages et regards croisés*, Aubert, I., Jobin, C., Kletz, F. (eds). Presses des Mines, Paris.

---

9 This was made possible by Ordinance No. 2021-584 of May 12, 2021 on territorial health professional communities and health centers.

Fournier, C. and Clerc, P. (2021). La construction d'une organisation regionale des acteurs de soins primaires face à l'épidémie de COVID-19 : apports d'une étude de cas à l'échelle d'un canton [Online]. Available at: https://doi.org/10.4000/rfst.869.

Fournier, C., Michel L., Morize N., Pitti L., Suchier M., Bourgeois I., Schlegel V. (2021). Les soins primaires face à l'épidémie de COVID-19. Entre affaiblissement et renforcement des dynamiques de coordination regionale [Online]. Available at: https://www.irdes.fr/recherche/questions-d-economie-de-la-sante/260-les-soins-primaires-face-a-l-epidemie-de-covid-19.pdf.

Gautier, S. (2019). Les conditions de l'action collective dans le cadre des communautés professionnelles regionales de santé : une approche qualitative exploratoire. PhD thesis, Université de Paris Cité, Paris.

Gautier, S., Ray, M., Rousseau, A., Seixas, C., Baumann, S., Gaucher, L., Le Breton, J., Bouchez, T., Saint-Lary, O., Ramond-Roquin, A., Bourgueil, Y. (2021). Soins primaires et Covid-19 en France : apports d'un réseau de recherche associant praticiens et chercheurs. *Santé Publique*, 6(33), 923–934.

Monziols, M., Chaput, H., Verger, P., Scronias, D., Ventelou, B. (2020). Trois médecins généralistes sur quatre ont mis en place la téléconsultation depuis le début de l'épidémie de Covid-19. Report, DREES, Paris.

Ray, J.F., Gautier, M., Seixas, C., Bourgueil, Y. (2020). Enquête nationale maisons de santé et centres de santé face au COVID-19. Résultats des deux vagues d'enquête. Report, IJFR, Paris.

Saint-Lary, O., Gautier, S., Le Breton, J. (2020). How GPs adapted their practices and organisations at the beginning of COVID-19 outbreak: A French national observational survey. *BMJ Open*, 10, e042119.

Valentijn, P., Schepman, S.M., Opheij, W., Bruinzeels, R.H. (2013). Understanding integrated care: A comprehensive conceptual framework based on the integrative functions of primary care [Online]. Available at: https://doi.org/10.5334/ijic.886.

Dynamic Capabilities and Resilience of a Health Organization: The Case of an EHPAD-Medicalized Retirement Home

While management research over the last 20 years has focused on the economic impact of reforms on healthcare institutions in France, there is still little research on the organizational learning dynamics that these reforms have generated in order to make hospitals more innovative in the long term. We carried out a case study about an EHPAD (*Établissement d'hébergement pour personnes âgées dépendantes*), which is a medicalized retirement home for the elderly, located in the south of France. We are interested in ways in which a series of signals linked to the turbulence of its environment will lead this structure to mobilize internal resources, previously unexploited, initially to absorb and improvise in the face of the crisis, and then to rapidly engage in a structured learning process with a view to innovating. We mobilize a framework – the concept of dynamic resilience capacity – that has not yet been widely used in the health sector .

3.1. Background context and questions

The crisis facing French health organizations at the beginning of the 21st century cannot be understood without reference to the two major currents of reform that have been imposed on them. The first reform, brought about by the hospital ordinances of 1996 and inspired by the principles of new public governance, affirms competition as a source of efficiency, transforming the patient-user into a patient-client. The second reform, carried out in 2010 by the law on *Hôpital, patients, santé, territoires* ("Hospitals, Patients, Health and Territories") emphasizes cooperation

Chapter written by Benoît NAUTRE.

between the various stakeholders in the healthcare system, shifting the locus of power from institutions to new coordination entities, which are supposed to represent the collective interest. In less than 30 years, healthcare organizations have gone from being a stable and protective environment to dealing with turbulent conditions for which they were not really prepared. Therefore, as the media tell us every day, "hospitals are in crisis".

While management research over the last 20 years has focused on the economic impact of reforms on healthcare organizations, and in particular their consequences in terms of site consolidation or resource transfers, there is still little research on the real dynamics of organizational learning that these reforms have produced, and on the capacity of this learning to transform their routines in a sustainable way, to make them more dynamic and innovative.

Beyond the resilience that hospitals and EHPAD-medicalized retirement homes demonstrate on a daily basis, the question here is how these organizations could take advantage of crises, in terms of learning, to sustainably strengthen their positioning and their capacity for innovation.

To support this study, we use research conducted at an EHPAD-medicalized retirement home in the south of France. A series of disruptive events have occurred in the external environment of the establishment, leading the managing association to resort to a transitional management. As field-based researchers, we study longitudinally the different stages of the crisis that this organization is going through. While the organization demonstrates a relatively natural resilience in absorbing successive shocks and then improvising solutions to withstand them, the questioning and analysis of our work focuses instead on the rest of the process. Once the first shock has passed, the structure will reveal an unexpected capacity to mobilize new resources, to take advantage of the signals coming from its environment and then to evolve its routines in order to reinforce its resilience in a sustainable way.

For our analysis, we make use of a concept that has not yet been widely used in management research in the field of health organizations, that of dynamic resilience capacities.

3.2. Conceptual framework

3.2.1. *Resilience in the field of health organizations*

The concept of resilience is naturally mobilized by the management sciences in crisis management research. In this respect, its application to the world of healthcare must take into account two factors that are specific to it: the passage in a few years from a protected environment to a highly turbulent environment, and the poor change readiness of this type of organization (Mintzberg 1996; Denis et al. 2004). Hospitals and EHPAD-medicalized retirement homes are thus described, not as collective actors endowed with strategy, but rather as political arenas within which strategies are naturally unstable, power games are omnipresent and the capacity to adapt to changes in their environment is always problematic.

However, the field in which hospitals and EHPAD-medicalized retirement homes evolved was stable until 1985 and, particularly in the public and associative sectors, relatively pro-protective. The charitable values inherited from history, which were still present in the care professions, and the logic of the Welfare State carried by the public authority, carried the meaning of collective action through a set of values and schemes: the public service mission in hospitals, mutualist militancy in EHPAD-medicalized retirement homes and solidarity action in the associative world. The first closures of maternity hospitals, then the arrival on the market of powerful private groups of clinics and EHPAD-medicalized retirement homes, and more recently the emergence of new coordination entities such as CPTS (*Communauté professionnelle territoriale de santé* – "territorial health professional community" in France), bear witness to the powerful transformation of this environment.

This transformation has a profound impact on the meaning of collective action. Hospitals and nursing homes, just as schools and town halls, have a natural legitimacy linked to their involvement in one of the main regalian missions of the State. The meaning of the action is based on a set of dimensions, some of which are quantitative (number of beds, number of doctors), and others are based on a more or less explicit system of values (the hospital, the largest employer in the municipality, proximity of a maternity hospital, permanence of care in an emergency department). Activity-based financing initiated by the 1996 reform changes these representations, with value now being measured by the production of care and no longer by private or public status or the number of beds.

In the same way, the 2010 law redefines the performance of care and dependency services, no longer on the basis of equipment, know-how or the motivation of professionals working in these organizations. On the contrary, we must avoid institutionalization, give priority to prevention and transfer power to coordination structures. While these changes are entirely legitimate, in view of the need for efficiency and the demand for quality of care and treatment, the meaning of collective action is naturally disrupted by these changes, which no doubt explains the difficulties of hospitals, the lack of motivation of staff, and the criticism of the State's action in relation to the closure of beds or the creation of "medical deserts".

At the same time, it is important to note the resilience of healthcare organizations in the midst of a crisis. The Covid-19 pandemic revealed unexpected capacities to face the unexpected, to cobble together emergency solutions, to mobilize values and rules and to stand firm in the face of adversity.

In this context, the query regarding the resilience of healthcare organizations is of particular interest, in its capacity to analyze the way in which these structures organize themselves to resist the turbulence of their environment, but also the dynamic attitudes that they could adopt in order to go beyond their initial state and engage in innovation processes.

3.2.2. *From the concept of resilience to that of dynamic resilience capacity*

The issue of resilience is not new. The Louis XIV dictionary (Bely 2015) reports the King's words to his confidant, Marshal de Villars, in 1712, "God is punishing me, I deserved it, I will suffer less in the other world", analyzing this comment not as an act of bravery in the twilight of a reign, but as the manifestation of a resilience built by the King throughout his life with a view to "endure with patience the decrees of Providence" (author's translation). We are here in the realm of individual resilience, described by schools of psychology as an intrinsic quality of each individual, willing to take advantage of life's difficulties in order to strengthen their capacity to face the dilemma (Begin and Chabaud 2010).

Organizational resilience, on the other hand, mobilizes a relatively broad theoretical framework and offers different definitions, the most frequently used of which is "the ability of an organization to prevent and overcome a crisis situation" (Roux-Dufort 2003, author's translation).

Individual resilience and organizational resilience complement each other. The individual resilience of actors within an institution can contribute to its organizational resilience (Lengnick-Hall et al. 2011) through three dimensions:

– cognitive abilities, which call for the construction of meaning insofar as the unpredictable event must be interpreted in order to act on organizational routines;

– behavioral characteristics, which allow us to find responses to an unforeseen situation through creativity, tinkering and improvisation;

– the contextual conditions, insofar as the context of relations and interactions between actors, both internal and external to the organization, allow for the mobilization of resources which in turn allows for action on the problem to be resolved.

Other research distinguishes between passive and active perspectives of resilience (Altintas 2020). The passive perspective, still referred to as adaptive (Prayag et al. 2018), limits resilience to the ability of an organization to absorb a shock, without implementing major changes and with the sole objective of returning to an initial state (Borekci et al. 2015). The active perspective of resilience, also called strategic resilience (Hamel and Välikangas 2003), implies a proactive approach by the organization to develop new capabilities in the face of the disruptive event.

The notion of dynamic capacity introduces a complementary dimension. It is mobilized by management research, independently of resilience issues, as a way for an organization to maintain its competitive advantage through the continuous adaptation of its skills and resources (Teece 2007). Recent work (Altintas 2020) highlights a link between dynamic capability and resilience, defining dynamic capability as the creation of organizational routines, capable of continuous adaptation under the effects of recurrent events in the environment.

Dynamic capability would thus differ from simple problem solving by several conditions, including the recurrence of its process, its structured character and its effects on the modification of the organization's resources. It thus establishes the principle of the dynamic transformation of organizational routines. These same works speak of a dynamic capacity for resilience, in the sense of a process initiated by signals in the environment, which trigger a structured and permanent learning process through which organizational routines transform and adapt.

Can the concept of dynamic capacity make a contribution in the world of healthcare facilities?

Observation shows that in the face of the profound changes imposed by the reforms, hospitals and EHPAD-medicalized retirement homes have been able to rely on their organizational routines to withstand the shocks and have even shown ingenuity in improvising responses to new and unprecedented situations. In exchange, the ability of these structures to take advantage of signals from their environment in a recurring and structured way, to reinforce their strength in their ecosystem, is more open to discussion.

Hospitals are in crisis, as the media reminds us every day. However, while the hospital environment has settled into a state of permanent turbulence, due to multiple factors of which the reforms are the expression thereof, the question is whether it is merely resisting such shocks in the hope of better days. On the contrary, is it engaged in a stable and recurrent learning process, with a view to strengthening its organizational resilience?

Having completed this brief literature review, let us take our reader to the field, a provincial mutualist EHPAD-medicalized retirement home, in which a series of transformations in its environment plunges it into an internal organizational crisis.

3.3. Case studies

3.3.1. *The field of study*

The EHPAD des Cerisiers-medicalized retirement home is a private, not-for-profit institution owned by an association that manages a dozen similar organizations throughout France. The association was founded in 1930 by the social works of a state-owned company in order to make up for the inadequacy of the retirement pensions for their workers. As requirements evolved, these institutions opened up to the entire elderly populations within their respective territories.

The board of directors is composed of salaried or retired members of the original company, the majority of whom are from the trade union world. The headquarters of the association is located in the Paris region, on an independent site, and is limited to about 10 members. The governance model of the association is not very formalized. Relations, procedures and delegations between the head office and the institutions have been built up over time, are not reviewed or updated and are unanimously criticized by the site directors who only partially respect them.

The EHPAD des Cerisiers-medicalized retirement home is located in the heart of a spa town of 4,000 inhabitants, far from the main communication routes, train stations and highways. Until the middle of the 1990s, the thermal baths represented a significant job pool for personal care services. In addition to these thermal bath enterprises, several care institutions for the elderly were founded, a public EHPAD, the EHPAD des Cerisiers and a third private commercial EHPAD.

In 1990, health insurance companies decreased the coverage for thermalism, placing the employees who work there in difficulty, at the same time as all the actors indirectly associated with that industry: hotels, casinos, guest houses and leisure businesses. The EHPAD-medicalized retirement home, until then a secondary actor to the thermalism industry, now take a central place in the local economy.

Since 1930, the EHPAD des Cerisiers-medicalized retirement home has been located in the center of the city, in a former castle donated by the municipality to this mutualist organization. The establishment, called "*l'hospice des vieillards*" (the old people's home), benefits from a good image and strong support from the local elected officials as well as from the population, in spite of the dilapidated state of its premises. It has negotiated an agreement with the department that finances residents without resources, on the basis of a constrained daily rate, which favors the reception of elderly people of the commune, even those with few resources.

The EHPAD-medicalized retirement home has a total of 75 employees. The employees are generally attached to their position. Three reasons contribute to this: salary and social protection conditions are more advantageous than those offered by the two other EHPADs of the municipality; the perception that it is an interesting and envied job (the employer is solid); and finally a very competitive job market, especially compared with that of thermalism, which is reducing its workforce year after year.

The director, who has been in place for more than 15 years and is a nurse by training, has benefited from significant resources to develop the new EHPAD-medicalized retirement home. She supervised the entire construction and presents it as her "career project". She is surrounded by a small management team, a nurse manager, a coordinating doctor and two administrative agents who are responsible for HR and resident administration. Very involved, she is present in all areas of decision-making, care, relationships with families and residents, and external relations.

Employees are divided into three socio-professional categories:

– Half of the first group is made up of care service agents (the most senior staff, who entered the profession before the diploma requirements) and agents with a nursing aid diploma (short technical training). The vast majority of them are natives and residents of the municipality or the surrounding area and began their careers in the institution.

– The second group is made up of cleaning and kitchen staff. About half of this group are not directly employed by the association but depend on an autonomous employer group common to the three EHPAD-medicalized retirement homes of the community.

– Finally, the third group is made up of a dozen professionals, nurses, a doctor, a psychologist and a re-educator. They all have a higher level of education, have previously worked in other institutions and are unreservedly independent of a job market that is oriented in their favor. The nurse manager is in the middle of her career. She has received funding from the association for on-the-job training as a facility manager, which she is in the process of completing. The position of coordinating physician is a recurring problem for the three EHPAD-medicalized retirement homes in the municipality, as few professionals are interested in this function. The position has been filled for a few months.

The dilapidated state of the premises and the evolution of safety standards required the construction of a new building, which is now in operation.

Since this change, the establishment has experienced a series of difficulties and internal conflicts. Faced with economic and competitive constraints, the current director is trying to implement several organizational changes. The teams were increasingly opposed, and the managing association decided to dismiss her. After her departure, we were entrusted with transitional management.

As soon as we arrived, we noticed a difficult social climate and distinguished three groups within the employees of the EHPAD-medicalized retirement home, half of whom were in care positions and the other half in hospitality and activity functions:

– Two thirds of the staff, mainly service agents and care assistants, position themselves as "discussants". Their expectation, vis-à-vis the director of transition, is to stop the conflict. For them, the solution is to return to the previous situation: "All these projects and even the new building is the cause of the problems". The loss of meaning, the mistreatment ("the staff are no longer taken care of"), the divisions between two clans and the pros and cons of the former director come up in all the discussions.

– Some of the nurses and the coordinating physician adopt an attitude of disengagement. They threaten to leave: "There are jobs everywhere, but in the meantime, we do the job and nothing more".

– The third group, smaller in size, is composed of three nurses and the psychologist. They positioned themselves from the outset as "saboteurs". Outwardly aggressive, for this group "the transition is a hypocritical step, the association simply does not have the courage to manage, we are going to leave the EHPAD-medicalized retirement home, which will not find anyone in our place. The crisis stems from the director who did not see it coming, did not understand that we are no longer in the time of the old people's home".

3.3.2. The research process

The methodological choice made is that of intervention research (Yin 2012). As researchers integrated into the field (transition director), we act on the organization and support our analysis of the effects produced, based on back and forth between the field and theory. Despite the biases that this inevitably introduces into the analysis (David 2000), our position gives us privileged access to observing the mechanisms of transformation, a process that is often difficult to observe, since it requires time to step back and distance oneself from it, time that an incumbent manager rarely has or rarely has the freedom to take (Weick 1993).

We first present the field of this research, the institution, its management association and the environment in which it evolves. We then choose to isolate a few major events that occurred in the environment of the institution before and during our mission. Finally, we describe successively, in chronological order of their occurrence, these events and the signals they produce, with a view to analyzing their effects on the organization under study. We identify six events, chosen from among those that carry the highest threat signals to the historical functioning of the institution:

– a security constraint necessitated relocation to a new building;

– the director has responded to a call for projects, which will modify the organization of work;

– faced with economic constraints, the director imposed a sectorization of the residents;

– the institution joins an employer group to subcontract the cleaning function;

– the director is dismissed by the association;

– the association entrusts us with the transitional management of the EHPAD-medicalized retirement home for 6 months.

We then set out to record, in a factual manner, without trying to make any sense of it, the information gathered through observations, comments and reactions from our interviews, meetings with employees and stakeholders of the institution. We note in particular the discursive content (words, syntax) that these interviews contain. Finally, we set out to establish the links of cause and effect between these disruptive signals from the environment and their effects on the evolution of the perception of the actors concerned.

We structure these observations into two categories:

– An *ante* approach: this corresponds to the first few weeks of our mission. We collected all the information necessary for our analysis through documents, informal interviews with employees, but also with various stakeholders (local elected officials, city doctors, families and suppliers). We perceive it as a period of pre-learning in the sense that the threatening signals from the environment have generated a crisis situation, as well as a collectively shared feeling of social deconstruction (loss of meaning).

– A post approach: we are in a position of transitional leadership, and our various decisions, consultations and discussions generate reactions that we use for our analysis. We interpret it as a period of reconstitution. The power games have been transformed, and the organization is engaged in a learning process, under the influence of new leadership.

We summarize this in Table 3.1.

Changes	Perception *ante*	Perception *post*
(1) The managing association has decided to build a new building, and the EHPAD-medicalized retirement home is moving in without changing the number of beds or the nature of activities.	"We can't find our way around". "It feels like a private club". "Before, we used to do voluntary themed meals, shows, we felt like part of the village". "We're only going to have rich people".	"We are fortunate to have the association". "Today the residents and families want something new". "Tomorrow, it's home-based, we have to adapt". "The private sector is going to lose its jobs". "We have to be the only ones".
(2) The director initiates a PASA (*Pôle d'activités et de soins adaptés*) project and hires a dedicated team to provide activities, taking this role away from the caregivers.	"More time to do the care". "No more mutual aid between agents". "They do activities and we do the dirty work". "The families are not happy".	"If we want to stand out from the crowd, we need innovative projects". "PASA is a way to involve families". "We are all caregivers and facilitators, there is only one project: the resident".
(3) The management decides to sectorize the residents according to their dependence, and the residents with cognitive disorders are placed on the third floor. They do not have access to the restaurant nor the activities.	"No one wants the third floor, it's too hard". "At night, it's easier to monitor". "We can serve the third floor dinner earlier; they are all disoriented". "Facilitators, we're not there to do nursing". "I was hired to provide activities; I don't like dealing with the disoriented ones".	"The new logic is inclusion, not institutionalization, it's about reconstituting the ordinary environment, so there should be no sectorization".

Changes	Perception *ante*	Perception *post*
(4) The creation of the GIE: the three EHPAD-medicalized retirement homes of the territory create a structure for the shared provision of service and care personnel.	"The association was taking care of the staff, now we're just numbers". "MSE agents, you can't blame them for not being motivated and competent, that's exploitation". "If we can't recruit on our own, it's because the salaries aren't keeping up".	"We need to build an integration pathway and tutoring for the first week". "The GIE is a way to meet the employment needs of the community, that's our mission at the Association". "They have to feel integrated, it gives us an educational mission, it's interesting".
(5) In response to the internal social conflict, the managing association laid off without notice and then dismissed the director. Several key professionals resigned (coordinating doctor, psychologist), and the director of care experienced burnout.	"There are two cliques, we have to stop that or we'll all be out of a job". "We need to change the teams to avoid cliques". "Who do we ask without the coordinating physician?"	"The coordinating physician should be a general practitioner in the community, we need their expertise, not their authority". "For authority, the psychologist is the best, let's imagine a new model".
(6) The managing association sets up a transitional management. The group of nurses is structured as "change-entrepreneurs".*	"The nurse coordinator needs to be called back, if she is the director, she will restore order". "The nurses, they are the anti-director clan, it's normal that they get along".	"This is the first time we've had a possible dialogue". "We don't have to please just one person". "We can finally discuss projects together". "We work 'Taylorian', we have to get into project mode".

*The change-entrepreneurs are employees of the EHPAD-medicalized retirement home who have shown leadership skills during the health crisis and have succeeded in imposing themselves through innovation. This refers to the notion of the "visionary entrepreneur" (Brechet et al. 2009).

Table 3.1. *A collection of conversations illustrating the observations at the beginning and end of the mission*

3.3.3. *Building a dynamic capacity for resilience in a crisis context*

On the basis of testimonies and documents, we have reconstructed and described below, in chronological order, the six events (disruptive signals) from the environment that the EHPAD-medicalized retirement home will most likely be confronted with.

We then take up each of these events as we strive to identify, through our observations, the effects produced on the organization.

We study these effects from two perspectives:

– We first use the most classical approach to resilience (Weick and Sutcliffe 2007), with a view to isolating the reactions that contributed to the absorption of the shock, and then the adaptations, adjustments and improvisations that would have favored a form of renewal and appropriation in the phase of disorder, without modifying the routines in a lasting and structured way.

– We then look at, with reference to the concept of dynamic capacity (Altantas 2000), whether these same events are capable, beyond the sole objective of limiting the risk or re-establishing the initial order, of engaging the organization in a dynamic of innovation, through which it transforms the threat into an opportunity to develop, to strengthen itself or to distinguish itself (innovate) from the other players in its territory.

In 2010, the passage of a departmental safety commission threatens the establishment on the continuation of its activities, the building proving to be dangerous in the event of fire. The evolution of the standards requires the construction of a new establishment on the same site. The association accepted the principle, allocated funding, and a new EHPAD-medicalized retirement home opened its doors in 2019.

The new facility is modern and well equipped. The disruption is fundamental. The old chateau turned retirement home is vast and not very functional, offered a great deal of freedom of organization to the employees and consequently little possibility of control by the management.

The 75 places are now spread over three floors, each floor having 25 private rooms, a relaxation area with a television and a library.

The architect designed a vast entrance hall with a hotel-style reception desk. This hall opens on one side onto a glassed-in restaurant, and on the other side, onto the offices of the nurse, the coordinating doctor and the psychologist. A third space, slightly set back, houses a management office.

Well located in the center of the town, surrounded by a pleasant garden area, the complex gives the impression of modernity and comfort, as well as a standardized image of a "contemporary collective" for the elderly, as found in many towns and city districts. The old chateau retirement home, a few 100 meters away, is now closed and has a relatively dilapidated and sad appearance in comparison. The move to the new premises has changed the working atmosphere within the institution. The organization of the site allows the director to control more efficiently the execution of tasks, respect of schedules and even the individual attitudes of each employee toward the residents and their families.

Box 3.1. *Description of the new site*

In this first event, we observe a rapid structuring of the collective around historical principles, a disinterested action ("we did it voluntarily"), a mission within the city ("we felt part of the village") and a specificity that carries meaning ("we don't look after the rich"). Mobilized during this change, these principles, although not very rational – during our exchanges, the employees admitted that the three EHPAD-medicalized retirement homes in the community shared the same market, both geographically and in terms of the socio-economic status of the residents – had the same meaning for collective action, contributed to accepting a series of unwanted changes (e.g. the new premises allow for better management control) and generated various forms of adaptation (improvised or alternative strategies), with a view to recreating spaces of freedom.

Then, after several weeks of discussions, the discourse changed. We organized a series of meetings with the employees and presented the new visions of care for the elderly in France and Europe. The next generation of residents will not have experienced war, they are the heirs of the "Trente Glorieuses"[1], they have traveled, have pensions and assets. They will prefer to stay in their own homes. These are new challenges to take up. The group of "saboteurs", at first very opposed, gradually became interested in this discourse, and even developed new arguments (the advent of digital technology to bring the elderly out of isolation, connected apartments in the heart of the community where the EHPAD-medicalized retirement homes could intervene from a distance). The discourse is clearly innovative, the interest is no longer focused on a return to stability, but seems to admit the reality of a universe that has begun moving and within which innovation is necessary. Our saboteurs have become "change-entrepreneurs". We refer here to the notion of the "visionary entrepreneur" of Brechet et al. (2009), wherein the authors describe the way in which a transformation project within an organization favors the emergence of new leaders, motivated by the concern that their vision be understood and accepted by the actors through whom the project will be formed and materialized.

---

1 *Les Trente Glorieuses* was a 30-year period of economic growth in France between 1945 and 1975, following the end of the Second World War.

The PASA project (*Pôle d'activités et de soins* s *adaptés*) was imposed on the three EHPAD-medicalized retirement homes in the commune by the RHA. The PASA benefits from dedicated funding in exchange for compliance with specific requirements, in particular the hiring of activities staff. Three facilitators and an occupational therapist trained in activities were recruited.

The activities are installed in the relaxation areas on the floors, which are redesigned for this purpose. The new team engages in different activities that quickly conflict with the existing set up. The new team is used to working in pairs, room by room, nursing, cleaning and taking residents to the restaurant. The whole process is a mix of care, individual contact with the resident and coffee breaks between rooms. The activities last all morning, with a standardized sequence of tasks, which suits both the caregivers and the residents relatively well. In contrast, the facilitators want the residents to be able to choose their activities (reading the newspaper, bingo and choir) and criticize the "Taylorian" manner in which the caregivers operate. The employees criticize the director for giving preference to these newcomers to the detriment of the caregivers and agents: "the residents need to be washed, to have their beds made and cleaned, not to have songs sung to them", "they know us, they ask us for lots of *services*".

Box 3.2. *An example illustration of the PASA project*

Here, the Taylorian logic of hospital work is first mobilized as a means of coping with the crisis; it standardizes and reassures around collectively shared routines. It justifies the rejection of the new facilitators. We observe, in reaction to this project, a strengthening around efforts that had been progressively put aside (systematic room rounds in the evening, for example). Complaints about the time spent on care, which was considered insufficient, and the dissatisfaction of the families were often cited as reasons for collective dissatisfaction. We note here forms of improvisation in order to resist the project.

Then, in the post-crisis period, the discourse was oriented toward a new revolutionary and meaningful dimension, and the PASA was a way of standing out from the competition, of involving families. During the interviews, the group of change-entrepreneurs repeatedly says: "We are all caregivers and activity facilitators". We take time to discuss this idea and note the mobilizing utopia carried by this slogan. The group even refuses to give it a more specific content, thus increasing its mobilizing and innovative character: "Only one project: the resident".

The director is committed to a project that she presents as support for a new strategy, which she believes is essential to resilience in a context "that has become very competitive, economically constrained and full of threats for the future".

She decided to sectorize the residents according to their level of dependence. The third floor was allocated to residents who are no longer autonomous. The structure of the work changed, with a concentration of nursing care and round changes for incontinent residents, while the other floors saw a reduction in case load. The director's rationale is to reduce costs (no need for dependent care equipment on each floor) and improve quality (monitoring disoriented residents will be easier): "We need to finance construction, we can no longer create positions as was done in the past, patients are entering the system later in their old age due to advancements in home care, so they are more and more dependent [...] and furthermore, we have to be wary of competition, today, public authorities advocate home care".

Box 3.3. *An illustration describing sectorization*

We are here in an opposition, which serves first of all as a support to face the shock: the opponents refuse the floor of the dependent persons, and others confess to having invented excuses. The group of change-entrepreneurs joins this opposition to the project, but by mobilizing again the dynamic concepts of inclusion, by maintaining an ordinary environment. A nurse, a member of this group, during one of our interviews said that from her own research online, "in Montreal, disability and old age are not a deficiency but a condition, and it is up to us to adapt so as to allow everyone to do everything".

Thermalism, in difficulty for many years, was strongly impacted by the Covid-19 crisis. The thermal baths are not authorized to open their season and doubts circulate around their ability to survive this event. The question agitates the employees concerned, mostly service agents and care assistants. The management of the three EHPAD-medicalized retirement homes is taking advantage of the tension in this market to promote the hiring of temporary workers from an employer alliance, created recently under pressure from their boards of directors, with a view to reducing the costs of human resource management and to homogenizing remuneration.

The competing establishments reproach the EHPAD des Cerisiers-medicalized retirement home for offering, with equal qualifications, superior conditions to the other institutions; however, the association did not want to get involved in the local political conflict this caused. This principle quickly impacted the social climate at Les Cerisiers. The temporary staff complained about being stigmatized as "precarious employees", while the other employees recognized the injustice of their status and denounced the lack of competence and motivation of these "temporary employees".

Box 3.4. *An illustration explaining the employer alliance*

Throughout this affair, the historical paradigm of belonging (the employees made available are different) is strongly mobilized (mythologized) in order to face the crisis (the staff must be taken care of, the others are neither competent nor motivated, their presence is a disruption). In exchange, the post-crisis learning phase rebuilds another vision, that of building a path of integration, of taking on a pedological mission.

The dialogue between the EHPAD team and the director is becoming increasingly conflictual. The latter deflects on the insufficiencies of the head office and openly criticizes the general management and policies of the association. Anonymous letters were sent to the head office, then, in the absence of a reply, a letter signed by a group of 20 employees was sent to the president, with a copy to the Labor Department and the RHA. The letter also denounced abuse and moral harassment. The nurse manager then took sick leave.

The general management, after having sought the agreement of the president, decides to lay off the director. The decision to lay off the director and the termination of the nurse manager destabilized the institution in a brutal way. The coordinating doctor resigned.

Box 3.5. *An illustration describing the dismissal of the director*

In order to allow for the continuation of programs, the association decided to install a transitional management team. This transitional phase was set to last 6 months.

Box 3.6. *An illustration explaining the transition management*

These last two events, as well as the reaction they induce, are of definite analytical interest here. The dismissal of the director generates a loss of meaning, fear for the future ("we're all going to be unemployed"), as well as a collective feeling of guilt. The capacity for renewal is materialized by the search for an immediate solution, and the nurse coordinator could become director. We questioned the teams several times about this idea, in particular about the governance project that this nurse could carry, and the teams' expectations of her. The answers were limited to the need for authority, and the nurse's position (including the office she would occupy) was necessarily the same as that of the outgoing director. The shock is absorbed. A solution has been improvised, but the objective is clearly to return to the initial situation.

The interviews we conduct with teams on the subject of leadership have a significant bias because transitional leadership provides a solution. It recreates an authority on which the teams can rely. Moreover, the exchanges regularly deviate to the past, to the expression of suffering at work linked to the authority of the outgoing director, or to the political games between the two clans, which is a temporary distraction for the method we have chosen to follow.

During a team meeting, we introduced the word "dialogue" and associated it with two other ideas: "no longer depending on a single person" and "considering emerging projects, we start with ideas and needs on the ground, we consult, discuss and negotiate with a view to making them happen". We observe a dual reaction: the group of change-entrepreneurs is fully committed and takes ownership of this idea of emerging projects. Conversely, the other employees express fear in the form of a power grab by their fellow leaders. The discussion then evolved toward the idea that before the recruitment of a new leader, there should be a collective reimagining of the "management role". The discussion was lively: "what do we expect from a director?", "in their office or at the EHPAD-medicalized retirement home reception desk?", "should they have a monopoly or should they share the dialogue with the families", "why not a dedicated group per project?" The dynamic dimension seems to us to be particularly present here, both through the words and concepts used (projects, project groups, sharing) and in the attitudes of the participants themselves. In fact, we accept the emergence of new leaders, but we fear that they will settle down (and we will be back at square one), as testified by the words of an employee: "If we let them do it, we fall back into the old way of working".

3.4. Lessons learned

In a study conducted on a single organization, the multiple biases that could be introduced by our position as a researcher integrated into the field are all factors that encourage the greatest modesty as to the lessons that could be conferred. However, our privileged access to information and the openness with which the teams cooperated with our approach lead us to formulate a few proposals likely to enrich the academic debate, as well as to participate in the progress of knowledge management on the ground.

First, the study highlights the nuance between resilience and dynamic resilience capacities. The analysis of the six disruptive events reveals two relatively distinct mechanisms. Faced with the disruptive signals from its environment, the EHPAD-medicalized retirement home was able to cope, without any disruption to its activity or any sequence of events of increasing severity. Let us recall here France Telecom, wherein the 2010s, a social crisis was followed by a wave of suicides within the company. In the same sense, the association was able to demonstrate its ingenuity, as shown by the do-it-yourself mentality and improvisation mobilized by the employees, for which the observations on each of the events have been described. It is easy to make the comparison with the way in which French hospitals were able, against all odds, to adapt their practices in the face of the unpredictable

Covid-19 crisis. The number of intensive care beds doubled in two months, a makeshift tent hospital was set up in three days on the parking lot of a university hospital in the east of France, and the historical divide between private and public hospitals was temporarily blurred, with the latter forced to cease its programmed activities, making its intensive care equipment and specialized personnel available to the former. Healthcare organizations are thus resilient, and it would no doubt be interesting to study the reasons for this, even given the fact that many contemporary studies already provide part of the answer.

In exchange, the construction of dynamic capacities, as we have highlighted through this short study, seems to us to open a vast door for research into the management of healthcare organizations. In response to each of the six events described, the EHPAD des Cerisiers-medicalized retirement home went beyond the simple objective of returning to the initial state, through post-crisis learning. This followed a double-loop model (Argyris and Schön 2001), in the sense that it did not only act on the operating modes but also revisited the frames of reference: the perception of a new site, the transformation of the corporate culture to open up to the support of external personnel, care beyond the walls as a means of innovation and the new vision of the management role. In the same sense, the study sheds light on the two specific conditions that seem to us to have been indispensable for the development of these dynamic capacities. The first was the internal resource, available and revealed by the crisis of leadership (our change-entrepreneurs) capable of imposing themselves through innovation in a governance process for which they were not expected, and the second was a sufficient level of intensity of disruptive signals from the environment to encourage the transformation of existing routines. Let us transpose this last aspect to the post-Covid situation of the French public hospital, which, after the remarkable agility it showed in overcoming the crisis, now seems to have returned to its initial state, "the hospital is in crisis". This statement opens the door to new debates, such as hospital governance, which is said to have a recurring leadership problem, or the fact that the environment is still too protective, and that there are insufficient incentives to force these structures to engage proactively in a structured, long-term learning process. These are all subjects for further research.

Healthcare institutions in the broadest sense of the term, hospitals, nursing homes and community structures, are of interest to management research because of their organizational complexity, the difficulty in constructing strategies, the many paradoxes related to their history, the interference from the political sphere and the permanent search for meaning related to the nature of their activities. Numerous works are progressively contributing to knowledge in this very specific field, mobilizing different theoretical frameworks, paradoxes, models of proximity and today the construction of resilience. The contemporary context of ransformation of hospitals and EHPAD-medicalized retirement homes, the evolution toward new approaches to care, the opportunities of digital health and the crisis of meaning expressed by care professionals are all realities that make this organizational field a real laboratory, at the same time as it opens up new avenues for research in management.

3.5. References

Altintas, G. (2020). La capacité dynamique de résilience : l'aptitude à faire face aux événements perturbateurs du macro-environnement. *Management & Avenir*, 115, 113–133.

Argyris, C. and Schon, D. (1978). *Organizational Learning: A Theory of Action Perspective*. Addison-Wesley, Reading.

Begin, L. and Chaubaud, D. (2010). La résilience des organisations, le cas d'une entreprise familiale. *Revue française de gestion*, 1(200), 127–142.

Bely, L. (2015). *Dictionnaire Louis XIV*. Robert Laffont, Paris.

Borekci, D.Y., Borekci, D.Y., Rofcanin, Y., Sahin, M. (2015). Organizational resilience and relational dynamics in triadic networks: A multiple case analysis. *International Journal of Production Research*, 53, 6839–6867.

Brechet, P., Scheib-bienfait, N., Desreumaux, A. (2009). Les figures de l'entrepreneur dans une théorie de l'action fondée sur le projet. *Revue de l'entrepreneuriat*, 8, 37–53.

David, A. (2000). La recherche intervention, un cadre général pour les sciences de gestion. *Actes de la 4ème conférence de l'AIMS*, Montpellier.

Denis, J.L., Langley, A., Rouleau, L. (2007). Strategizing in pluralistic contexts: Rethinking theoretical frames. *Human Relations*, 60(1), 179–215.

Hamel, G. and Valikangas, L. (2003). The quest of resilience. *Harward Business Review*, 81, 52–65.

Lengnick-Hall, C.A., Beck, T.E., Lengnick-Hall, M.L. (2011). Developing a capacity for organizational resilience through strategic human resource management. *Human Resource Management Review*, 21, 243–255.

Mintzberg, H. (1982). *Structure et dynamique des organisations*. Eyrolles, Paris.

Prayag, G., Chowdruhy, M., Spector, S., Orchiston, C. (2018). Organizational resilience and financial performance. *Annals of Tourism Research*, 73, 193–196.

Roux-Dufort, C. (2003). *Gérer et décider en situation de crise*. Dunod, Paris.

Teece, D.J. (2007). Explicating dynamic capabilities: The nature of micro-foundations of (sustainable) enterprise performance. *Strategic Management Journal*, 28, 1319–1350.

Weick, K.E. (1993). The collapse of sensemaking in organizations: The Man Gulch Disaster. *Administrative Sciences Quarterly*, 38, 628–652.

Weick, K.E. and Sutcliffe, K.M. (2007). *Managing the Unexpected: Resilience Performance in an Age of Uncertainty.* John Wiley & Sons, New York.

Yin, R. (2012). *Case Study Research: Design and Methods.* Sage Publications, Newcastle.

The Health Pathway: A Resilient Model for Transforming the Governance of Health Authorities?

In recent years, the healthcare pathway has become the new paradigm at the heart of reforms aimed at transforming our healthcare system. This reference framework is underpinned by the implementation of a decompartmentalized health organization, which must promote better coordination between health professionals, with a view toward a regional approach. It also implies a renewed conception of the role of the health authorities, in particular the role of Regional Health Agencies (RHAs), located at the interface of national health policies and the territories. From a regulatory position, they must progressively evolve toward becoming supervisory partners, implying a reexamination of their relationship with the actors in the field. Our objective will therefore be to analyze how a form of cooperation between "supervisory authorities and field actors" can be a mechanism, or even a necessity, for the RHA today, in order to support the deployment of the healthcare pathway paradigm across the territories.

4.1. Background context and questions

Over the past 30 years, the use of the term "pathway" has been multiple across many sectors of public action. Whether in social and professional integration policies, health policies or even in the field of training, it has gradually become ubiquitous and is now the new reference framework (Bouquet and Dubéchot 2017). Within national health policies, this concept made its first appearance in the mid-2000s alongside the structuring of primary care (Law of August 13, 2004 on

Chapter written by Laëtitia BOREL.

health insurance). At that time, we spoke of a care pathway, with the primary care physician as the gateway. From the 2010s onwards, national actors have been making increasing use of the care pathway in their actions (Féry-Lemonnier et al. 2014), under the impetus of the work of HCAAM, France's "High council for the future of health insurance". The latter have highlighted the pressing need to improve the pathways of patients in complex situations, which is also a source of greater economic efficiency in our healthcare system (HCAAM 2012). They have therefore been included in every social security financing law since 2012, as well as in numerous public health plans. The optimization of healthcare pathways is at the heart of the national health strategy announced in 2013. In the same perspective, in 2016, the law on the modernization of our healthcare system positioned this notion as the new paradigm at the center of the reforms.

Having started with an initial medical representation, we are evolving toward a global dimension by talking about a healthcare pathway, or even a life pathway, aiming to increase the efficiency, fluidity and continuity of care through a transversal vision that covers both the medical and social needs of the sick person. The challenge of using the health pathway is twofold. It should make it possible to better control expenditure (in a context where our healthcare system is facing a significant structural deficit, a situation which is likely to increase due to the epidemiological transition linked to the aging populations and the development of chronic diseases), while at the same time guaranteeing the quality of the healthcare offer and equal access to care. However, how can it be a mechanism for this transformation?

It is often pointed out that one of the significant causes of the deficit in the health system is linked to its very functioning: compartmentalization and cultural differences between the health, medico-social and social sectors, but also between the city and the hospital, the multiplicity of guardianship, etc. (Bourgueil, in Féry-Lemonnier et al. 2014). This organizational problem generates a lack of links between the different care and support services put in place around the patient, particularly those concerning the most complex situations that require multiple interventions. In the absence of a coordinated response, the impacts are multiple: redundancy of acts, risk of disruption in care and so on. As a result, the pathway is seen as the new logic to adopt in order to structure the healthcare system on the basis of patients' needs so as to develop the offer. This concept is underpinned by the implementation of a decompartmentalized local health organization, with the aim of encouraging cooperation and the pooling of practices between healthcare providers.

The territory is one of the pillars of the new architecture of the health system, recently reaffirmed by the *Ségur de la santé* in 2020. We cannot therefore discuss the healthcare pathway without associating it with the territory, both of which seem to be closely intertwined. The healthcare pathway is above all a paradigm shift, in that it reinterprets professional practices and positions, modes of reasoning and the behavior of the actors, and more particularly the relational system that is associated with it. In order to become operational, it must take shape in a territory, that is, in a space where health professionals can meet to forge links and team up to work collectively around the patient and common projects (Desaulle, as cited in Féry-Lemonnier et al. 2014). This convergence between pathways and territory is explicitly expressed in the 2019 Health Law[1], which aims to create "care collectives" within the territories, a combination of the health, social and medico-social worlds. The change that is taking place must allow for the implementation of a new human organization, the success of which depends on the ability of these actors to cooperate and combine their respective skills in local areas defined by the RHA.

This new situation has led to a change in the way public action is thought of. The HPST (*Hôpital, patients, santé, territoires*) law[2] of 2009 marks, in our opinion, a first milestone with the creation of the RHA. Intrinsically linked to the development of the healthcare pathway and to the evolution of local representation, they must embody this new paradigm that is gradually taking place. The establishment of the RHA is justified by the need to decompartmentalize, unify and bring transversality between the hospital, medico-social, prevention and town medicine sectors, in order to break up the "organ pipe" organization (Evin 2019) and improve the fluidity of patient pathways. In addition, this reflects the desire for health policies to be anchored at a regional level, which appears to be the relevant level for ensuring their deployment and adaptation to local needs and specificities.

In 2016, the law on the modernization of the French healthcare system had the objectives of developing the participation of all local actors and coordination between healthcare structures and professionals, making pathways more fluid and improving coherence between public policies. This approach seems to be based on the gradual emergence of a new form of health governmentality (Aubert et al. 2020) introduced by the public authorities. It is based on a principle of co-construction of public action, concerning subjects related to healthcare pathways, where the initiative is left to the actors to organize themselves in the territories.

The State relies on several pillars to establish this model of regional self-organization: shared governance and population responsibility, local events, the use of digital tools to promote information exchange, experimental financing methods, notably via Article 51 of the French Social Security Financing Act, which promotes innovative cooperation projects and so on. The role of the State then lays out the

---

1 Law of July 24, 2019 on the organization and transformation of the healthcare system.
2 Law of July 21, 2009 on "hospital reform and patients, health and territories", commonly known within France by its acronym HPST.

general course, that is, the key waypoints, puts in place the conditions and tools (incentives and/or coercive measures) necessary to encourage collaboration between all stakeholders, with the operationalization ultimately being placed in the hands of the actors on the ground. For example, we can cite the creation of a CPTS (*Communauté professionnelle territoriale de santé* – "territorial health professional community") DAC coordination support systems, GHT and so on, initiated by France's 2016 Health Law[3] and reinforced by the 2019 law[4]. The plan for equal access to care in the territories, announced on October 13, 2017, also states as its Priority 4 "A new method: trusting the actors in the territories to build projects and innovate".

To support these transformations, the reinforcement of local events facilitated by the RHA seems to be a mechanism for the legislator. The *Ségur de la santé*, in 2020, devotes a section to the evolution of the RHA, indicating the need to strengthen the departmental level and their capacity to support projects. From this perspective, the RHA must support the transformations underway in the territories, support health actors in their projects and promote links between these projects. The RHA is positioned in a new role as a facilitator and interweaver of connections, while at the same time exercising its function as a fully embedded State authority. The function of the departmental delegations appears to be a key issue in the strategy of the RHA, with the *Ségur de la santé* report on health recommending that their role be consolidated and recognized. The RHA must now move from being a regulator to becoming a supervisory partner of health actors, of which the departmental delegations appear to be one of the mechanisms. The health pathway model is therefore becoming a resilient model that could help transform the governance of health authorities.

In light of these issues, the following question arises. In what way can a form of cooperation between "supervisory authorities and actors in the field" be a mechanism, or even a necessity, for the RHA today, and in particular the departmental delegations, to support the deployment of the paradigm of health pathways in the territories?

4.2. Conceptual framework

As we have seen, the introduction of the health pathway into health policies has led to the definition of a new form of health governmentality by the State (Aubert

---

3 Law of January 26, 2016 on the modernization of the French healthcare system.

4 Law of July 24, 2019 on the organization and transformation of the healthcare system, commonly known as *Ma santé 2022*.

et al. 2020) and to a strengthening of localization. But how has this materialized in practice thus far?

In the Ile-de-France region (our field of study), the RHA 2018–2022 regional health project was broken down into five areas of transformation that are based on a localized dynamic, driven by healthcare professionals. To this end, the operational level chosen by the RHA for the mobilization of health actors is the "coordination territory" (a sub-departmental area covering the entire region), within which a "coalition of actors" in the health, medico-social and social sectors must emerge, organized with the support of digital tools and on the basis of shared local governance. In order to better characterize the future health organization of the territory and to perceive the issues related to its deployment, we have chosen to compare it to the holographic organization model, developed by Gareth Morgan, using the metaphor of the brain. Here, the author examined whether it is possible to design organizations with the same capacities for flexibility, resilience and creativity as the brain (Morgan 1989). To support this view, Morgan defines four main principles for the development of a self-organizing type of structure: redundancy of functions, required variety, minimal critical specification and double-loop learning.

According to Morgan's principles, each member of the organization must have one or more specific areas of expertise, a source of diversity and complementarity (variety required). These must be coupled with a form of versatility in terms of available skills, the knowledge common to all actors and shared values (redundancy of functions), vectors of homogenization and continuity. The aim is to give the organization a form of flexibility, cohesion, reactivity and the ability to reorganize itself. In the end, it is a question of finding a balance between homogenization and diversity in order to improve adaptability and inventiveness. The level of internal variety must be just as important and complex as the environment in order to deal with the problems posed by it. In the case of healthcare pathways, this implies bringing together the health, social and medico-social sectors, as well as the city and hospital sectors, via obligations shared between health professionals (coordination and organization of healthcare pathways), which require the mobilization of specific skills and resources (medical, paramedical, social, etc.) for their implementation, which will have to be articulated and shared.

A flexible and non-prescriptive framework is required to facilitate self-organization (minimal critical specification). It is advocated that "organizational designers should primarily adopt a facilitating or orchestrating role, creating 'enabling conditions' that allow a system to find its own form." (Morgan 1989, pp. 109–110). This has a parallel that can be drawn with the State's declared desire to establish a new way of thinking about public action, through a different form of health governmentality. Therefore, in this health system reform project, the State seems to want to position itself as the project manager, setting the scope and objectives, delegating the project management to the actors in the field who are, in a way, the craftspeople in charge of building this new organization in each territory. This is based on a desire to institutionalize the co-construction between actors in the field and the collective development of responses in order to deal with the organizational problems of the territories. At the interface of national policy guidelines and the field is the RHA, a kind of "frontier actor" (Latour 2007, as cited in Aubert et al. 2020) or "relay translator" (Bloch and Hénaut 2014). The mobilization of RHA resources in support of these local projects is based on two axes: the consolidation of local coordination and the strengthening of change management capacities. The role of the departmental delegations, in particular, appears to be a major mechanism within a coordination territory, with the recommendations of the *Notat* report (2020), pertaining to the *Ségur de la santé*, recommending the generalization of "activity facilitators" within the latter.

The main challenge is therefore to change the current operating methods of professionals, who are still highly compartmentalized, toward a global and collective perception of the response to health needs. This change, which is above all human, requires the identification of "the way in which we succeed in obtaining the convergence and coordination indispensable to effective cooperation" (Crozier 1994, p. 62, author's translation), which in fact requires work on professional positions and the co-construction of "new common frames of reference" (Aubert et al. 2020, author's translation). This presupposes an explicit strategy for supporting change, which is underpinned by the implementation of an organizational learning process (learning to learn). Schön (1978) goes further by specifying that beyond the capacity to change institutions in response to environmental change, we must strive for the development of true "learning systems" capable of self-transformation. This means continuously re-examining the limits set by the organization in order to adapt them to changing needs, in a mechanism known as double-loop learning (Argyris and Schön 2002). In this approach, learning is no longer simply a mechanism for appropriating and anchoring change but is itself the very source of change.

With regard to these four basic principles that represent the foundations of self-organization through Morgan's perspective, the role of the RHA would be:

– To encourage the "stimulation of collective exploration" (Cazin 2017, as cited in Aubert et al. 2020, author's translation) between actors in the territories. This means, among other things, fostering inter-knowledge, dialogue and connections between actors belonging to different cultures, uniting them around a common goal (the patient pathway), providing meaning and setting up areas for comparing ideas and points of view, at the same time allowing for the regulation of possible conflicts.

– To establish a basis conducive to the emergence of such an approach, that is, a framework that is both versatile and sufficiently flexible, which provides a minimum foundation for structuring.

– To accompany the operational implementation of the results of this collective exploration, which should lead to a genuine reorganization of regional health actors.

– To facilitate the reconciliation between national public policies and problems on the ground.

– To be the guarantor of a form of overall coherence, at the local level, but also with regard to national guidelines.

Nevertheless, an important step remains to be taken, as it appears that the functioning of the RHA is part of a bureaucratic type of structure, which is still highly compartmentalized and verticalized to this day. Moreover, beyond the technical know-how inherent to the functioning of the RHA, these new obligations raise the question of the evolution of skills: technical know-how, which has been predominant up until now, must now be combined with the development of relational and even political skills, based more on interpersonal skills. A question arises: how can a bureaucratic type of structure, based on technical know-how, manage to support the formation of a flexible and organic type of self-organization?

Among the mechanisms on which the departmental delegations could rely to strengthen their role as regional facilitators and facilitate integration and connectivity between actors, we distinguish the transversal functions present in the territories (project managers, coordinators, regional facilitators, etc.). Indeed, with the rise of the pathway paradigm and a new form of public management that stems from it, these transversal functions have materialized through the appearance and structuring of new types of professions (Bloch and Hénaut 2014; Aubert et al. 2020). They are similar to "professional promoters" or facilitators intervening in a given territory (Bloch and Hénaut 2014), also taking the form of coordination mechanisms created to foster links between actors. Examples include the MAIA pilots, the PAERPA experiments, the Alzheimer's referents within the RHA in the elderly sector, the *E-parcours* project managers to support the use of digital tools, and mechanisms such as *communautés 360* ("360 communities") in the field of disability, the PTSM for mental health and the CPTS local professional health community for the organization of primary care in cities and so on. A multitude of actors and mechanisms have appeared in the healthcare ecosystem to support this organizational and regional dynamic, resulting in a "thousand-layer" effect of numerous entities with local coordination obligations, at various regional levels and with diverse borders.

In this chapter, we will focus more specifically on one of them: the DAC (*Dispositif d'appui à la coordination*) is a coordination support system in France, brought into being following the introduction of the 2019 Health Law. The creation of a DAC coordination support system for each coordination territory in the Ile-de-France region, resulting from the grouping of existing mechanisms (mainly health networks and MAIAs for the Ile-de-France region), should make it possible to facilitate complex healthcare pathways and organize care to support urban health professionals. They are also responsible for local coordination and for observing disruptions in care. The public authorities intend to set up the DAC coordination support systems as a true territory coordinator in order to compensate for the redundancy of existing mechanisms. We will assimilate them to the "reform entrepreneurs" as per the typology of Bloch and Hénaut, carrying out the dual function of team management internally and network facilitator externally.

A more specific analysis of the relationship between the departmental delegations and the DAC seems particularly relevant to us for several reasons. First, the DAC coordination support system is a new mechanism to be deployed by the RHA, whose local management in Ile-de-France is entrusted to the departmental delegations. This will make it possible to question the methods of change management implemented by the supervisory authorities, and the way in which they support the DAC coordination support systems in order to take their place in the healthcare ecosystem. Second, the DAC coordination support system has an obligation to coordinate at the level of the coordinating territory, since a department in the Ile-de-France region is made up of two or three coordinating territories on average. We will see what links are established between the supervisory authority (the departmental delegations) and the actors in the field (the DAC coordination support system), both of which are characterized by a certain type of professionalism, as highlighted by Bloch and Hénaut (2014): the translator for the departmental delegations (or facilitator within the *Ségur de la santé*) and the reform entrepreneur for the DAC coordination support system. The combination of these two professionalisms may constitute a mechanism for departmental delegations, in order to strengthen their position as local event facilitators in support of the DAC coordination support system.

4.3. Case studies

Our research work led us to focus on the case of the Ile-de-France region. The objective was to gain a better understanding of the relationships that currently exist in the territories between the two main parties, the RHA departmental delegations and the DAC coordination support systems (a new unified system to be set up, based on the convergence of already existing entities with a local coordination obligation), through the cross-analysis of four distinct "pairings" in different departments. These elements were put into perspective with the regional positioning of the RHA, with regard to the process of internal change led by the RHA, with the evocative title: "transforming oneself, in order to transform", on the one hand, and the nation-centric guidelines, on the other. The way in which the departmental delegations view these different elements can be characterized as the central axis of our analysis. It should be noted that this study was conducted during the Covid-19 health crisis. The impacts of this particular situation are highlighted.

The general management of the Ile-de-France RHA has decided to launch a change process in 2019, the particularity of which is that it is internally oriented and externally oriented. The objective is, as the name of this strategy indicates, to "transform ourselves in order to transform"[5]. The premise is that, in order to enable the operational deployment of the healthcare pathway paradigm throughout the territories, the State's regional health authorities must first be able to change their attitudes and the ways in which they operate, particularly with regard to those working in the field. Two priorities are put forward, internal decompartmentalization and localization, as well as new relationships with the actors: "to be the partners in the projects", "to listen to the actors in the territory" and "to have more confidence in the actors". The implementation of this strategy, impacted in 2020 by the arrival of Covid-19, involves a process known as the "double movement", consisting of a regionalization of certain activities and a change in the role of the departmental delegations in charge of local event facilitation and territory management. The aim is to give them more autonomy, more room to adapt, and a greater capacity for commitment so as to deploy the solutions they deem most relevant for their territory, with the support of more sustained recognition. In 2015, the reform that led to the merger of the regions had a strong impact on the RHA, reducing their number and establishing much larger geographical perimeters. This had accentuated the need to delegate more responsibilities locally to the departmental delegations (Evin 2019); however, Ile-de-France had not encountered this at the time of this research. Today, the national framework requires us to work differently with local actors in order to implement a new cross-sectoral health organization and more intensive coordination between stakeholders. This requires the RHA to be on the ground more, in contact with the operators, through the departmental delegations, which are at the heart of this dual movement. However, in practice, this is not so easy to implement, since the dual movement is more of a perspective than a clearly established process. In addition, it represents a real cultural shift for the RHA, as delegations have often taken a back seat to the headquarters' directorates. The aim is to reverse this trend by strengthening their function as local facilitators.

The ways in which the departmental delegations characterize their local event obligations are, on the surface, quite similar, suggesting the association of two complementary functions. These are analogous to those of an "orchestra conductor", whereby the delegations coordinate the "musicians", in this case the field workers, in order to guarantee overall coherence with regard to a "score" similar to the guidelines of public health policies, and that of the "weaver", in the sense of linking the players in order to encourage better knowledge between them and their

---

5 "Se transformer pour transformer", ARS Ile-de-France (June 2019).

rapprochement around a common work. Where variations appear between the departmental delegations is in the way they play this role, the resulting relationship with the actors in the field and the level of synthesis between these two functions.

Two of the departmental delegations interviewed put particular emphasis on the function of the conductor, reporting that, to date, there has been a profusion of actors and mechanisms, created by the legislator and the institutions, with a local event obligation, making this notion confusing and unclear. We are witnessing both overlapping phenomena and a type of dispersal of resources with a significant risk of competition between actors. For Delegation 1, which is more in line with a directive approach, the fundamental actors who must be in charge are the funders, that is, the supervisory authorities. The role of the delegation is therefore to define the strategy, to coordinate the sharing of a local diagnosis, to bring the actors to the table, and to define their scopes of action. The legitimacy of the supervisory authority comes, according to Delegation 1, from this function as "orchestra conductor", reinforced by the ability to issue authorizations and finance. Delegation 1 is not in a position of co-construction with the DAC coordination support systems: it believes that this is an important obligation of the latter, provided that they define the scope. It will be more of a controlling type relationship with the DAC coordination support system. Local coordination is a major issue for Delegation 1, expressed through a strong desire to manage and steer this aspect, which is a key element in the internal and external strategy of this delegation to establish its position vis-à-vis the RHA headquarters and health actors. From an operational point of view, it relies on the gradual recruitment of transversal local project managers, working together in close proximity.

Delegation 3 agrees with this desire to structure and clarify the scope of intervention for each. On the other hand, they feel that greater autonomy has been left to the actors. The delegation will be invited to represent the actions carried out by the DAC coordination support systems and will be kept informed of projects and their progress. However, the delegation expresses a point of vigilance, regarding the place of localized coordination in the obligations of the DAC coordination support system: it must not take precedence over coordination and individual support of the patients' health pathways. This delegation indicates that the current period, which has been marked by the Covid-19 health crisis, has not been conducive to the implementation of genuine, in-depth reflection on localized coordination. This role seems to be less embodied by the latter, as may be the case for the other three delegations we encounter.

In the case of Delegation 2, as with Delegation 1, localized coordination is a crucial issue, as shown by the choice of direct management by the Directorate. The added value of such an option is that it places localized coordination at a strategic level, representing a major symbol and making this issue of coordination and cooperation more credible, in order to convince and encourage the actors within the territory. She sees her role as that of a facilitator and promoter, this collective work appearing as an imperative, with regard to the paradigm of the healthcare pathway accentuated here by a particular territory context: a less urbanized department and a limited healthcare offer when compared to the other departments in the Ile-de-France region, in terms of structures and professionals. "I have the impression that they consider that the job requires them to define the ways in which they want to do it and that the RHA is there to help them work together and define themselves". This is based on a recognition of the role of the delegation in creating and interweaving connections, on the benefit perceived by the actors in taking part in such a process, and on the establishment of a trusting relationship on both sides. In this perspective, Delegation 2 sees itself as a "meta-coordinator" at the departmental level, wishing, at the local level, to strengthen the position of "opinion leaders or facilitators who are able to carry a public policy and listen to the actors: that there be some intermediaries in the cross-cutting process", such as the DAC coordination support system. While Delegation 1 puts more emphasis on the use of internal relays (territory project managers), Delegation 2 seems to want to rely on "operators", promoting their roots within the territory and legitimacy with actors on the ground.

The vision of Delegation 4 is quite similar in this respect, even if the relationship with the DAC coordination support system seems to be somewhat different (as we shall see later). The delegation places itself in the position of supporting the emergence or consolidation of communities of actors, such as the CPTS local professional, collective practice structures for example, constituting the basic supports of the new local organization of health, and it is the responsibility of workers on the ground to link them together by establishing, as it were, a network of connections. The positioning of these two delegations particularly echoes Morgan's model of self-organization in which they play a systemic coordination role, with the DAC coordination support systems acting as sub-departmental relays, intervening with the sub-systems that make up this complex organization of actors.

These various statements should be weighed against the period during which this survey was conducted. It took place during the Covid-19 health crisis, which mobilized the RHA teams enormously. Therefore, the statements made by the actors in the delegations often correspond to the ways in which they "idealized" and conceived of their role after the pandemic, even if they all note two main means of action that stand out and allow them, to date, to further affirm the real added value of their function, both with professionals in the field in their territories and with the regional level of the RHA. In several of the interviews we conducted, we sensed the ambiguity and complexity of the relationship with the regional level of the RHA, sometimes with the feeling that there was little room for maneuver.

The first of these mechanisms came from the State itself in the context of the latest 2019 Health Law, already mentioned above. Delegation 1 stated that it "really took some time to understand what role a local delegate could play", as policy definition was the prerogative of headquarters and they did not have control at the local level over the traditional regulatory mechanisms available to the supervisory authorities, particularly financial management: "Fortunately, *Ma santé 2022* came along and that was a turning point [...]. The DAC coordination support system, and then the CPTS in particular, boosted the delegation's position". Delegation 4 emphasized that mechanisms such as the CPTS and DAC coordination support systems perfectly illustrate this current trend: "They are more texts, laws that provide toolboxes, frameworks". This gives real room for the actors on the ground and the delegations to maneuver. On the other hand, one has to be weighed against the other. This autonomy of the delegation is not representative of all subjects, some of which lend themselves to it more than others. In addition, some interviewees note that Covid-19 has led to the recentralization of other issues. Finally, it is also dependent on the structure of the different business units at headquarters. At the regional level, the management of the DAC coordination support system is the responsibility of the Innovation Directorate, and more specifically of the DAC Convergence Obligations. The delegations interviewed recognize that the latter has lent itself to the game of dual movement, leaving it to the delegations to ensure local management, once the framework has been established. The latter was co-constructed with the actors, through the organization of working groups involving professionals from the coordination mechanisms and delegations, and resulted in the formalization of a regional reference framework. The intervention by head office is now limited to certain subjects only, and modulated according to the needs of each delegation.

The measures created by the *Ma santé 2022* Law forced the supervisory authorities to work differently in the territories and to shift the cursor to the departmental delegations. According to the RHA head office, "we would never have carried out the double movement if we did not have objectives and measures that obliged us to do so", because in order to achieve this, it necessitates working differently internally. In fact, these measures are based on a logic of decompartmentalization and co-construction between the actors in the field and are based on a strong territory-based approach. This requires the RHA to play a more supportive and coordinating role, which can only be done at a very local level. It is a matter of facilitating convergence between actors, encouraging the emergence of local initiatives, helping to structure them and supporting project leaders. From this perspective, the delegation plays a central role. Delegation 4 stated, in this sense: "We were often prescribers of many things. I find that, now, we are moreover collaborators". Here, the traditional regulation tools are no longer exclusively the only modalities of actions of an authority. They must be balanced with other types of relational mechanisms. Cooperation between actors, which is at the heart of the guidelines of the *Ma santé 2022* Law with mechanisms such as CPTSs, DAC coordination support systems, the creation of healthcare collectives and so on, cannot be decreed, can hardly be based solely on coercive mechanisms, or on the position of a "directive" chief of staff. We note that beyond the simple creation of mechanisms or structures, it is essentially a question of putting in place a support system to encourage collective work between actors, and this is where the added value of the delegation lies, as the classic regulation tools are of little use under these circumstances. The RHA can no longer work alone; it is obliged to lead, alongside the "musicians", and to develop new capacities similar to those of the "weaver" or "weaver of connections", if it hopes to deploy a new local health organization that is truly sustainable and efficient, corresponding to a profound cultural change. This invites the supervisory authorities to invent new mechanisms for mobilizing the actors who are fully responsible for the departmental delegations.

In this context, we note that the delegations interviewed adopt quite different behaviors with regard to the DAC coordination support system and use different coordination mechanisms. For two of them, the DAC coordination support system clearly appears to be an instrument of their strategy. This is particularly true of Delegations 1 and 2, where the delegation directors are directly linked to the DAC coordination support system. Nevertheless, their objectives are not the same. For Delegation 1, this consists of establishing and legitimizing its role as "orchestra leader" by taking control of mechanisms such as the DAC coordination support system. For Delegation 2, it is more a question of setting up some kind of external relay operator(s) to support its role as a territory coordinator, and of relying on the DAC coordination support system to bring about a change in its own internal organization, by integrating the transversality induced by the piloting of polythematic systems. The resulting relationship modes differ greatly.

Delegation 1 is part of a managerial approach to the DAC coordination support system, resulting in tighter control and a desire to control the internal organization of the programs, which is seen as interference by the latter, who are generally associations. The director of this delegation claims this directive management of the DAC coordination support system, who perceives it very negatively and judges it as too top-down, making it more difficult for the actors to adhere to it and get on board. We are part of a power struggle in which the DAC coordination support systems are trying to develop strategies for circumvention, in particular by grouping together the DAC coordination support system to form an alliance with the supervisory authorities, by relying on a strong board of directors, or by seeking external funding to develop their own projects, independent of the RHA.

Delegation 2, on the other hand, favors a logic of collaboration and support for the DAC coordination support system. This relationship seems to be based on a reciprocal mechanism. Delegation 2 emphasized the fluidity of relations with the

DAC coordination support system and a bond of trust, elements confirmed by the DAC coordination support system. A real form of convergence can be felt, where everyone seems to benefit: a "win-win" logic, where the delegation relies on the DAC coordination support system as a local facilitator within the territories, and where it allows the DAC coordination support system to be legitimized in their role, facilitating their local roots within the territories. This is reinforced by mutual recognition of the legitimacy of each role.

On the other hand, the lack of initiative on the part of the DAC coordination support system was regretted by Delegation 4 in its territory. This delegation is surprised that the DAC coordination support system did not seize the Covid-19 crisis as an opportunity to play a role and be recognized by other actors within the territory: they did not know how to "jump on the bandwagon" and "stand out". The delegation expects a form of proactivity, even entrepreneurship, from the DAC coordination support system. On their side, we do not perceive a great proximity with the delegation, the actors essentially left to their own devices and to organize themselves. Delegation 4 affirms the desire for a non-rigid framework, where the latter is in support. The DAC coordination support system seems to have room to maneuver and develop projects, this delegation referring, on several occasions, to the actors in the field as partners. This liberal system can quickly reach its limits, especially in the case where certain DAC coordination support systems, as is the case here, require reinforced support, to be evaluated according to the level of maturity of these systems, and the profiles and skills of the teams that comprise them. In the same way, the question as to the type of profiles needed by delegations to play the role of supporter and facilitator arises, which we will return to later.

This freedom for actors on the ground to self-organize has another facet, as illustrated by the presence of conflicts in certain territories between the actors of the DAC coordination support system, resulting from the merger of multiple entities. The delegations often intervene late, not always taking a clear position, which is a source of ambiguity and leaves room for power games. The RHA sometimes seems to have difficulty acting as an arbitrator, resulting in stagnant situations and making it more difficult to resolve the conflict. It seems vital for the delegations to find the right balance between the role of regulator and that of partner, since the RHA remains, above all, a guarantor for the implementation of public policy. Coercive and directive management does not, however, appear to be the solution, as we have seen in the case of Delegation 1, because in view of the spirit of the reforms to be carried out at present, this cannot be done without the support and participation of actors in the field. Innovations emanating from the field and public policies are intimately linked and self-sustaining. In this context, Bloch and Hénaut (2014) speak of "reciprocal prescriptions".

Furthermore, we note that the notion of operators to qualify the DAC coordination support system comes up in the speeches of several delegations. For example, Delegation 3 entrusts the young DAC coordination support system, still in the process of being structured, with the task of carrying out additional measures dedicated to the management of the Covid-19 crisis. Although the DAC coordination support system claims that this has allowed them to strengthen their local roots and recognition by the actors in the field and institutions, there is a real risk of weakening these DAC coordination support systems, which have not yet consolidated their internal foundations. We can clearly see that the DAC coordination support system is a sort of instrument of the delegation, which will choose, according to its strategy and current projects, to entrust certain subjects to the DAC, sometimes at the risk of diverting them from their initial obligations. This leads to a more central questioning of the guarantee of equality of service to patients throughout the regional territory (and even nationally), through shared obligations, while incorporating a certain level of flexibility to adapt to specific local needs. In this context, the regional level of the RHA has a major role to play in ensuring this balance and preventing possible abuses linked to an overly ambitious integration of the DAC coordination support system by certain delegations or to local policy issues, which would be to the detriment of their core obligations, the objectives defined by the legislator and the implementation of a national health policy. Through these elements, we return to the notion of a balance to be found for the supervisory authority, which must support and lead the implementation of a local health self-organization in the sense of Morgan (1989): a balance between its position as regulator and partner, a balance between regulatory and coercive coordination mechanisms and relational coordination mechanisms, and finally a balance between regional integration and local differentiation. This highlights the complexity, even ambiguity, of this new role.

Beyond these points of vigilance, it should be noted that for three of the delegations interviewed, Covid-19 was also an accelerator that allowed them to truly establish their place as territory coordinators, through better interaction with actors in the field and especially through the establishment of vaccination centers, which brought about genuine empowerment. For some, this was an opportunity to take a step forward: to go into the field and see first-hand the objective of the double movement. Delegation 2 went on to highlight how the context of the health crisis allowed them to foster a *rapprochement* between the DAC coordination support system and the actors in the hospital and private health field, who come from different cultures: "It's something we had never managed to do before". Covid-19 has enabled the delegation to promote links between these actors, leading to the formation of cooperation in the form of patient management protocols. Other delegations insist on the unprecedented nature of these initiatives: "This is the first time we have succeeded in doing this", "I would not have had the legitimacy to bring them together like this without the urgency provided by the pandemic".

The management of the Covid-19 crisis can be likened to a "mobilizing challenge" (Crozier 1994) due to which the actors became aware of the need to unite collectively. Crozier, illustrating this concept with the example of a company that had to make a profound change in strategy in order to guarantee its survival, states that: "The awareness of the crisis and the collective capacity to face it made the challenge plausible. [...] The impact was all the greater because what before seemed impossible, from the point of view of changing habits, turned out to be reasonable". It remains to be seen whether the delegations will be able to capitalize on these initial milestones and continue to sustain the dynamics that have been set in motion, with a view to bringing about this cultural change brought about by the healthcare pathway paradigm.

Three of the delegations interviewed emphasize the notions of legitimacy, credibility and recognition that this has given them, particularly with regard to health actors. For them, this constitutes an element to be put forward to the head office, which has much greater assets than before Covid-19, even if the delegations recognize that this depends on the subjects and that some of them are managed by the head office: "The crisis makes me say that it is obviously within territories that things are achieved", "the partners and then the elected representatives: we have a relationship that is without comparison, reinforced and given credibility". This is where the RHA's organizational flexibility and ability to readjust appears to be indispensable, in order to determine the most relevant level (regional, local or a combination of the two) for conducting a project, depending on the subject, its size, the issues at stake and the nature of the skills to be mobilized. The effective implementation of such a form of agility still seems difficult given the complexity of the relationship between these two levels, with delegations often expressing a lack of recognition from headquarters. Several of them have recourse to this perception, which, although it may seem stereotypical and is tending to evolve, is still a prevalent representation, assigning to delegations the role of executor and headquarters the role of elite strategist: "The head in headquarters and the legs in the delegations". For a certain number of the delegations interviewed, their voice is still not taken into account enough. However, all of the delegations interviewed emphasize that their role is far more complex than simply implementing policies. They describe the mobilization of very specific skills through local events: "This work requires reflection, a light touch that is not just a matter of field skills", "it requires the mobilization of skills, agility, identifying opportunities, the right moment". This echoes our previous comments, which compare the traditional regulatory mechanisms of the supervisory authorities with the complementary use of other types of relational mechanisms to mobilize the actors in the field, in light of the new rules of the game established by the healthcare pathway paradigm.

In addition to the legal and administrative expertise of the RHA and the traditional regulatory instruments, new skills must be incorporated that are related to interpersonal skills, with collaborators who are more like transverse and polythematic project managers with strong coordination skills. In our view, this is compounded by the need to be able to adapt to different contexts and types of stakeholders, ranging from healthcare professionals to local elected officials, and the ability to bring together and involve multiple stakeholders with different issues, which implies a high degree of relational skills. This implies profiles at the crossroads of politics and networking, with an intuition for seizing or creating opportunities, and a keen perception on the interplay of actors in a given territory. Several delegations highlighted the complexity and challenges encountered at the local level: links with elected officials, prefectures, ensuring exchanges with and between actors, ensuring the consistency of health democracy and so on, are among the difficulties of working in territories that are insufficiently described or accounted for.

Two of the delegations interviewed emphasized the ultimate abstract nature of their local coordination obligations and the competencies it underlies: "We have local coordination, which is a bit vague, while they [the regional level of the RHA] have the hard stuff: authorizations, finances". Here, we find the metaphor of the hard sciences (physics, mathematics, etc.), which are generally highly valued, versus the soft sciences (humanities and social sciences), which had to justify their credibility and gain legitimacy. This impression is all the more reinforced when we consider that alongside the delegations, multiple actors have this obligation: the DAC coordination support system, the CPTS and other regional mechanisms such as the *e-Parcours*. As one delegation pointed out, this single term is becoming a sort of "catch-all" that is difficult to interpret. The context in which the delegations were created in 2009 undoubtedly helps us to understand this situation, as the HPST law was not very specific about them, and the boundaries of the delegations' work appeared to be unclear. There is therefore a real need to conceptualize local coordination, which in our view can be a driving force by which delegations can demonstrate their added value, in the light of current policies structured around the healthcare pathway paradigm. In concrete terms, this means defining and describing what is currently involved in leading a local policy and the skills required in order to better recognize and characterize the role of the delegations and their complementarity with the skills of headquarters.

The difficult recognition of the delegations is also due to power issues with the actors at the regional level of the RHA. We will not describe them in this study, even though this is a component to be taken into account, as it could represent a decisive obstacle to this change in the stature of the delegations, which aims to enhance their value and give them more autonomy (on certain subjects). This implies questioning the place of each person on this chessboard and the relational system in effect. We are facing a profound cultural shift. As per the case study, the delegations are still very dependent on the regional level, which is organized into business units (care services, autonomy, etc.). This same structure is mirrored by the delegations, making it particularly likely that their human resources will be vertically integrated and that they will find themselves under the functional authority of the activity-based departments. In order to counter this form of control, some delegations are tending to develop more matrix-based structures by changing and decompartmentalizing their organizational charts, which may generate some resistance and generate uncertainty at headquarters.

Beyond a simple strategy of actors to gain autonomy, the introduction of transversality in organizations responds to the current challenges of transformation with the emergence of very open, polythematic, multi-professional and multi-sectoral systems, which the RHA must ensure the deployment and management thereof. The current structure of the RHA seems unsuited to this change. The introduction of transversality is not a new subject, but it is not so simple to implement in a concrete way, given the very great compartmentalization of extra-sectoral public policies. For several of the actors interviewed, the local delegations can be a decisive mechanism, based on the assumption that it is from these delegations that transversality could be introduced within the RHA. Indeed, performing their role as local facilitators, in line with the healthcare pathway paradigm, depends on the decompartmentalization of their skills and their subjects internally, local events and transversality being intrinsically linked.

4.4. Lessons learned

As we have seen, the RHA is faced with a reversal of its positioning. From being a prescriber, it must now become a partner in support of actors in the field, in order to give substance to the health pathway paradigm in the territories, while retaining its role as a State authority. Strengthening the local roots of the RHA appears to be a *sine qua non* condition for carrying out this function in the best possible way, which is underpinned by a detailed knowledge of actors in the ecosystem and the establishment of a close relationship with them. The departmental delegations, through the reaffirmation of their role as local coordinators, are on the front line to occupy what we will call this border post, seen as a determining point of passage, through which to ensure balance:

– between integration by the RHA headquarters, through the definition of a regional policy, and differentiation embodied by the departmental delegations, resulting in organizational diversity between territories due to specific local differences and contexts;

– between exploitation and exploration, that is, a form of organizational ambidexterity (Johnson et al. 2017) aimed at reconciling the consideration of resources, skills and alliances between actors existing in a territory and the implementation of a new form of local health organization, calling for a change.

The progression toward a form of cooperation between the departmental delegations and the actors in the field should, in theory, be the basis for a means of action for the latter to establish this position and facilitate the deployment of the transformations in progress, adapted to each territory. The initial insights provided by this research show us that support for mechanisms such as the DAC coordination support system can, first of all, appear to be an internal instrument for the departmental delegations to move the lines, by gradually integrating transversality into their organizations. This is justified by the management of this type of scheme, which is based on complex, very open courses of action, requiring the mobilization and combination of different expertise within delegations. Externally, the RHA must support and facilitate the implementation of self-organization among actors in the territories. The DAC coordination support system can, in this context, be considered a disseminator for the RHA, which would encourage connections between actors at the sub-departmental level, based on a principle of joint development that can hardly be decreed or imposed. This requires a change in the relationships between actors in the field and supervisory bodies, but also a questioning of the representations of each, via the construction of a shared-culture meeting zone, on the basis of collective organizational learning.

In our opinion, this depends on several prerequisites, referring in particular to the principle of "minimal critical specification" of the self-organization model defined by Morgan (1989), mentioned above. As a reminder, the person supporting the change, in this case the supervisors, must put in place favorable conditions to encourage the emergence of such a model. In this particular case, it seems to us that this requires financial security and the organizational stabilization of coordination mechanisms. In the past, the latter may have suffered from uncertainties toward the durability of their existence. It appears that one of the fundamental elements for initiating a change in the "supervisory authorities–actors in the field" relationship lies in making these sometimes fragile structures more reliable, often under associative status, carrying out public service obligations without having the status, and remaining subject to the dangers of changes in political orientations. The internal security of these structures would undoubtedly be a springboard for changing the relationship between the actors in the field and the authorities: as the vital requirements for the survival of these structures are assured, it is easier to project themselves into a logic of local projects. In fact, this changes the representation of the supervisory bodies by the actors in the field: from a regulatory supervision that "tightens the screws on the budget", to a supervision that supports the actors projects, as is the case with the CPTS, for example. That being said, this raises another question: how can structures be secured and stabilized without falling into a form of institutionalization and excessive standardization that could hinder the agility and flexibility specific to these structures and the need for a form of autonomy, a source of innovation?

Another factor comes into play, the national level, which is still very compartmentalized. This leads to the creation of overlapping guidelines and mechanisms that do not make the system easy to understand, or coherent, as we have seen with the function of local coordination, which the RHA must juggle, and in turn, so must the actors in the field. Beyond the compartmentalization specific to the RHA, this does not facilitate the relationship between the RHA and the actors in the field, which can be a source of tension.

In order to make these local coordination mechanisms genuine mechanisms for delegations to deploy the healthcare pathway paradigm, the profiles and skills present within these mechanisms must also be examined. In addition to the support that a delegation can provide, to facilitate their local roots and legitimacy, it appears that the DAC coordination support systems must also be actors in their own development, able to make proposals and enter into a form of "constructive" confrontation with the RHA. For its part, the RHA is positioned more than ever as the supporter of the change to be undertaken, while at the same time being subject to its own transformation since it is itself one of the stakeholders in this new local organization of healthcare. As we have seen, the regional delegations appear to be the relevant link for interaction with actors on the ground. The consolidation and recognition of their role, both by actors in the field and by RHA headquarters, require, in our opinion, the conceptualization of local event facilitation, which appears to be still too abstract a notion. To this must be added the description of the corresponding competencies, and the implementation, where necessary, of a real human resources policy to support the evolution of practices and to equip themselves with profiles in line with the new challenges facing the RHA. The departmental delegations are assets through which to promote the added value of their role: the national guidelines, through the *Ségur de la santé* and *Ma santé 2022*, and the Covid-19 health crisis have enabled the first milestones to be set, which must now be capitalized on.

Would the conclusion not be that it all takes time? The healthcare pathway paradigm poses a new way of understanding the healthcare system, relying essentially on the ability of actors to collaborate at all levels. This desire and intention are clearly reflected in institutional speeches and texts. It is now a question of moving from the professed theory to the theory of practice (Argyris and Schön 2002), which implies re-examining the relational system and the practices in place. It is above all a human, and therefore cultural, change that we are facing.

4.5. References

Argyris, C. and Schön, D.A. (2002). *Apprentissage organisationnel. Théorie, méthode, pratique*. De Boeck, Paris.

Aubert, I., Kletz, F., Sardas, J.C. (2020). Les nouvelles professionnalités au service de la territorialisation des politiques publiques sanitaires : l'exemple des chefs de projet e-parcours. *Colloque AIRMAP*, Montpellier.

Bloch, M.A. and Henaut, L. (2014). *Coordination et parcours. La dynamique du monde sanitaire, social et médico-social*. Dunod, Paris.

Bouquet, B. and Dubechot, P. (2017). Parcours, bifurcations, ruptures, éléments de compréhension de la mobilisation actuelle de ces concepts. *ERES*, 2(18), 13–23.

Crozier, M. (1994). *L'entreprise à l'écoute. Apprendre le management post-industriel*. Le Seuil, Paris.

Evin, C. (2019). 10 ans d'ARS : quel bilan d'une forme de déconcentration régionale ? *Regards*, 2(56), 105–116.

Fery-Lemonnier, E., Monnet, E., Prisse, N. (eds) (2014). Parcours de santé – Enjeux et perspectives. *ADSP*, 88, 11–56.

Johnson, G., Whittington, R., Regnér, P., Angwin, D., Scholes, K. (2017). *Stratégique*. Pearson, Montreuil.

Morgan, G. (1989). *Images de l'organisation*. Les Presses de l'Université Laval, Quebec.

Gray literature

ANAP (2009). La loi HPST à l'hôpital : les clés pour comprendre. Document, Ministère de la Santé et des Sports.

Agence Régional de la Santé Île-de-France (2022). Projet Régional de Santé 2018-2022. Document, Ministère de la Santé.

European Commission (2004). Loi No. 2004-810 du 13 août 2004 relative à l'assurance maladie.

European Commission (2009). Loi No. 2009-879 du 21 juillet 2009 portant réforme de l'Hôpital et relative aux Patients, à la Santé et aux Territoires, dite loi HPST.

European Commission (2016). Loi No. 2016-41 du 26 janvier 2016 de modernisation de notre système de santé.

European Commission (2019). Loi No. 2019-774 du 24 juillet 2019 relative à l'organisation et à la transformation du système de santé, dite Ma santé 2022.

HCAAM (2012). Rapport sur "l'Avenir de l'assurance maladie : les options du HCAAM". Report, HCAAM.

Ministère des solidarités et de la santé (2017). Plan national d'égal accès aux soins. Report, Ministère des solidarités et de la santé.

Ministère des solidarités et de la santé (2020a). Ségur de la santé : les conclusions. Report, Ministère des solidarités et de la santé.

Ministère des solidarités et de la santé (2020b). Rapport Notat "Ségur de la santé – Recommandations". Report, Ministère des solidarités et de la santé.

PART 2

Collective Intelligence and the Resilience of Healthcare Organizations

Introduction to Part 2

This section explores the interaction between collective intelligence and resilience in healthcare organizations. In order to do so, it draws on different yet complementary readings from researchers, health professionals and institutional actors from health authorities. It combines theoretical readings on the challenges of collective intelligence in the field of healthcare, with case studies on the manifestations of such intelligence and the challenges that accompany it.

In Chapter 5, Jan Mattijs and Vincent Mabillard focus on the trends of co-creation and collective intelligence in relation to e-health, as well as on the issues related to them, notably concerning the transformation of the relationship between patients and practitioners, the changes in the practices and organization of work in the healthcare field, the ethical and legal challenges, as well as those related to the involvement of patients or citizens. After noting that there is little literature on the intersection between co-creation and the digitization of healthcare, the authors embark on an empirical research work that does not aim to deepen the existing literature, but instead to complement it, in particular by exploring any incompleteness or contradictions that appear within it. Specifically, the tensions between exciting technological prospects and concerns about governance linked to ethical and relational concerns, the need to envisage multiple and interdisciplinary approaches, as well as a co-creation dynamic wherein the question of e-health is addressed, and even the absence of the patient from technological developments in e-health that only attribute to them the role of consumer.

In Chapter 6, Fatima Yatim looks at the figure of the patient educator emerging in France, following the *Ma santé 2022* reform, which institutionalizes the integration of patients in the training of health professionals. She shows that this role, which aims to change the place of users in the health system by questioning its

Introduction written by Aline Courie-Lemeur.

functioning, is placed at the crossroads of multiple identity issues, which are at once professional, political and social. It attributes professional identity to the role of the patient educator who draws their legitimacy from experiential expertise, the experience of illness and knowledge of the healthcare system, without coming into conflict or competition with the scientific and clinical legitimacy of health professionals. It links political identity to the promotion of democracy in health and raises, at the level of social identity, the issue of acceptance that users/citizens have of the relationship between healthcare providers and patients.

In Chapter 7, Béatrice Pipitone and Hélène Marie present the case of *Alliance Santé 77*, which deals with the organizational changes that occurred at the Ile-de-France Regional Health Agency (RHA) in connection with the management of the Covid-19 pandemic, both internally and with respect to its partners. They point to the fact that in order to manage the pandemic, RHA staff had to work on new public policies, which led to organizational changes. An atypical organization was created during this crisis period and made possible strategic and operational consultation and cooperation with local health actors. They show that this organizational innovation can be a mechanism for improving the efficiency of the healthcare system, by allowing for the implementation of public actions that are more localized and better adapted to the needs of patients and professionals, while facilitating their local appropriation. They highlight an innovative role for the RHA, as a local coordination structure. They conclude on the major role of partnership relations and mutual aid in the resilience of the healthcare system, and on its solidity in the face of new challenges, such as the Covid-19 pandemic. They identify points of vigilance and mechanisms that can be used to facilitate the deployment of such organizational innovations.

In Chapter 8, Laurent Cenard discusses the case of the "alliance-maker", presented as a future key actor dedicated to orchestrating collective action and the implementation of healthcare coordination mechanisms to become more resilient. This function already exists in large international companies and even within very small companies. The author seeks to show its necessity for the construction and piloting of DAC (*Dispositif d'appui à la coordination*) coordination support systems, where managers will have to rethink their methods of collaboration in order to create links, allowing for more fluid and effective relationships between actors. He points out that this function already exists in the DAC coordination support system, predominantly attached to the director, who may not be very aware of it, and that is why it is not very well structured. He expresses his interest in the qualities of the "alliance-maker" and focuses on their training. He identifies the skills and abilities necessary to ensure such a function, which can be perceived as a mechanism to improve resiliency, and which is structured around knowledge, know-how, and interpersonal skills.

Co-creation, Co-production and Collective Intelligence in Digitized Healthcare Policies

In recent discussions about management in the public sector, co-design and co-production of services are a very significant trend, both theoretically and practically. These co-creation efforts aim at simultaneously improving service delivery and legitimacy. At the same time, digitization is extending in public services. Beyond using information technologies (IT) for production, public organizations are increasing their use of social media and other citizen- or service-oriented platforms, not to mention the burgeoning use of artificial intelligence (AI). This chapter focuses on the combination of these trends – co-creation, collective intelligence and digitization – in the field of healthcare. Emerging themes revolve around technological developments, the transformation of patient–practitioner relationships, changes in care working practice and organization, ethical and legal challenges and ultimately challenges about involving patients or citizens in e-health. The latter aspect indicates a discrepancy between the promises of co-creation, the prevailing optimistic approach to digitization in healthcare and the low level of involvement of patients in technological developments.

5.1. Context and issues

Digitization is a core feature of our societies, and the last few decades have been influenced by the strong development of new information and communication technologies (ICTs). These technologies have a direct impact on our lives, through a wide range of activities that now depend on them. The opportunities presented by

Chapter written by Jan MATTIJS and Vincent MABILLARD.

this shift have been touted all over the world, for practically all sectors, in a surge of technological optimism. New technological systems and platforms are increasingly adopted by public administrations to better interact with their citizens, provide services more efficiently and modernize their daily operations. They are creating an ecosystem in which governments are connected to almost all stakeholders. In this vein, being absent from digital networks or not using digital tools would place them in a critical situation. This has a significant impact on public policies since citizens may be more deeply involved in policy implementation. Finally, decision-making processes will also be affected by digitization, especially through algorithms that guide or automate decision-making.

In healthcare, this surge of technology-driven optimism is also visible. For example, a report from the OECD (2019) states that "health lags far behind other sectors in harnessing the potential of data and digital technology, missing the opportunity to save a significant number of lives and billions of dollars". There is a hope that digitizing healthcare can help meet its numerous challenges, including a decrease in human resources (we have seen a decrease in the number of physicians, especially in primary care, in multiple countries); an increasing number of patients, due to chronic diseases and an increase in life expectancy; and a decrease in financial resources (Menvielle et al. 2017). Against this backdrop, the alleged benefits and expectations raised by the new technologies are the key factors leading the current digital transformation. They include economic and efficiency gains for multiple stakeholders, better quality care, high levels of patient trust, as well as better doctor–patient coordination and data security. The Covid-19 pandemic has accelerated this digitization drive.

However, the digital transformation has raised several challenges related to organizational change, privacy, the transformation of the patient–doctor relationship (Mabillard et al. 2021) and patient involvement in the development of ICTs. For instance, the recording and sharing of personal data holds promises of more efficiency, but it automatically poses the question of data protection and IT security. The use of algorithms aims at improving decision-making processes, but issues of discrimination and inequality arise. The technology-intensive health services risk disempowering both healthcare workers and patients. Specifically, the creation, implementation and usage of connected devices raise a debate about the actual engagement of patients. Consequently, the aim of this chapter is to provide a systemic view of the issues raised by digitization in healthcare policies, and to disentangle the tensions between user involvement, (collaborative) modes of governance and technological progress.

First, in our theoretical overview, we will compare definitions and conceptualizations about the design and management of collaborative digitization. Starting from mainstream public administration (PA)/public management (PM) research, we will retrace the history and dialectics of salient conceptualizations of governance, co-creation, co-production, collective intelligence and digitization. Second, in our literature review, we will focus on healthcare policies more specifically, leading to categories of emerging issues and illustrating the knowledge gaps and tensions that remain between these connected concepts. Finally, these gaps and tensions will be discussed, providing scholars with new insights, and inviting them to work on an interdisciplinary research agenda.

5.2. Theoretical and conceptual overview

The expected benefits of digitization in democratic societies are directly connected to two phenomena: technological developments, of course, but also (and perhaps more importantly) the redefinition of the relationship between authorities and citizens, and the respective roles assigned to them. Digitization, co-creation and collective intelligence therefore fit into a changing context of state administrations. Since the late 1970s, there has been an evolution from traditional public administration to new management and governance models, where the focus shifted from political compliance and legality to performance, from a taxpayer and service user perspective (the "new public management" (NPM) movement), and then to stakeholder involvement based on networks, social practices and activities (Bevir 2012). For this latest evolution, Osborne (2006) coined the term "new public governance" (NPG) in which trust and/or relational contracts are central in networks of actors forming "the plural world that now comprises the environment of public services and of [public sector organizations]" (p. 384).

These general governance approaches are now influenced by technological change. The shift from NPM to a period marked by the predominance of technology was seminally summarized by Dunleavy et al. (2006) as follows: a focus on (A) *regeneration*, through agencification rollback, re-governmentalization and the reengineering of back-office functions; (B) *needs-based holism*, through agile government processes and interaction-based relationships with citizens; and (C) *digitization processes*, through electronic services, automated processes and increased co-production. Recent contributions (e.g. Meijer et al. (2021)) added the rise of AI. In all cases, new behaviors seem to derive from social norms and changing cultural administrative traditions rather than technological determinism per se, justifying the status of "digital-era governance" (DEG) for this technology-driven evolution.

We will first review the elements of public governance that operationalize the active involvement of multiple stakeholders in public policy: co-production, collective intelligence and co-creation. In a second step, we will see in what way digitization impacts these collective processes, before proposing a synthesis that will guide the literature review.

5.2.1. *Co-creation, collective intelligence and co-production of public services*

According to Ansell and Torfing (2021), new forms of public governance are needed to address four main challenges of our time: (A) a public service problem (*increasing citizen expectations vs. limited resources*), (B) a policy problem (*political and institutional factors vs. robust policy solutions to complex societal problems*), (C) a community problem (*erosion of social cohesion and social capital vs. self-organized solution for local communities*) and (D) a democratic problem (*political polarization and disenchantment vs. liberal representative democracy*). Co-creation, defined as "the process through which a broad range of interdependent actors engage in distributed, cross-boundary collaboration in order to define common problems and design and implement new and better solutions" (Ansell and Torfing 2021, p. 6), may well provide an answer to these challenges.

The cautious condition is worth noting at this point: while the engagement of customers, users or citizens seems *prima facie* a good idea that might be defended on its own symbolic or political grounds, there remains a dearth of evaluation. This is all the more important if, as shown in the Introduction, digitized co-creation faces tensions and contradictions or may even backfire. Furthermore, our analytical perspective requires conceptual clarity. However, the terminology is inconsistent: authors use different conceptualizations across co-creation, collaborative governance, co-production and collective intelligence. Significant differences arise notably from the scope of affected activities and the underlying definition of value. These aspects deserve clarification for the purpose of our discussion.

Ostrom et al. (1978) pioneered the work on co-production of public services. But co-creation also emerged in the private sector, since "co-creation between firms and consumers has the potential for creating value because value creation is increasingly focused on user experience rather than on the product per se" (Ansell and Torfing 2021, p. 33). In this regard, an authentic relationships between companies and consumers was sought, and consumers were to be seen as joint problem solvers with businesses. This evolution from a goods-centric to a service-centric logic can also be found in the public sector. Alford (2014) extends Ostrom's preliminary work by pointing out that the production of goods (products), and not only services, should still be considered. This remains consistent with the more materialistic overtone carried by "production", where co-production emphasizes the implication of users in the final delivery. Value then implicitly lies in everyday use, experience and outcomes.

Bovaird and Loeffler (2012) insist on the potential of co-production for creating public value, that is, trigger behavior change or prevent societal problems from happening in the future. They define co-production as "the provision of services through regular, long-term relationships between professionalized service providers (in any sector) and service users or other members of the community, where all parties make substantial resource contributions". Interestingly, they provide examples of diverse types of co-production, for example, co-planning of policy (*deliberative participation*), co-managing of services (*parents–school governors*) and co-delivery (*nurse–family partnership*). Nabatchi et al. (2017) go on to distinguish different phases of the service cycle: co-commissioning, co-design, co-delivery ("which is most in line with the traditional view of co-production") and co-assessment. As we can see, although Bovaird and Loeffler or Nabatchi and her colleagues have a wide scope in mind, they stick to "co-production" as the general umbrella concept, consistent with Ostrom's seminal work.

In their literature review on co-creation and co-production, Voorberg et al. (2015) explain that they are often defined in similar terms but note that the literature on co-creation puts more emphasis on strategic value creation. Torfing et al. (2019) further argue that although co-production may improve service delivery, it does not engage in broader innovation dynamics.

How can collective intelligence be situated with respect to the co-creation/ co-production debates within the PA/PM literature? It originates from diverse research and practices: social psychology and organizational research on group performance, more applied work on strategic consultancy or IT-supported organizational learning, and sectoral applied research (notably in social work intervention: Foudriat (2021)). Some of these strands have been weaved into a cross-cutting, interdisciplinary collective intelligence research program (Malone and Bernstein 2015). While this body of knowledge did not originate in PA/PM, it does find immediate applications there (Mair et al. 2019). In many ways, this collective intelligence program overlaps with the discussion about co-creation processes, but with an emphasis on the exploration and deliberation stages. It also adds a distinctly pragmatic perspective, focusing on the design of decision-making rules, purposeful collective processes, with a view to decision-making effectiveness and legitimacy. Co-production in the sense of joint service delivery is less the focus of collective intelligence, except in activities in which exploration and decision-making are inseparable from core operations (e.g. medical diagnosis).

In what follows, we will use co-creation as the "umbrella concept" that encompasses shared agenda-setting, co-design, collective intelligence and co-production in all their various scopes. In doing so, specific attention should always be given to defining the specific process through which co-creation occurs, depending on its expressed purpose, its place in a design and delivery sequence, the implied actors and its procedural and technical infrastructure.

5.2.2. Digitization in the public sector

The current practice of "digitization" (or "digitalization") has roots that go back to the early days of IT after World War II. Computing has historically been presented as a disruptive reform instrument that would by itself deeply impact the structure and operations of organizations, originally to bring more efficiency and improve both individual and organizational performance (Kraemer and King 2006). Later calls for opening up governments (McDermott 2010) refer to a more encompassing agenda, including transparent administrations, increased collaboration within the public sector, increased citizen participation and an improved citizen–state relationship, now labeled "collaboration". This mode of governance built on the open government notion relies on networks, the concept of "government as a platform" and a strong focus on support, dialogue and collaboration (De Blasio and Selva 2016).

Collective intelligence also has a digital avatar that emerged from the hope that the availability and interactivity of knowledge through the Internet would automatically improve collective intelligence – the catchword "crowdsourcing" illustrated that optimism. Later authors recognized that the procedures had to be right so the "wisdom of crowds" did not turn into foolishness (Bonabeau 2009). This technology-driven optimism has recently blended into a more general recognition of the importance of digitization for collective intelligence: Malone and Bernstein's (2015) handbook devotes two chapters to tech, and it is tightly embedded into Mulgan's (2018) presentation.

Current digitization processes claim to be different from earlier e-government propositions. The term "digitization" as it is understood here encompasses the uptake and usage of multiple technologies, including tracking devices in healthcare, digital self-service and new systems of data collection and diffusion. The digitization process goes beyond the adoption of a particular technology, since it extends to public management and governance principles, including the improvement of the state–citizen relationship (Dunleavy et al. 2006). Even so, digitization remains dependent on the political, institutional and organizational contexts that determine its effectiveness; there is no technological determinism (Castelnovo and Sorrentino 2018).

With a more analytical perspective, digitization takes on various (technical) shapes and has different scopes and produces diverse consequences depending on the stakeholders. General assertions are difficult to defend. In his review of the main technological developments that influence co-production and co-creation in the public sector, Lember (2018) warns that the overall highly optimistic mood should be questioned and debated, since the effects of the digitization can vary greatly according to the context, the type of technology and the issues at stake. Sound, analytical discussion and assessment are made all the more difficult by the conceptual heterogeneity in the field of e-government. Aceto et al. (2018) set out to clarify the categories in the field of e-health, suggesting taxonomies that are of wider relevance, distinguishing actions with different scopes for IT services: those aiming "merely" to communicate, those also adding sensing, those including processing, or extending to actuation, that is, producing effects in the physical world (p. 133). Lember (2018) shows that social media have been extensively investigated, as well as the technologies traditionally associated with the development of smart cities (e.g. devices such as sensors). But additional technologies can also affect co-production indirectly or hold the potential to transform co-creation and co-production. Hence, the discussion needs to consider not just the technical scope, but also indirect organizational and social effects.

Let us take three examples of critical discussion of social effects. First, the digital transformation should empower citizens. Indeed, it is expected that new technologies will generate more shared sovereignty and responsibilities between public organizations, companies and especially citizens. However, Kitchin (2016) writes that "automated management facilitates and produces instrumental and technocratic forms of governance and government". Second, digitization promises more participation and inclusiveness. However, the digital divide and digital literacy often pose underdiscussed problems. Third, new technologies are also often praised for their potential to increase efficiency. This is the case for electronic health records, which can establish fast and accurate communication. Nevertheless, successful implementation still relies on political willingness, leadership, the uptake of compliance reports and so on (Silow-Caroll et al. 2012).

Finally, co-creation can play a role of its own within digitization. As noted above, digital services can support co-creation processes, but is this just a matter of providing co-creators with the right digital tool out of the box? A distinction needs to be made between co-creation supported through digitization, and the more upstream or concurrent *co-creation of the digital services themselves*. While these can be conceptually and practically held apart as a special case of the co-design/ co-delivery distinction (Nabatchi et al. 2017), they are interdependent when the involvement of users in the design process becomes a prerequisite of the digital service's effectiveness (Mettler et al. 2020).

5.2.3. *Co-creation and digitization in healthcare*

In the healthcare sector, there are elements of the landscape outlined above for co-creation and digitization in general government. In healthcare also, co-creation and/or co-production have been identified as essential to effectiveness and legitimacy, independently of digital services. Concerns span the scope from health policy definition (Rantamäki 2017) and service design (Donetto et al. 2015) to professional practice and patient empowerment (Singh et al. 2017), and include various stakeholders, both on the professional and patient or citizen sides (Hardyman et al. 2015; Eriksson and Hellström 2021).

As for digitization in healthcare, the issue is so broad that it has been studied in diverse fields and addressed in many different ways. Reference books squarely on the subject of digitization have been published (see McLoughlin et al. 2017; Menvielle et al. 2017). In the public administration and management literature, digitization in healthcare is primarily addressed as a tool to further reinforce partnerships and encourage more participation from citizens, with the State playing the role of a facilitator (Simonet 2011). It has also been studied through international comparisons (Kizito and Magnusson 2020). The coordination between multiple stakeholders is also underlined by Cucciniello et al. (2015), since complex innovations require efficient coordination between the actors involved. Beyond these fairly familiar concerns, a wealth of highly technical literature also quickly becomes apparent, with specific publication outlets (*International Journal of Medical Informatics*, *Journal of Medical Internet Research*, *Perspectives in Health Information Management*, etc.) on top of general medical or policy journals.

It emerges that adding healthcare as the empirical field presents us with a specific context that needs to be made explicit: the sensitivity of health as a matter of lived experience, the importance of professions, the ethical implications, the institutional structures and so on. We cannot assume that the intersection of co-creation and digitization here is just a smaller-scale image of the general discussion about digitization and co-creation in government. The discussion above has allowed us to identify major topics, mainly:

– the scope and various forms of co-creation in public policies and services;

– the legitimizing or democratic potential and effectiveness of co-creation;

– IT-driven technological optimism versus the complexities of policy implementation;

– the significance of user involvement, both in design and delivery;

– the organizational and social consequences of digitization.

However, each of these now needs to be re-examined in the context of healthcare.

5.3. Literature review

Starting from a more inductive method, the literature review complements the theoretical overview and pursues two main objectives: (A) create categories to better understand how digitization in healthcare is developed in the literature and (B) compare the findings with the elements highlighted above. This will allow for the identification of potential gaps, the critical discussion of these gaps and the provision of possible paths for future research in the field.

Given the breadth of the topics outlined at the close of our theoretical discussion, our literature review cannot be comprehensive. It can still be systematic enough to limit selection bias and yield significant results, if combined with careful reading and analysis. Our eligibility criteria include: (1) *Publication status*: due to the proliferation of technical reports and official documents on digitization in healthcare, we narrow down the search to papers published in peer-reviewed journals only. (2) *Publication year*: the recent development of e-health and the technological (re)evolution led us to focus on the last decade – our literature review concentrates on contributions published between 2011 and 2021. (3) *Language*: only publications in English were selected in our literature review, especially due to the difficulty in translating certain key terms. (4) *Topic of digitization in healthcare*: the keywords should include digitization AND healthcare policies, co-creation or collective intelligence. Using digitization in healthcare would have only led to the compilation of contributions with a purely technical focus. (5) *Study design*: empirical, conceptual and theoretical studies are included in our literature review, since we are interested in the material that will allow us to better draw a global picture and identify paths for future research. The research has been conducted on Google Scholar using the keywords mentioned above.

The search yielded 38 relevant contributions, as shown in Table 5.1. Based on the analysis of their content, we clustered them into four categories that reflect the central issues addressed: (A) transparency and privacy, (B) interactions with patients (digitization and care), (C) innovation, devices and technology and (D) new jobs and organizational change.

(A) The first category, counting $n = 9$ articles, revolves around privacy and transparency. In this regard, DesRoches (2020) argues that "information transparency in healthcare has become a pressing legislative and regulatory issue" (p. 533). Access to information is easier nowadays for patients because of third-party apps on which they will find consultations, discharge history, laboratory and pathology reports and so on. Studies in the United States have shown that consulting such information helped most patients to remember their care plans, to better understand their medication, and make them more likely to take their medication. However, this push for transparency, especially through increased digitization, has raised many privacy concerns. Theodos and Sittig (2020) argue that the privacy of patient information has been mostly regarded as an ethical rather than a regulatory issue up to now, so legislation on privacy did not evolve as quickly as new technologies, so much so that "many consumers are never aware that their information is breached, shared or sold to a third party" (p. 4). Harvey and Harvey (2014) add that key principles such as confidentiality, integrity and availability should always be included in technological development and use of mobile apps to ensure privacy. In the same vein, Azad et al. (2019) affirm that issues of data storage, access, acquisition and analytics, as well as communication protection, should always be guaranteed for privacy to be protected in healthcare. More generally, transparency and privacy more particularly are often regarded in the literature as key concerns of digitization processes, systems and devices in healthcare policies.

(B) The second category (n = 5) relates to digitization and care in the relationship between patients and healthcare professionals. This theme can also be related to transparency issues, since devices and new technologies, while they promise more transparency, can also negatively impact the patient–doctor relationship. Indeed, the knowledge deficit and patient's appetite for better understanding (and empathy) remains often addressed by physicians through a close relationship with their patients (Mabillard et al. 2021). Regarding quality of care, useful, relevant, but cautious integration of digital technologies can better individualize therapies. While the beneficial effects of digitization are discussed, Steinhubl and Topol (2015) argue that "the digitization of healthcare can eventually help build a markedly improved physician–patient relationships, allowing greater time for interaction when a patient requires the care of a physician" (p. 7). From a slightly different perspective, Menendez et al. (2020) point to the pitfalls of digitizing health services for patients, especially for the neediest patients, who often appear to be digitally illiterate, have no access to new technologies, or who are not willing to engage with ICTs. More generally, potential benefits and downsides of digitization for the patients and healthcare professionals is discussed in the literature, despite the relatively low number of papers in which it is the main issue.

(C) The third category (n = 16) gathers contributions that focus on innovation, devices and technology. It refers mainly to technological development, system interoperability, efficiency gains related to progress in ICTs, the creation of new devices and coordination issues, which are envisaged from a technology-oriented angle in most cases. For instance, Raghavan et al. (2021) explain that cloud computing is being increasingly adopted by governments to deliver citizen-centric services. This translates into cloud-based mobile apps, and healthcare is no exception to this development. The main issues addressed concern technology policies, readiness and data management. Data privacy is also tackled, showing that our categories can overlap in certain ways and that transversal topics are discussed by scholars with various backgrounds and skills. Indeed, privacy can also be addressed through a more technological focus, as shown in Ben-Assuli's 2015 article, which focuses on electronic health records and information exchange networks. In line with most contributions mentioned above, advantages as well as pitfalls of the digitization of healthcare are presented: "Promising as it may have appeared, the transition from paper-based medicine to computerized, digital formats over the last decade have been fraught with practical, legal, medical and financial difficulties that can dramatically undercut potential increases in efficiency and quality" (p. 287). In addition, innovation in healthcare can be seen as a complex implementation process that requires close coordination (Cucciniello et al. 2015).

(D) Finally, the fourth category ($n = 8$) covering new jobs and organizational change gathers the most articles relating to collective intelligence (five out of six). Digitization's impact on healthcare stakeholders starts with healthcare professionals themselves. Haag et al. (2018) state that students in medicine are often under-equipped to address the future challenges of digital medicine and to make "meaningful use of digital teaching and learning technologies" (p. 1). The global change in the sector results from "technological innovation along with new expectations and perceptions of healthcare services, inter-professional relationships and profession–state relations" (Bossen et al. 2019b, p. 77). Digitization has led to the emergence of new professions (mainly technicians) and role changes that have been summarized by Nancarrow and Borthwick (2005) as follows:

– diversification (new and/or complementary tasks performed by professionals);

– specialization (increased level of expertise);

– vertical substitution (tasks adopted across hierarchical boundaries);

– horizontal substitution (tasks adopted across same-level professional boundaries).

5.4. Lessons learned

Our review of a sample of the literature has limitations that need to be acknowledged, such as the use of a single search engine and use of a simple set of search terms. A wider and more flexible search does return additional and very relevant articles (some of which have already been used in the theoretical and conceptual discussion). Nevertheless, the literature at the intersection of co-creation and digitization in healthcare is not that abundant, and our review paves the way for a discussion that will also rely on additional, less academic sources. Our discussion will be illustrated with empirical evidence that is starting to emerge from our current research (see the cases in Mabillard and Mattijs (2022)), since we are convinced that empirical work will be the next most fruitful research step rather than deepening the existing literature.

5.4.1. *From multi-disciplinarity to interdisciplinarity*

The literature review points to the necessity of considering multiple approaches when we address the issue of digitization in healthcare. The low number of contributions in the field of PA/PM on the issue of digitization in healthcare compared to articles published in journals from other disciplines (ethics in medicine, medical informatics and information systems, mainly) highlights the need to confront key public (digital) governance concepts with theoretical and empirical developments observed in other fields. Technological issues, for instance, lead to problems and challenges that can be better addressed by specialists, and that can shed a different light on digitization as it is currently tackled in the PA/PM literature. However, certain aspects are also addressed in most categories presented above and partly in PA/PM research, such as privacy, legal aspects and ethical considerations about the development of digital tools and services. Based on our findings, interdisciplinarity is therefore needed to better understand the phenomenon of digitization in healthcare and to design better policies.

5.4.2. *Tensions between bright technological prospects and governance worries*

Contradictions in the literature appear when we confront the positive, enthusiastic perspective on digitization with ethical and relational concerns. This is for instance the case for automation of data treatment and telemedicine versus the physician–patient relationship, and more broadly the position of the "care" issue in the digital transformation of healthcare. The co-creation aspect also potentially conflicts with privacy: how do we deal with patient data when engaging the patients in innovation? In this regard, our findings highlight a clear gap between researchers and practitioners that enthusiastically embrace new technologies and those who insist on the downsides of technological evolutions. The downsides are mostly divided into two categories: the digital divide (no access or lack of digital literacy) and opacity in the development of technological tools (especially algorithms). They are rooted in political and/or business interests that clash with ethical and privacy concerns. Such downsides can be regarded as threats to the democratic aspirations of the governance rationale as described in the PA/PM literature. However, these worries do not seem to be key concerns in our review of the literature. The technological determinism identified in certain contributions carries the risk, in our opinion, of removing democratic or legitimacy concerns that can impede policy implementation and/or the adoption of certain devices. Broader discussions about achieving sustainable "computer-supported collective action" (Valetto et al. 2015) go some way toward bridging psycho-social needs and technological possibilities, but still tend to discuss them as separable steps, hinting again at the difficulty of empirically grounded transdisciplinary work.

5.4.3. *Lack of discussion on co-creation in e-health*

The dynamics of co-creation and co-production are more absent than expected when we focus on digitization in healthcare. In recent key theoretical contributions on the digital shift in public administration, stakeholders are a central concern (see section 2.1). However, the narrower literature on healthcare digitization policies and management is dominated by privacy–transparency and technical concerns. This phenomenon can be partly explained by two factors: on the one hand, the enthusiasm surrounding the promises of digitization leads to focus on uptake issues, leaving certain parties (e.g. citizens) out of the picture; on the other hand, the salience of the privacy issue leads to an overrepresentation of this aspect in the current literature, trumping the co-creation/co-production issue. Empirically, the lack of co-creation points to the rather closed processes of digital development in the healthcare sector, as can be seen in the design of the unified Electronic Health Record in Belgium. This raises the issue of users' involvement in these processes, even though healthcare professionals are much better represented than patients in e-health developments.

5.4.4. *What is patient involvement?*

Finally, in the literature we review, the patient is either absent from technological developments or regarded as a final beneficiary of such developments. The focus on service providers and purely technological considerations eludes the issue of the digital divide and leaves the question of patient involvement in innovation unanswered. Casual empirical evidence suggests that the lack of patient involvement in co-creation is not just an academic artifact that can be noticed in a literature review. For example, Nicholas and Broadbent (2015), in a report for a UK nonprofit, stress the importance of patient organizations as knowledge brokers and discuss the supporting digital tools. The European Patients Forum (2015) advocates for more patient involvement in the EU medical devices legislation, and the Belgian League of healthcare users reports on the digital divide (LUSS 2019).

As a tentative conclusion, our results point to a broader issue of a lack of strategic and policy thinking about the digitization of healthcare. Existing e-health policies tend to be focused on specific service development and led by professional perceptions (by IT and medical staff) that ongoing IT developments are useful. Indeed, they probably are, but patients and citizens take the back seat (there are exceptions, like the process led in the French National Health Conference about connected health (Conférence Nationale de la Santé 2018). Of course, the scientific publications we mainly reviewed are not a direct reflection of government practice, but given the relatively good coverage of neighboring topics, the gap we observe is significant. A lack of analysis of user needs and social effects is difficult to square with a consistent strategy, especially in the context of contemporary public governance models that emphasize co-creation. Scientific research needs to catch up with user involvement in e-health.

5.5. Appendix

Category	Articles	Main focus	Main discipline(s)
Transparency and privacy (A)	Angst, C.M. (2009). Protect my privacy or support the common-good? Ethical questions about electronic health information exchanges. *Journal of Business Ethics*, 90, 169–178.	Balancing the public good aspect with individual interests (ethical issues)	Management
	Azad, M.A. et al. (2019). A privacy-preserving framework for smart context-aware healthcare applications. *Transactions on Emerging Telecommunications Technologies*, 38, e3634.	Protection of sensitive user data	Computer science
	Chang, J. (2018). Privacy and security concerns in online health services. *Applied Economic Letters*, 25(19), 1351–1354.	Link between use of e-health and security concerns	Economics
	DesRoches, C.M. (2020). Healthcare in the new age of transparency. *Seminars in Dialysis*, 33(6), 533–538.	Can transparency help strengthen communication, trust in clinicians, and engagement?	Medicine
	Harvey, M.J. and Harvey, M.G. (2014). Privacy and security issues for mobile health platforms. *Journal of the Association for Information Science and Technology*, 65(7), 1305–1318.	Examination of some of the key challenges facing mobile health with a focus on privacy and security	Computer science

Transparency and privacy (A) (cont'd)	Hausfeld, J.N. and Zimmerman, R. (2018). Your organization can and should be cyber secure! *The Journal of Medical Practice Management*, 33(6), 389–391.	Creation of a roadmap to ensure cybersecurity (practitioner perspective)	Management
	Jennath, H.S. et al. (2020). Blockchain for healthcare: Securing patient data and enabling trusted artificial intelligence. *International Journal of Interactive Multimedia and Artificial Intelligence*, 6(3), 15–23.	Addresses security and privacy issues in blockchain (transparency and traceability)	Computer science/ management
	Serenko, N. and Fan, L. (2013). Patients' perceptions of privacy and their outcomes in healthcare. *International Journal of Behavioural and Healthcare Research*, 4(2), 101–122.	Develops a measurement instrument of patient perceptions of privacy in the healthcare sector and empirically investigates the outcomes of privacy	Sociology
	Theodos, K. and Sittig, S. (2020). Health information privacy laws in the digital age: HIPAA doesn't apply. *Perspect. Health. Inf. Manag.*, 18(1), 1–9.	Legal framework and its shortcomings	Health studies/law
Interactions with patients (digitization and care) (B)	Andreassen, H.K. et al. (2018). Digitized patient–provider interaction: How does it matter? A qualitative meta-synthesis. *Soc. Sci. Med.*, 215, 36–44.	Exploration of studies that can illuminate important aspects of social relations in contemporary society	Sociology/ technology
	Mabillard, V. et al. (2021). How can reasoned transparency enhance co-creation in healthcare and remedy the pitfalls of digitization in doctor–patient relationships? *International Journal of Health Policy and Management*, 11, 1986–1990.	Reasoned transparency and issues of communication/trust in the doctor–patient relationship	Management/ medicine
	Menendez, M.E. et al. (2020). The telehealth paradox in the neediest patients. *Journal of the National Medical Association*, 113(3), 351–352.	Recognizing the opportunities provided by telehealth do not suffice/Need to engage patients	Medicine
	Steinhubl, S.R. and Topol, E.J. (2015). Moving from digitalization to digitization in cardiovascular care: Why is it important and what can it mean for patients and providers? *J. Am. Coll. Cardiol.*, 66(13), 1489–1496.	Digital technologies in healthcare can improve the doctor–patient relationship through more time dedicated to human interaction	Medicine
	Vaagan, R.W. et al. (2021). A critical analysis of the digitization of healthcare communication in the EU: A comparison of Italy, Finland, Norway, and Spain. *International Journal of Communication*, 15, 1718–1740.	Organizational communication and interactions between institutions, providers, and patients	Communication

Innovation, devices and technology (C)	Ali, S.A. et al. (2020). Global interest in telehealth during COVID-19 pandemic: An analysis of Google trends. *Cureus*, 12(9), e10487.	Interest in the connection between e-health and Covid-19	Medicine
	Atasoy, H. et al. (2019). The digitization of patient care: A review of the effects of electronic health records on health care quality and utilization. *Annual Review of Public Health*, 40, 487–500.	Determination of future paths for digitization in healthcare (electronic health records)	Management
	Ben-Assuli, O. (2015). Electronic health records, adoption, quality of care, legal and privacy issues and their implementation in emergency departments. *Health Policy*, 115(3), 287–297.	Review of the electronic health records and health exchange tools: What are the benefits, concerns, and obstacles?	Management
	Bhavnani, S.P. and Harzand, A. (2018). From false-positives to technological Darwinism: Controversies in digital health. *Personalized Medicine*, 15(4), 247–250.	Analysis of patient and clinician engagement, sustainability, creation of new models, cost savings	Medicine
	Briganti, G. and Le Moine, O. (2020). Artificial intelligence in medicine: Today and tomorrow. *Frontiers in Medicine*, 7(27), 1–6.	Discussion of the recent literature on digitization and overview of the pros and cons of digitization	Medicine
	Chakraborty, S. et al. (2021). Analysis of digital technologies as antecedent to care service transparency and orchestration. *Technology in Society*, 65, 101568.	Necessity to clarify the outcomes of digital technology adoption on healthcare services/orchestration	Management
	Cucciniello, M. et al. (2015). Coordination mechanisms for implementing complex innovations in the health care sector. *Public Management Review*, 17(7), 1040–1060.	Contribution to the debate on coordination in healthcare policies	Management
	Greenstein, S. et al. (2013). Digitization, innovation, and copyright: What is the agenda? *Strategic Organization*, 11(1), 110–121.	Copyright law/economics of commons/intellectual property	Economics
	Kooman, J.P. et al. (2020). Wearable health devices and personal area networks: Can they improve outcomes in hemodialysis patients? *Nephrology Dialysis Transplantation*, 35(Supp. 2), ii43–ii50.	Cybersecurity and data privacy must be addressed, as well as adequate models based on AI and mathematical analysis	Medicine
	Onaya, T. et al. (2015). ICT trends in Japan's healthcare policy. *Fujitsu Sci. Tech. J.*, 51(3), 10–17.	Latest policy trends and importance of ICT to address issues of aging society and costs	Management

Innovation, devices and technology (C) (cont'd)		Pianykh, O.S. et al. (2020). Improving healthcare operations management with machine learning. *Nature Machine Intelligence*, 2, 266–273.	Analysis of AI use for predicting events and identifying key workflow drivers	Medicine
		Prainsack, B. (2020). The value of healthcare data: To nudge, or not? *Policy Studies*, 41(5), 547–562.	Policymakers should facilitate the use of healthcare data to build better institutions	Management
		Raghavan, A. et al. (2021). Public health innovation through cloud adoption: A comparative analysis of drivers and barriers in Japan, South Korea, and Singapore. *Int. J. Environ. Res. Public Health*, 18(1), 334–364.	Identification of the drivers and barriers to the adoption of cloud tech in healthcare and policy recommendations	Management
		Secundo, G. et al. (2021). Digital technologies and collective intelligence for healthcare ecosystem: Optimizing Internet of Things adoption for pandemic management. *Journal of Business Research*, 131, 563–572.	Analysis of some technical elements of the Italian healthcare system from a collective intelligence perspective and proposition for a model for allocating connected diagnostic devices in the Covid-19 pandemic context	Management
		van Velthoven, M.H. et al. (2019) Digitization of healthcare organizations: The digital health landscape and information theory. *International Journal of Medical Informatics*, 124, 49–57.	Understanding of the digital health landscape and initiatives from competitors	Medical informatics
		Winter, J.S. and Davidson, E. (2019). Big data governance of personal health information and challenges to contextual integrity. *The Information Society*, 35(1), 36–51.	Data governance challenges for ensuring value for individual, organizational, and societal stakeholders as well as individual privacy and autonomy	Management
New jobs and organizational change (D)		Bossen, C. et al. (2019a). Data work in healthcare: An introduction. *Health Informatics Journal*, 25(3), 465–474.	Healthcare organizations must re-organize around data production, through new resources	Management/ information studies
		Bossen, C. et al. (2019b). The emergence of new data work occupations in healthcare: The case of medical scribes. *International Journal of Medical Informatics*, 123(1), 76–83.	Investigation of emergent occupations focused on "data work", growth and stabilization of medical scribes	Management/ information studies

New jobs and organizational change (D) (cont'd)		Camacho, A. et al. (2017). Collective intelligence and databases in eHealth: A survey 1. *Journal of Intelligent & Fuzzy Systems*, 32(2), 1485–1496.	Literature review of collective intelligence in e-health, specifically defined as information collected in databases	Computer science
		Galmarini, C.M. and Lucius, M. (2020). Artificial intelligence: A disruptive tool for a smarter medicine. *Eur. Rev. Med. Pharmacol. Sci.*, 24, 7571–7583.	Analysis of the potential contribution of AI to biomedical research	Computer science
		Haag, M. et al. (2018). Digital teaching and digital medicine: A national initiative is needed. *GMS Journal for Medical Education*, 35(3), 1–5.	Digital teaching and learning technologies should be updated	Medicine
		Hernández-Chan, G.S. et al. (2012). Knowledge acquisition for medical diagnosis using collective intelligence. *Journal of Medical Systems*, 36(S1), 5–9.	Design of IT diagnosis decision support systems (DDSS) based on collective intelligence and consensus methods	Computer science, operational research
		Hernández-Chan, G.S. et al. (2016). Collective intelligence in medical diagnosis systems: A case study. *Computers in Biology and Medicine*, 74, 45–53.	Case study/experiment on diagnosis decision support system based on medical consensus methods supported by shared databases	Computer science, operational research
		Waidyanatha, N. and Dekker, S. (2011). The RTBP – Collective intelligence driving health for the user. *International Journal of User-Driven Healthcare (IJUDH)*, 1(2), 57–65.	Case study of a shared public health database pilot project. Highlights collective intelligence by connecting previously disconnected healthcare operations and epidemiological tracking	Public health

Table 5.1. *Findings from the literature review by category, N = 38*

5.6. References

Note that this reference list includes only entries not already included in Table 5.1.

Aceto, G., Persico, V., Pescapé, A. (2018). The role of information and communication technologies in healthcare: Taxonomies, perspectives, and challenges. *Journal of Network and Computer Applications*, 107, 125–154.

Alford, J. (2014). The multiple facets of co-production: Building on the work of Elinor Ostrom. *Public Management Review*, 16(3), 299–316.

Ansell, C. and Torfing, J. (2021). *Public Governance as Co-creation. A Strategy for Revitalizing the Public Sector and Rejuvenating Democracy*. Cambridge University Press, Cambridge.

Bevir, M. (2012). *Governance: A Short Introduction*. Oxford University Press, Oxford.

Bonabeau, E. (2009). Decisions 2.0: The power of collective intelligence. *MIT Sloan Management Review*, 50(2), 45–52.

Bovaird, T. and Loeffler, E. (2012). From engagement to co-production: The contribution of users and communities to outcomes and public value. *Voluntas: International Journal of Voluntary and Nonprofit Organizations*, 23(4), 1119–1138.

Brown, A.W., Fishenden, J., Thompson, M. (2014). *Digitizing Government: Understanding and Implementing New Digital Business Models*. Palgrave Macmillan, London.

Bryson, J.M., Crosby, B.C., Bloomberg, L. (2015). *Public Value and Public Administration*. Georgetown University Press, Washington.

Castelnovo, W. and Sorrentino, M. (2018). The digital government imperative: A context-aware perspective. *Public Management Review*, 20(5), 709–725.

Conférence Nationale de la Santé (2018). Faire en sorte que les applications et objets connectés en santé bénéficient à tous : avis adopté en assemblée plénière, le 08.02.18 [Online]. Available at: https://solidarites-sante.gouv.fr/ministere/acteurs/instances-rattachees/conference-nationale-de-sante/avis-et-recommandations/mandature-2015-2019-10665/article/faire-en-sorte-que-les-applications-et-objets-connectes-en-sante-beneficient-a [Accessed September 24, 2021].

De Blasio, E. and Selva, D. (2016). Why choose open government? Motivations for the adoption of open government policies in four European countries. *Policy & Internet*, 8(3), 225–247.

Dunleavy, P. and Margetts, H. (2015). The second wave of digital-era governance: A quasi-paradigm for government on the web. *Philosophical Transactions of the Royal Society A*, 371, 20120382.

Dunleavy, P., Margetts, H., Bastow, S., Tinkler, J. (2006). New public management is dead: Long live digital-era governance. *Journal of Public Administration Research and Theory: J-PART*, 16(3), 467–494.

Eriksson, E. and Hellström, A. (2021). Multi-actor resource integration: A service approach in public management. *British Journal of Management*, 32(2), 456–472.

European Patients Forum (2015). Lack of patient involvement in the Council position on medical devices [Online]. Available at: https://doi.org/10.1002/poi3.118 and https://www.eu-patient.eu/news/News-Archive/lack-of-patient-involvement-in-the-council-position-on-medical-devices/ [Accessed 9 May 2021].

Foudriat, M. (2021). *La co-construction en actes*. ESF Editeur, Paris.

Hardyman, W., Daunt, K.L., Kitchener, M. (2015). Value co-creation through patient engagement in health care: A micro-level approach and research agenda. *Public Management Review*, 17(1), 90–107.

Kraemer, K. and King, J.L. (2006). Information technology and administrative reform: Will e-government be different? *International Journal of Electronic Government Research*, 2(1), 1–20.

Lember, V. (2018). The increasing role of digital technologies in co-production and co-creation. In *Co-production and Co-creation: Engaging Citizens in Public Services*, Brandsen, T., Steen, T., Verschuere, B. (eds). Routledge, Abingdon.

LUSS (2019). Inventaire 2019 fracture numérique et e-santé. *Ligue des usagers des services de santé* [Online]. Available at: https://www.luss.be/classement/inventaire-e-sante-et-fracture-numerique/ [Accessed September 24, 2021].

Mabillard, V. and Mattijs, J. (2022). Digitization and co-production of healthcare: Toward a research agenda. *Working Papers*, 21(21), 1–48.

Mair, D., Smillie, L., Placa, G.L., Schwendinger, F., Raykovska, M., Pasztor, Z., van Bavel, R. (2019). Understanding our political nature: How to put knowledge and reason at the heart of political decision-making [Online]. Available at: https://doi.org/10.2760/910822 [Accessed September 24, 2021].

Malone, T.W. and Bernstein, M.S. (eds) (2015). *Handbook of Collective Intelligence*. MIT Press, Cambridge, MA.

McDermott, P. (2010). Building open government. *Government Information Quarterly*, 27(4), 401–413.

McLoughlin, I.P., Garrety, K., Wilson, R. (2017). *The Digitalization of Healthcare – Electronic Records and the Disruption of Moral Orders*. Oxford University Press, Oxford.

Meijer, A., Lorenz, L., Wessels, M. (2021). Algorithmization of bureaucratic organizations: Using a practice lens to study how context shapes predictive policing systems. *Public Administration Review*, 81(5), 837–846.

Menvielle, L., Audrain-Pontevia, A.F., Menvielle, W. (2017). *The Digitization of Healthcare. New Challenges and Opportunities*. Palgrave Macmillan, London.

Mettler, T., Daurer, S., Bächle, M.A., Judt, A. (2021). Do-it-yourself as a means for making assistive technology accessible to elderly people: Evidence from the ICARE project. *Information Systems Journal*, 33, 56–75.

Moore, M.H. (1995). *Creating Public Value: Strategic Management in Government.* Harvard University Press, Cambridge, MA.

Mulgan, G. (2018). *Big Mind: How Collective Intelligence Can Change Our World.* Princeton University Press, Princeton.

Nabatchi, T., Sancino, A., Sicilia, M. (2017). Varieties of participation in public services: The who, when, and what of coproduction. *Public Administration Review*, 77(5), 766–776.

Nancarrow, S.A. and Borthwick, A.M. (2005). Dynamic professional boundaries in the healthcare workforce. *Sociology of Health and Illness*, 27(7), 897–919.

Nicholas, L. and Broadbent, S. (2015). Collective intelligence in patient organisations [Online]. Available at: https://www.nesta.org.uk/documents/441/collective_intelligence_in_patient_organisations_v8.pdf [Accessed March 14, 2021].

Novak, J.D. and Cañas, A.J. (2006). *The Theory Underlying Concept Maps and How to Construct Them.* Florida Institute for Human and Machine Cognition, Pensacola.

OECD (2019). *Health in the 21st Century: Putting Data to Work for Stronger Health Systems.* OECD Publishing, Paris.

Osborne, S.P. (2006). The new public governance? *Public Management Review*, 8(3), 377–387.

Ostrom, E., Parks, R.B., Whitaker, G.P., Percy, S.L. (1978). The public service production process: A framework for analyzing police services. *Policy Studies Journal*, 7(1), 381–389.

Plesner, U., Justesen, L., Glerup, C. (2018). The transformation of work in digitized public sector organizations. *Journal of Organizational Change Management*, 31(5), 1176–1190.

Rantamäki, N.J. (2017). Co-production in the context of Finnish social services and health care: A challenge and a possibility for a new kind of democracy. *VOLUNTAS: International Journal of Voluntary and Nonprofit Organizations*, 28(1), 248–264.

Silow-Caroll, S., Edwards, J.N., Rodin, D. (2012). Using electronic health records to improve quality and efficiency: The experiences of leading hospitals. *Commonwealth Fund*, 17, 1–40.

Simonet, D. (2011). The new public management theory and the reform of European health care systems: An international comparative perspective. *International Journal of Public Administration*, 34(12), 815–826.

Singh, J., Owens, J., Cribb, A. (2017). What are the professional, political, and ethical challenges of co-creating health care systems? *AMA Journal of Ethics*, 19(11), 1132–1138.

Sørensen, E., Bryson, J., Crosby, B. (2021). How public leaders can promote public value through co-creation. *Policy & Politics*, 49(2), 267–286.

Torfing, J., Sørensen, E., Røiseland, X. (2019). Transforming the public sector into an arena for co-creation: Barriers, drivers, benefits, and ways forward. *Administration & Society*, 51(5), 795–825.

Torfing, J., Andersen, L.B., Greve, C., Klausen, K.K. (2020). *Public Governance Paradigms: Competing and Co-existing.* Edward Elgar, Cheltenham.

Valetto, G., Bucchiarone, A., Geihs, K., Buscher, M., Petersen, K., Nowak, A., Rychwalska, A., Pitt, J., Shalhoub, J., Rossi, F. (2015). All together now: Collective intelligence for computer-supported collective action. *2015 IEEE International Conference on Self-Adaptive and Self-Organizing Systems Workshops*, Cambridge, MA.

Voorberg, W.H., Bekkers, V.J.J.M., Tummers, L.G. (2015). A systematic review of co-creation and co-production: Embarking on the social innovation journey. *Public Management Review*, 17(9), 1333–1357.

6

The Patient Educator: A Profession, A Political Mandate or A Social Mandate?

This chapter focuses on the patient educator role as it emerges in France, following the *Ma santé 2022* reform, which institutionalizes the integration of patients into the training of health professionals. The analysis is based on the results of an exploratory survey of key actors involved in the implementation of reforms in medical schools. We show how the new role of the patient educator is at the crossroads of a multiple identity issue: a professional identity, a political identity and a social identity.

6.1. Background context and questions

The Latin root of the term "patient", *patiens*, refers to suffering, passivity and resignation. The patient would thus represent "an ignorant and passive subject of a treatment, decided and prescribed by another, the one who knows" (Lagrée 2004, author's translation). However, the emergence of chronic diseases and, with them, an increase in patients' skills during the 1930s and up to the present day have gradually led to the appearance of a certain autonomy delegated by the physician (Klein 2012). This partial autonomy was a first step in a profound evolution toward greater real autonomy for patients (Hibbard et al. 2004). In France, the patient, who is the subject of their own care, went on to be qualified as a user in the March 4, 2002 Law pertaining to patients' rights, and they will progressively become a social and political actor because of the strengthening of the legislative and regulatory framework.

Chapter written by Fatima Yᴀᴛɪᴍ.

Indeed, it is because of the 2002 law that the first foundations of health democracy were laid. The 2002 law and the subsequent health reforms of 2000 and 2010 have all strengthened the individual and collective rights of users and institutionalized the expression of user-citizens (Lefeuvre et al. 2018). Health democracy thus becomes, in the words of Demailly (2014), a joint undertaking of political democracy and social democracy. The rights to individual and collective expression have been progressively consolidated and have been continued in two ways. On the one hand, they have gone beyond simple expression to the field of more active participation. On the other hand, health democracy has gained social depth by becoming health democracy.

At the same time, a new stage in the empowerment of patients has been reached, both politically and in terms of health knowledge. New patient roles have emerged, because of the support of patient associations, to the tools deployed by the public authorities, but also to the daily work done by patients themselves in conjunction with health professionals in the wake of evidence-based medicine (EBM) (Sackett and Rosenberg 1995). With EBM, the role of the expert patient or partner patient has appeared, referring to a patient with expertise in their illness and health, a patient whose experience guides therapeutic choices and complements the physician's clinical expertise and medical scientific knowledge (Sackett and Rosenberg 1995).

In addition, over the past few decades, society's view of the patient has evolved. This evolution has given rise to a social construction that first identified the patient through their health problem, then through their status as a social security recipient, then as a user-citizen with rights and a political voice and finally as an expert or partner of professionals. Today, the role of patients is being called upon in other areas, including training, through the *Ma santé 2022* reform, which makes the patient an actor in the training of professionals. Alongside the roles of the political patient, the patient as an actor in their own health, the patient as an expert/partner, the role of the patient educator has now emerged. The latter must personify the knowledge and expertise they possess, but they must also, and above all, show the perspective of all the other patients in the relationship they have with professionals and within the healthcare system. This raises a number of questions: how should this new role of patient educator be understood? How should this new actor be positioned? What is their distinctive skillset? And what contribution can they make to professionals, to other patients and to the healthcare system as a whole?

This chapter will attempt to provide answers to these questions by presenting the results of an exploratory qualitative survey conducted among different categories of actors involved in the implementation of the reform of health studies in French medical schools. The following section will present and analyze the foundations that led to the emergence of the new role of the patient educator. We will explain and justify the problem and the questions raised. In section 6.3, after indicating the methodology used, we will present and analyze the results of the survey conducted. Section 6.4 will focus on the lessons learned, highlighting the issues underlying the emergence of the patient educator role and, more particularly, the issues in terms of the multiple identities of this new actor.

6.2. Conceptual framework

6.2.1. *From patient to expert patient*

Distanced for decades from health issues, civil society was called upon to take a very active interest in them during the human immunodeficiency virus (HIV) epidemic that affected France as well as all countries in the early 1980s. Patient associations played a central role throughout, more specifically the fact that the citizen action was structured and organized to confront the epidemic, but also to confront decision-makers, whether they be professionals or public authorities (Saout 2015). In this context, and because of the support of the media, the role of the active patient emerged, and with it, recognition of their associative expertise (Saout 2015). The HIV epidemic has thus come to concretize, on a societal and political scale, a trend that began in the 1930s that sought to empower chronic patients. However, this time, it is not only the patients who are affected but the whole of society.

Since then, the new roles taken on by patients and by all users of the health system have continued to develop. This evolution has been driven by patients themselves, but it has also been largely encouraged and reinforced by the public authorities through sustained legislative and regulatory support. The most emblematic step was the law of March 4, 2002 on patients' rights (Cardin 2014). In addition to the individual rights recognized for each patient, the main ones being the right to information and the right to share in the decision-making, the 2002 law established a philosophy, a public policy known as health democracy. The law recognizes the collective rights of all user-citizens, guaranteeing them representation in decision-making bodies in public health, in healthcare institutions and within a large number of decision-making bodies at the local, regional and national levels, such as the National Health Conference (Favre et al. 2012).

At the same time, in the scientific world, a similar evolution has taken place, this time for non-political reasons. Indeed, the patient's point of view will be promoted from the 1990s onward as an important component of what is called EBM. In addition to the clinical experience of the professional and the data from scientific research, the patient's experience and feedback will be considered key factors in the success of medical management (Richards et al. 2013). In addition, while EBM has not taken the ultimate step to incorporate patient values and preferences (Richards et al. 2013), it has nevertheless emphasized the importance of patient experiences and the collaborative potential between patients and professionals. Most importantly, it has greatly promoted the integration of the patient's perspective and enriched care processes to look beyond pathology and to consider the person.

In France, this evolution has been translated into legislation and has reinforced the existing framework. The 2009 law on patients, health and territories introduced a new practice in the care of patients suffering from chronic pathologies through the introduction of therapeutic education. In addition to putting EBM findings into practice and improving clinical outcomes for patients, the introduction of therapeutic education will be an additional form of recognition of patient expertise (Grimaldi 2010). Therefore, a significant evolution in care relationships has occurred through a dual movement of the desacralization and appropriation of medical knowledge by patients (Grimaldi 2010).

Therefore, over recent decades, in addition to the roles of the patient as spokesperson for users and the patient as expert on their illness, a third role has emerged. This third role is that of the "expert patient for others", in the words of Grimaldi (2010). Because of a certain political maturity and a rise in therapeutic competence, patients, helped by patient associations and health professionals in particular, have been able to engage in a process of objectivization of acquired experience and knowledge (Domecq et al. 2014). This last evolution will be, in France as in many other countries, the tipping point toward a new paradigm known as the "patient-centered care approach" as opposed to "biomedical" medicine, centered on the disease (Fahey and Nicliam 2014).

In addition to the emphasis on personalizing care and developing patients' skills, this approach is based on the desire to affirm in principle and equip in practice a real complementarity between the expertise of professionals and the experience of the patient (Sebai and Yatim 2018). What is at stake, in fact, is the establishment of partnership relationships between patients and professionals. Therefore, according to the French National Health Authority, which has clearly included it at the heart of the conditions for certification of health establishments in 2020, this is an approach that is part of a "partnership relationship with the patient, [their] relatives [...] to lead to the construction together of a care option, the monitoring of its implementation and its adjustment over time"[1]. This paradigm shift will be another important step in

---

1 Patient-centered approach, information, advice, therapeutic education, follow-up [Online]. Available at: https://www.has-sante.fr/portail/upload/docs/application/pdf/2015-06/demarche_centree_patient_web.pdf.

a silent revolution that is making patients central actors in areas that were previously very detached, including the training of healthcare professionals.

6.2.2. *A health system enhanced by expertise*

With the recognition of patients' skills and expertise, patients have rapidly moved into new key areas such as professional training, especially for physicians (Flora 2013). The investment by patients in training facilities alongside future health professionals began with the introduction of therapeutic education, mentioned above. In fact, the first university therapeutic education courses were created in 2009, bringing together both health professionals and patients among the trainees and trainers. However, it is with the *Ma santé 2022* reform that the involvement of patients in the training of professionals becomes a clear political commitment to "rethink the professions and training of health professionals" (Ministry of Health, author's translation)[2].

The *Ma santé 2022* plan announced the objective of rethinking health training and student evaluations by taking into account the patient's point of view and perspective in order to develop the personalization of care as well as the human and relational capacities of professionals. To this end, it plans to mobilize expert patients to participate in the training programs of health professionals. These experts will be involved in both practical and theoretical training and invert the various educational fields. With the *Ma santé 2022* reform and the emergence of the new role of the patient educator, France is part of a global dynamic with a growing number of initiatives.

The most commonly cited model is the Montreal model that identifies different levels of patient involvement, ranging from involvement in care to significant involvement in training   (Flora 2016). Within the Faculty of Medicine at the University of Montreal, patient educators or trainers emerged as early as 2010 with the establishment of a *Direction de collaboration et de partenariat patient* jointly piloted by a patient and the Dean of the Faculty of Medicine at the University (Flora 2016). Their role is to intervene during the first 3 years of study with all health professions, psychology, social work and health administration training audiences to ensure the awareness and acculturation to patients' experiences and perspectives (Flora 2014). The patient trainers' objective is to "raise awareness of the necessary complementarity of scientific knowledge in health and experiential knowledge from living with illness" (Flora 2014, author's translation) to foster the construction of a

---

2 Ministère des Solidarités et de la Santé (2018). *Ma santé 2022* [Online]. Available at: https://solidarites-sante.gouv.fr/IMG/pdf/ma_sante_2022_pages_vdef_.pdf.

common culture of care partnering. They intervene alongside clinician-teachers for theoretical and practical teaching, providing mentoring to students and, significantly, investing in key fields such as clinical ethics (Flora 2016).

In France, there are also pioneering initiatives that preceded the *Ma santé 2022* plan. The most significant of these is the patient-teacher program at the University of Paris 13 (PEP13), which was set up in 2016 and is heavily inspired by the approach of the Faculty of Medicine in Montreal. In its objectives, this program aims to integrate patients into the teaching provided to future general practitioners as part of their postgraduate studies, with the aim of developing a culture of patient-centered care among these professionals and promoting the bio-medico-social paradigm of health (Gross et al. 2017). The patient perspective is integrated primarily in ethics and care relationships courses, but their contribution is also extended to courses mobilizing simulation techniques and to student assessment (Gross et al. 2017).

With the implementation of the *Ma santé 2022* plan, initiatives such as that of the University of Paris 13 have been developed to meet the requirements of the reform. The various programs set up to date in the different medical faculties have something in common with the program at the University of Paris 13, with the experience at the University of Montreal, and other experiments conducted at the international level. All of these programs share the same primary objectives. The aim is to develop a culture of patient–professional cooperation, to encourage consideration of the expertise and perspective of patients, and to promote a biomedical and social approach and patient-centered care. The common challenge is thus to go beyond the paternalistic model and to enrich the dominant bio-medical approaches.

However, if there is a common base in terms of philosophy, there are also numerous divergences that concern more particularly the operational methods of implementation, but which have significant impacts on the position of these new actors. For example, interventions can target the first years of training, be ongoing throughout the training, or target specific moments in the training, such as the specialization period. The audiences are therefore equally diverse: all health professions, future doctors, certain medical specialties and so on. Similarly, there are differences in the profile of patient educators or patient-trainers and their positioning with respect to the other actors in training. Therefore, while there is a certain consensus on the importance and relevance of patient educators' interventions to change the training and practices of health professionals, this consensus does not exhaust the questions relating to the prerequisites and consequences of calling into question a historical model of training, which is that of the transmission of knowledge by peers (Amsellem-Mainguy 2014).

Indeed, the various existing programs make it possible to better understand the philosophy behind patient educators and to better identify the boundaries of their obligations in medical schools in France and elsewhere. However, current knowledge does not allow for a clear understanding of how these new actors position themselves in relation to traditional training actors and how they appropriate this new role that has become theirs. The main issue raised is therefore that of the place of these new actors within a historically compartmentalized training model.

The patient educator embodies an additional level of skill development and is the culmination of a process that began with the role of a patient as the object of their care, passing through the role of a social user of the health system, a political actor representing users and then a patient expert/partner of other patients and health professionals. Its arrival in the field of training therefore raises many questions at different levels.

– How can its action be linked to that of traditional health training actors? What legitimacy and what levers of legitimization?

– What is the political mandate of the patient educator in France? And is it intended to extend the path begun toward greater democracy in health?

– What are the contributions for future health professionals? What are the benefits for users? And what is the impact on the health system as a whole?

In section 6.3, we will look at the position of patient educators in medical education and attempt to propose answers to the questions posed by mobilizing the results of an exploratory qualitative survey.

6.3. Illustrations

The *Ma santé 2022* reform is distinguished by its scope and by the many innovations it brings to improving the functioning and performance of the French healthcare system. A number of projects have been launched: the fight against inequalities in access to care, the quality and relevance of care, digital healthcare, the financing of institutions and the management of institutions. Innovations in these areas have consolidated the efforts made in recent years. However, there is a new and ambitious area of reform, namely the training of health professionals. In addition to the abolition of *numerus clausus* and other changes in terms of access to health studies, the reform introduces a major innovation by institutionalizing the integration of patients as actors in the training provided to future health professionals.

Although it is part of a long list of initiatives undertaken in recent years to promote the role of patients, as explained above, the integration of patients as stakeholders in health education remains an important innovation with various challenges. The survey whose methodology and results are presented below seeks to identify and analyze these issues.

6.3.1. *Methodology*

The survey was based on 11 semi-structured interviews with key actors involved in the implementation of the *Ma santé 2022* reform in French medical schools. The sample consisted of three user representatives who are members of patient associations working with health profession training institutions, two medical school deans, a director of a university hospital center (commonly known in France as a CHU) in charge of patient relations, two university professors who are hospital practitioners and three medical students.

The interviews were conducted on the basis of an interview guide structured into three parts:

– the place of patients within the healthcare system (their involvement in their own care, with other patients, with professionals, etc.) and new obligations for the training of healthcare professionals;

– the steps taken in French medical schools to implement the *Ma santé 2022* reform (their methods, relevance, advantages and difficulties encountered);

– the prospects for the evolution or emergence of a French model in this area, taking into account the specificities of the training of health professionals in France.

All interviews were conducted via telephone or video conference. Eight were recorded, but all were partially transcribed and a detailed report was made. The analysis was based on manual thematic coding in accordance with the structure of the interview guide.

6.3.2. *Results*

The integration of so-called patient educators into the various health training programs, and more particularly into medical studies, represents a major change for patients, health professionals and the entire health system. One of the issues that seems to be emerging is that of a challenge to a training model historically based on the transmission of knowledge from scientific research by peers, due to the legitimacy, also recognized by peers. In this context, the positioning of these new actors seems complex, as it raises questions about a multitude of identities, three of which emerged clearly from our results: a professional identity, a political identity and a social identity.

6.3.2.1. *The professional identity*

What positioning, what legitimacy, and which levers of legitimization?

The first question raised by the integration of patient educators relates to their positioning in relation to the scope of traditional actors within training, namely physicians, peers recognized for their scientific legitimacy and clinical expertise. What is the legitimacy of patient educators and what status should they be given? On this question, all of the people we spoke to agree on the specific legitimacy of patient educators, based on their experience of the disease. Their added value is that of experiential knowledge, a situated knowledge that results from the objectification of lived experience because of exchanges with other patients and health professionals: "The patient has knowledge, they have know-how. It doesn't come from books but from a life with the disease, with their own body, in hospitals and with doctors" (University Professor-Hospital Practitioner, PU-PH).

Therefore, it is the complementarity between the scientific and clinical knowledge held by health professionals and the experiential knowledge held by the patient that is sought from patient educators. The latter must enrich the teaching provided by integrating the patients' perspective. The goal is twofold. On the one hand, it is a matter of making people aware of the singularity of individual cases and the need to adapt care: "We do not treat everyone in the same way. A 60-year-old person has nothing to do with a 30-year-old man or woman. They do not experience the same disease in the same way" (Medical School Dean). It is hence a matter of bringing professionals to delve further into their reflective position, to question the knowledge they have received, to challenge it and to even question it case by case: "There is what is in the anatomy books and what the patient tells you. If you have to choose, it's the patient you have to listen to first" (PU-PH).

As a result, if the position that could be described as "patient profession" is rejected, this is also the case for the position of "teaching profession". The question of pedagogical skills is revealing in this respect. According to our interviewees, patient educators are not required to have specific pedagogical skills, since the issue at stake is essentially their ability to provoke reflection and to transmit experience, not knowledge as understood in the common sense. However, all of the people we met emphasized the importance of personal qualities and, more specifically, the ability of patient educators to foster positive relationships and to understand the social representations at work within health professions: "You have to be diplomatic in order to get your message across. You have to find future allies among these students. We are looking for the trigger first and the change of position afterward, when they will be handling patients in the field" (User Representative).

These exploratory results show that it is not a question of developing a distinctive professional identity, but rather of clarifying a professional position. The patient educators are in fact patients first, but also patients with objectified and situated knowledge that must be complementary to the formal knowledge transmitted to future professionals by their peers. As one interviewee put it: "It must not become a profession. If they become institutionalized, they will talk like professionals. In which case, they lose what they really bring to the table and that's not the point" (Facility Director).

In this context, the programs implemented in the faculties of medicine present great diversity in terms of the modalities of intervention (in pairs with teachers or alone), the pedagogical tools (theoretical courses, simulations, debates) and the target audiences (different levels in the training curriculum). Neither the practical modalities nor the content of the interventions seem to be the object of tension. While this can be explained by the youth of the reform and by the work in progress to develop a model applicable at the national level, the explanation can also be found in the aims underlying the integration of patient educators. The questions are more about political and social identities.

6.3.2.2. *The political identity*

What is the political mandate and what is the extension in the promotion of democracy in health?

In France, the institutionalization of user representation within the bodies of healthcare institutions dates back to the end of the 1990s and has since been extended to all healthcare bodies at local, regional and national levels. User representatives, who are members of approved healthcare associations, play important roles in health democracy. Their role is to express the views of all user-citizens and to defend their rights. The emergence of the patient educator can be seen as a new arena to accommodate the expansion of their role. The political identity of the patient educator thus refers to the superposition or, on the contrary, to the necessary distance between the role of the user-representative and that of the patient educator.

Our results are consistent with this, although our respondents had strong reservations. All of the people interviewed recognize the role that user representatives can play as patient educators. They all emphasize their legitimacy in promoting individual and collective rights to future health professionals: "We must keep this hat on, this role of defending rights" (User representative); "Finally, the goal is to go and find future professionals on the school benches and not to wait to 'brush shoulders' with them in the institutional bodies and when there are problems or complaints" (Medical School Dean).

However, with the exception of one user representative we met, who considers the patient educator mandate to be the natural continuation of the representative mandate, our interlocutors insist on the fact that there is a distinction to be made between the role of the representative and the patient educator. More than the official mandate and the formal status of user representative, it is membership in an association that seems to be a prerequisite for the patient educator. It is a matter of defending the rights and expressing the voice of users in the name of their experience and that of an associative group: "It is true that there is a challenge of acculturation. However, it is not only the mandate of the representative that allows this acculturation. When you are a volunteer in an association, you are part of a collective. You are aware of your rights and of health democracies. And consequently, patients can be trained" (PU-PH).

Although understood as a representative of users, the patient educator is a specific representative. They represent other users through a shared experience, discussed and reflected upon within the framework of an associative group and not through a formal mandate of representation: "If I can speak on behalf of other patients, it is not because I am a representative. It is because I have an experience that I share with other patients [...] I learned to accompany patients thanks to the association and that also helped me. You put your personal experience into perspective in relation to others. That's the role of associations" (User representative).

Therefore, while the formal role of the representative is recognized in terms of advocacy and the promotion of health democracy, the role of the patient educator integrates and goes beyond it by putting more emphasis on the experience of access to rights and the experience of the health system. According to our interlocutors, although they represent a political role, the patient educator should not be identified as a political actor. Several reasons were given for this:

– The first is the necessary neutrality with respect to the public authorities that rely on approved associations[3]. This neutrality is considered essential to reassure health professionals but also to allow patient educators to remain autonomous.

– The second reason is related to the issue of proximity to the field. Some interviewees consider that user representatives, because of their political mandate, are relatively distant in their position from places of care: "Representatives sit in institutions, it's political, and often, they are distant from the daily reality of patients and caregivers. And that's what we're going to look for in the patient educators" (PU-PH).

---

3 In France, only members of associations approved at the national or regional level can exercise a mandate as user representatives. These approved associations receive public funding to support their obligations.

The role of the patient educator can thus be situated as an extension of the representative position, but it is more a social representation that is expected rather than a political one.

6.3.2.3. *The social identity*

What contributions and what societal impact?

While the political identity of patient educators may be the subject of debate, and sometimes disagreement, their social identity is clearly identified. Our results show that in this respect, patient educators have a social and societal ambition. All of the participants agree that the ultimate goal is to challenge, in a profound way, unbalanced care relationships and a medical model considered inefficient and ineffective. The aim is to align three targets with different timeframes: to change practices by working with health professionals during training, to improve health outcomes and the quality of care by relying on the actual experience of patients with their caregivers, and finally to change the behavior of patients and all user-citizens.

Regardless of how patient educators are integrated, all of the people we spoke to insisted that their priority area of intervention is the care relationship. The main challenge is therefore to change professional practices in this area: "It's not specific to a disease or a specialty, what we're looking for is for future doctors to change their outlook towards patients and question the doctor–patient relationship" (Medical School Dean). In addition, it is the acculturation to new approaches to care and caregiver–patient relationships that is targeted in order to promote patient-centered care approaches, the integration of the patient's perspective, co-decision or even the collaborative or partnership logic: "We cannot talk about patient-centered care without the patients. Do you understand? Changing professional practices tomorrow starts with changing the teaching practices of today" (PU-PH).

Therefore, in line with the principles of EBM, the objective through the evolution of professional practices in terms of care relationships (encouraging listening, empathy, the collection of experience and preferences, etc.) is to improve the clinical results of patients and the quality of care. It is therefore a question of accompanying patients toward more open, horizontal relationships. As one medical student put it: "I think trust is important, the placebo effect is an example of this. And then, there is information that we can't have if the patient doesn't say it. We can adapt and personalize care better" (Medical student); "That's the whole point of collaboration, of partnership, we adapt care and in addition we empower the patient to become capable of *doing* instead of *undergoing*" (User representative). This is also a point of distinction between patient educator and representative. Our interviewees stressed the importance of patient educators being representative of all patients and of the diversity of experiences of users of the healthcare system, more so than the representatives, who are mostly retired people with serious pathologies and sometimes painful experiences that motivate their involvement in associations.

However, the impact of changing professional practices in terms of care relationships does not stop at individual therapeutic care but goes beyond it to affect the whole of society. In fact, all of the people we spoke to emphasized the expected impact of the evolution of practices in terms of the evolution of the social roles of caregivers and those being cared for. As one interviewee put it: "Knowledge is power. A caregiver has scientific knowledge and it is a power that the cared-for person is subjected to. So, we need to emancipate ourselves. Empowerment" (User Representative). The patient educators therefore also have a social and societal role to play by providing recognized knowledge and power that participates in the emancipation of other patients from health professionals: "Doctors will always keep the power but, at least, we are introducing mechanisms to balance this" (PU-PH).

The evolution of professional practices is therefore, because of the emergence of patient educators, an additional, important step in the progress of health actors. However, this step cannot be analyzed without understanding the social and societal implications: for health professionals, on the one hand, who are moving from the role of the *knower* to that of the *companion*, and for patients, on the other hand, who are moving from the condition of *objects of care* to a role as *actors in their own well-being*.

6.4. Lessons learned

Through these initial exploratory results, the institutionalization of the role of the patient educator appears to be a further step in the process started in France two decades ago to change the place of users in the healthcare system. From being an active patient in the wake of the HIV epidemic in the 1980s, they evolved into a real political role, a user-citizen with individual and collective rights, because of the 2002 law and a legal and regulatory arsenal that has been expanded upon ever since. The emergence of the patient educator role is a natural part of this process. However, the emphasis placed on the evolution of professional practices calls for particular attention when analyzing the position of the patient educator, insofar as it involves a profound questioning at the very heart of the functioning of healthcare activities and the healthcare system. Our results show that this new phase can be seen as a leap, a changeover, insofar as the identity issues at the professional and political levels are underpinned by a social identity issue and a profound societal impact.

First, in terms of professional identity, our results make it possible to underline the role expected of patient educators. This role must be complementary to that of traditional training actors. Their legitimacy is that of experiential expertise, of living with the disease, of knowledge of the healthcare system, and it does not conflict or compete with the scientific and clinical legitimacy of healthcare professionals (Gross et al. 2017). In terms of political identity then, patient educators seem to fit well with what has been implemented in recent years, which seeks to promote health democracy (Cardin 2014). Our results show the importance of the representative role on behalf of an associative collective, the importance of knowing one's rights and the very importance of the role of advocate, or at the very least the awareness-raising actor, among future health professionals. However, the role of the patient educator goes well beyond these dimensions. More than a political representation, it is the social representation that is expected to accompany the development of professionals and all users of the healthcare system.

Indeed, in terms of social identity, patient educators are called upon to play a central role in the evolution of practices as the cognitive referential. While real progress has been made in recent years to facilitate the acculturation of professionals (Akrich et al. 2012), the acculturation of users remains a matter of discussion. A real social evolution presupposes a real transformation of the acceptance that user-citizens have of the relationship between *carers* and the *cared-for*. Without this, the evolution of professional practices would remain limited in terms of consequences for the functioning and performance of the healthcare system (Hassenteufel 2011).

Therefore, while the role of the patient educator does not seem to refer to a political role in the image of that of the user representative, there are underlying issues in terms of social and political democracy that encompass and go beyond the issues of democracy in healthcare (Demailly 2014). The questions raised are social and societal. It is a question of promoting the capacity and consent of user-citizens to be actors for their own care and actors within the healthcare system. In short, it is a question of promoting *empowerment* in the dual sense of the term, that is, promoting the emancipation of those being cared for with respect to the caregivers and promoting this very process of emancipation.

The principles of the *Ma santé 2022* plan and its initial operational implementation in medical schools provide two important mechanisms for activating this process. It facilitates this acculturation effort among professionals, on the one hand, and it establishes the legitimacy and recognition of patient educators, on the other. However, it cannot cover the entire social process necessary for such a project alone. Healthcare education, like the political education of citizens, continues to involve issues that go beyond the healthcare system; issues that are even more profound given the massive development of health technologies, which certainly contribute to emancipation, particularly in terms of healthcare but that also risk being a source of even greater social inequalities.

We are interested here in the role of the patient educator emerging in France following the *Ma santé 2022* reform, which institutes the integration of patients in the training of healthcare professionals. Based on an exploratory survey of key actors involved in the implementation of the reform in medical schools, we highlighted three main results. First, we have shown that the new role of the patient educator is at the crossroads of a multiple identity issue: a professional identity, a political identity and a social identity. We then highlighted the place that this new role occupies in the path toward greater democracy in health and the major differences with other emblematic roles such as the user representative. Finally, we have shown how, specifically, the social identity of the patient educator represents the main issue, given the necessary societal prerequisites. The evolution of the practices of health professionals is certainly indispensable, but its consequences are likely to remain limited if it is not accompanied by a profound change in the way user-citizens perceive the relationship between caregivers and patients.

6.5. References

Amsellem-Mainguy, Y. (2014). Qu'entend-on par "éducation pour la santé par les pairs"? *Cahiers de l'action*, 43(3), 9–16.

Cardin, H. (2014). La loi du 4 mars 2002 dite "loi Kouchner". *Les Tribunes de la santé*, 42(1), 27–33.

Demailly, L. (2014). Les médiateurs pairs en santé mentale. Une professionnalisation incertaine [Online]. Available at: https://doi-org.ezproxy.universite-paris-saclay.fr/10.4000/nrt.1952.

Domecq, J.P., Prutsky, G., Elraiyah, T., Wang, Z., Nabhan, M., Shippee, N., Brito, J.P., Boehmer, K., Hasan, R., Firwana, B. et al. (2014). Patient engagement in research: A systematic review. *BMC Health Services Research*, 14, 89.

Fahey, T. and Nicliam, B. (2014). Assembling the evidence for patient centred care. *BMJ*, 349, 4855.

Favre, M., Lainard, M., Loiseau, L. (2012). Participation des usagers dans les projets de santé publique : réalités et paradoxes. *Spécificités*, 5(1), 139–152.

Flora, L. (2013). Savoirs expérientiels des malades, pratiques collaboratives avec les professionnels de santé : état des lieux. *Éducation permanente*, 195, 59–72.

Flora, L. (2014). Le patient formateur, un nouveau métier pour accompagner un nouveau paradigme au sein du système de santé. In *Nouvelles interventions réflexives dans la recherche en santé : du savoir expérientiel des malades aux interventions des professionnels de santé*, Jouet, E., Las Vergnas O., Noel-Hureaux E. (eds). Archives contemporaines, Paris.

Flora, L. (2016). Le savoir des malades à travers un référentiel de compétences "patient" utilisé en éducation médicale. *La recherche en éducation*, 15 (20116), 59–75.

Grimaldi, A. (2010). Les différents habits de l'"expert profane". *Les Tribunes de la santé*, 27(2), 91–100.

Gross, O., Ruelle, Y., Sannié, T., Khau, C., Marchand, C., Mercier, A., Cartier, T., Gagnayre, R. (2017). Un département universitaire de médecine générale au défi de la démocratie en santé : la formation d'internes de médecine générale par des patients-enseignants. *Revue française des affaires sociales*, 61–78.

Hibbard, J.H., Stockard, J., Mahoney, E.R., Tusler, M. (2004). Development of the patient activation measure (PAM): Conceptualizing and measuring activation in patients and consumers. *Health Services Research*, 39(4), 1005–1026.

Klein, A. (2012). Contribution à l'histoire du "patient" contemporain. L'autonomie en santé : du self-care au biohacking. *Hist Médecine Santé*, 1, 115–128.

Lagrée, J. (2004). Patient. In *Dictionnaire de la pensée médicale*, Lecourt, D. (ed.). PUF, Paris.

Lefeuvre, K. and Ollivier, R. (2018). *La démocratie en santé en question(s).* Presses de l'EHESP, Rennes.

Richards, T., Montori, V.M., Godlee, F., Lapsley P., Paul D. (2013). Let the patient revolution begin. *BMJ*, 346, 2614.

Rothier Bautzer, É. (2012). Formation des soignants en France : la difficile émergence de nouveaux modèles. *Les Tribunes de la santé*, 36(3), 83–88.

Sackett, D.L. and Rosenberg, W.C. (1995). On the need for evidence-based medicine. *Journal of Public Health*, 17(3), 330–334.

Saout, C. (2015). La lutte contre le sida : le face à face des associations et de l'État. *Les Tribunes de la santé*, 46(1), 25–30.

Sebai, J. and Yatim, F. (2018). Patient-Centred Care model et New Public Management : confluence et paradoxe. *Revue Santé Publique*, 30(4), 517–526.

Sultan, S. (ed.) (2003). *Psychologie de la santé.* PUF, Paris.

The Emergence of an Innovative and Resilient Organization of Healthcare Actors: The *Alliance Santé de Seine-et-Marne*

The context in which the pandemic was managed by the Ile-de-France Regional Health Agency (RHA) led to organizational changes both internally and externally with their partnerships. RHA staff had to work across the board on new public policies (screening, tracing, vaccinations and new healthcare pathways), developed as the crisis evolved. New missions emerged. *Alliance Santé 77* was set up in the context of crisis management to enable strategic and operational consultation and cooperation on shared issues, such as the shared management of the Covid-19 pandemic between general practitioners (GPs) and the hospital, and support for long Covid-19 patients.

7.1. Background context and questions

The usual tasks of regulating the healthcare system have been amplified by an acceleration effect due to the emergence of new issues. The use of mobile communication tools (widespread use of teleconferencing and videoconferencing) has transformed the ways in which the healthcare system is managed. With regard to its partners, the RHA has been mobilized to listen to problems and tasked to try to respond in real-time. The RHA departmental delegation in Seine-et-Marne has supported collective action with the *Ordre des Médecins*, hospital operators (medical and administrative), the *Samu* emergency medical service, community

Chapter written by Béatrice PIPITONE and Hélène MARIE.

medicine (including private practice) and the DAC (*Dispositifs d'appui à la coordination* – coordination support systems. The approach has been to exchange information on issues and requirements on a regular basis, and then to rapidly build local strategies to meet the needs of all actors, based on a shared and evolving diagnosis. The respective knowledge and trust between actors, and the working habits established at the time of the crisis, have also made it possible to develop more structural actions, beyond the sole management of the Covid-19 pandemic. If there are structural obstacles to this type of initiative, whether institutional obstacles linked to the very organization of the healthcare system between general practitioners and the hospital for example, or to the organization of the institutions that regulate it, a change in the position of the actors themselves, deciding to mobilize together, and of the regulatory authorities, accepting a more horizontal role among peers, is decisive in making it possible to implement and develop a project and for healthcare professionals to work as a collective. The adaptation of the RHA's institutional positioning in Seine-et-Marne during the Covid-19 pandemic facilitated the emergence of a collective organization with the region's healthcare actors: *Alliance Santé 77*.

Alliance Santé 77 has been able to capitalize on specific regional features that have proved to be assets: the DAC coordination support systems have been positioned from the outset as facilitators and experts in coordination for all healthcare actors; the low medical demography has enabled a bias toward cooperation between a small but mobilized number of healthcare professionals. The RHA is thus breaking new ground in its role as a regional coordinator, working alongside professionals and listening to their concerns at all times, as one of the driving forces behind operational projects that bring added value to healthcare professionals, patients and healthcare pathways.

This atypical organization, founded on listening, trust and a lateral partnership between the supervisory authorities (RHA, *Ordre des Médecins*) and GPs-hospital-*Samu*-DAC actors, has been mobilized to provide solutions to problems arising from the health crisis in particular. It is beginning to demonstrate its resiliency in the longer term, with projects designed to alleviate the more systemic tensions in healthcare organizations that were highlighted by the pandemic. Lastly, it is demonstrating its capacity for innovation by deploying collective actions to improve GP–hospital healthcare pathways, and by taking into account the needs of patients and professionals better. As a catalyst for local initiatives to implement public health policy as closely as possible to the local level, it is an incubator for innovation and the emergence of collective projects between healthcare professionals and institutions who share a common diagnosis, the assets and problems of their region, common values and a shared commitment to improving health.

Innovative organizations such as *Alliance Santé 77* do not have the resources to permanently address the structural weaknesses of the healthcare system that became apparent in the wake of the Covid-19 pandemic, starting with the lack of human resources and the problems of public service management. This calls for strong structural measures. On the other hand, a number of mechanisms can be activated to remove regulatory, organizational and financial constraints, and thus facilitate the deployment of innovative organizations applying the same principles as *Alliance Santé 77*, while adapting them to the local context of each territory. These actions would support structural measures by helping to improve healthcare pathways.

7.2. Illustrations

7.2.1. *The emergence of a collective organization of healthcare actors in Seine-et-Marne*

7.2.1.1. *Adapting the RHA's position to the Covid-19 context*

A public administrative body created on April 1, 2010 and governed by the French Public Health Code and the Regional Health Authority is responsible for implementing a unified national health policy in the regions, in order to better meet the needs of the population and increase the efficiency of the system. In this capacity, it fulfils the role of financial guardian, in charge of setting objectives and allocating resources, steering and managing resources, issuing permits to health and medico-social establishments, monitoring and inspecting, monitoring health and so on. At the same time, it has a very specific role to transform the healthcare system, since it is also responsible for modernizing and rationalizing the healthcare service. The management of the Covid-19 pandemic tested the RHA's ability to fulfil this second mission. Faced with the short-term imperatives of pandemic management, the RHA had to do some heavy prioritizing, and thus had to limit its involvement in long-term projects to fundamentally transform the healthcare system, as defined in the *Projet Régional de Santé (PRS) II*, in order to be able to allocate more staff to crisis management.

At the same time, however, the RHA had to demonstrate a 10-fold agility in the day-to-day management of its old and new missions in order to cope with a system under extreme pressure. The challenge was to develop hospital capacity in real-time to provide logistical support to cope with the shortage of human resources, equipment and medicines, to organize the emergency response and outpatient care, to disseminate doctrines to adapt organizations, to organize patient transport between regions, to ensure the isolation of contact cases, to define and implement appropriate screening strategies and to rapidly deploy the national vaccination campaign. To achieve this, the RHA, in collaboration with the *Assurance Maladie*, France's national health insurance, had to rapidly and thoroughly transform its management, organization and relations with healthcare actors.

Indeed, the crisis has considerably changed the way the RHA operates internally. The risk of staff infection has led the RHA to develop telecommuting and to organize the rotation of agents in the workplace. This has accelerated the introduction and use of communication tools more commonly used in the private sector, such as videoconferencing and instant messaging. Also new, these tools were used for both internal and external communications, with the RHA organizing coordination meetings between the various actors in the healthcare system (city, hospital, medico-social) within local crisis units. In addition, the organization, management and decision-making timescales were challenged by the need to set up a crisis management organization based on crisis cells involving staff from different hierarchical levels and different *départements*, to make decisions quickly, to manage crisis communication and adaptation to an ever-changing context, and finally to organize remote working. In this way, the RHA has moved toward a more lateral management style, both internally and in its relations with the actors in the healthcare system.

Internally, teams from different *départements* have been working together in crisis units according to their skills, getting to know each other and making their interventions more complementary. For some Covid-19 projects, funding requirements were estimated on a global basis, rather than "by type of actor", that is, by department. Initiatives have been taken by staff at different hierarchical levels, and managerial innovations have facilitated the movement of staff between delegations, Covid-19 crisis units and the *département* head offices. For example, delegations were able to express their need for human resource reinforcements, the Human Resources Department organized a human resources reserve and put delegations in touch with interested agents to provide support; a business continuity plan was also set up to prioritize missions and dedicate time to crisis management; working conditions for employees on shared or back-up assignments were facilitated via the reimbursement of travel and meal expenses and so on.

Along with healthcare system actors, the RHA has moved toward a more partnership-based relationship, listening more closely to needs and monitoring the actions implemented, building solutions with partners, organizing more frequent and regular exchange times and continuously evolving the actions implemented. In other words, it has made use of *soft power* far more than a *carrot–stick* approach.

7.2.1.2. *A new dynamic between the RHA in Seine-et-Marne and healthcare actors*

As part of this dynamic, the Seine-et-Marne DD (*Direction Départementale*) departmental delegations supported the emergence of *Alliance Santé 77*, of which it is a full member along with the other institutions and actors in the Seine-et-Marne healthcare system, in the context of crisis management. This was done at a time when it was clear to professionals, both GPs and hospitals, who had been facing difficulties for over 3 months as a result of Covid-19, that there was an urgent need to talk to each other and work together to define and improve healthcare pathways, as patients with acute symptoms were being cared for both at home and at the hospital. In order to achieve this, the RHA drew on a detailed preliminary local diagnosis, carried out through discussions with the actors involved, which provided it with a global local vision and identified possible areas for improving healthcare pathways by better connecting actors. The RHA's action consisted of facilitating collective dialogues, by taking the initiative of convening conference calls and organizing meetings on the notion of healthcare pathways and joint city-hospital work setups, establishing a relationship of trust with each actor individually, and supporting the actors to trust one another; finally, it put its administrative engineering and project management skills at the service of actors by leading a work schedule and working groups dedicated to the projects that the alliance wished to implement.

In this way, the RHA has developed a more lateral and partnership-based relationship with the actors in the Seine-et-Marne healthcare system. It has provided them with an ongoing forum for collective discussion and mutual support. In this space, it has listened to needs and proposed actions to meet these requirements in order to enable their inception and implementation; it has sought to identify points of convergence and joint projects to be initiated between the various actors; it has facilitated inter-knowledge sharing and the articulation of missions and actions in the service of healthcare pathways; finally, it has made available to actors its expertise in the organization of the healthcare system, applicable rules and funding, as well as its capacity to mobilize resources. Through this action, the RHA has taken on a new role as an administrative supervisory body, which is neither that of a healthcare financing body (health insurance) nor that of a system actor (private practitioners, hospitals, health and medico-social establishments and services, etc.), but rather that of an "orchestra conductor", bringing together the various actors in the healthcare system to organize a response that is as adapted as possible to the pandemic. In so doing, it has demonstrated its singular and indispensable role in the local healthcare system, that of the "pilot" institution, able to bring all the actors together because of its knowledge of the system, management rules, funding and applicable legislation, the regulatory missions of the various actors, their assets and constraints and organization systems in place.

From the third wave onward, DD 77 departmental delegation took organizational innovation a step further, creating a small team dedicated to improving GP–hospital healthcare pathways throughout the region and by deploying digital tools to support pathways, reporting directly to the director, and choosing to make its pathway manager available to the alliance on a temporary basis, pending the hiring of a permanent staff member to lead the alliance. The RHA has thus taken on the role of local coordinator, offering its services to alliance members, to organize meetings, to lead the collective, to help professionals formalize their shared organizational processes and the various tools and documents produced by the alliance, to organize more operational sub-working groups enabling progress to be made on the various projects, without exhausting the group, and finally to report on progress to all members. This position is also the subject of an internal managerial innovation at the RHA, since it is shared part-time between the DD departmental delegations and RHA head office, the *Parcours 77* (Pathway 77) manager is also part-time responsible for the deployment of DAC coordination support systems for the Ile-de-France region.

In addition, a permanent dialogue has been established between the various relevant administrative levels of the healthcare system (the RHA DD at the field level, the head office at the regional level and the ministry at the national level), facilitated by the existence of a dual head office/delegation position and, on certain issues, enabling virtually instantaneous decision-making. This triple innovation has considerably accelerated the funding and implementation of initiatives such as the organization of a pathway for long-stay Covid-19 patients, the implementation of the *Terr-eSanté Melun* tele-monitoring platform, the deployment of digital sharing tools and the organization of an experimental SAS-like (*Service d'Accès aux Soins*) healthcare access service, by enabling the territory to quickly identify the regulatory and financial opportunities (*Ségur, eParcours* funding, etc.) that their local projects could benefit from.

At the same time, the position of town and hospital actors vis-à-vis the supervisory authority has evolved and several key actors in the region, such as the *Samu 77* emergency medical service and the Seine-et-Marne Medical Association, have chosen to join a collective organization and support a partnership with the RHA. Because of a relationship of trust that has gradually been established, each actor has been able to express itself transparently and share its constraints, difficulties and needs. This has made it possible to organize a collective reflection around solutions to the problems encountered, and to collaborate on projects to improve the healthcare system, representing not their individual interests but their sectoral/business interests for healthcare pathway services, the region and innovation. This is how an innovative organization – *Alliance Santé 77* – has emerged in the Seine-et-Marne region, based on a lateral partnership between GPs, who constitute the CPTS (*Communauté professionnelle territoriale de santé*) local professional health community, the *Samu* emergency medical service, public hospitals (directors and presidents of the CME), the RHA, the *Ordre des Médecins*, CPAM (*Caisse Primaire d'Assurance Maladie*, France's primary health insurance fund) and the DAC coordination support systems.

7.2.1.3. *Starting with action, concrete projects and collective structuring a posteriori*

Atypically, this collective organization initially came together around shared values, common projects and a shared vision of the regional evolution required to improve healthcare pathways. From the outset, it developed concrete, operational projects. It was only structured once with the drawing up and signing of a constitutive charter detailing the shared values and specifying the purpose and organization of *Alliance Santé 77* in order to perpetuate the alliance while maintaining the operational flexibility desired by its members. As a result, the alliance was set up and from June 2020 ran for a year, before its members signed a founding and operating charter in June 2021.

Another unique feature of *Alliance Santé 77* is that with the support of the *Ordre des Médecins*, it has brought together doctors from the outset, both from the town, through the leading doctors of the CPTS local professional health community under construction, and from hospitals, through the representatives of the medical directors (CME, *Commission médicale d'établissement*) of public hospitals, as well as the administrative directors of public hospitals (directors and/or their deputies). This common working space enables professionals to discuss and exchange information concerning their respective needs and organizations, on shared needs, difficulties encountered and possible solutions that could be implemented together.

7.2.2. **Concrete results in the fight against the Covid-19 pandemic and beyond**

7.2.2.1. *Alliance Santé 77, a key actor in the management of the Covid-19 epidemic in Seine-et-Marne*

Within *Alliance Santé*, tools for managing the Covid-19 pandemic were put in place as early as the second wave: the idea of working together on an integrated GP–hospital–GP protocol and recommendations for all healthcare professionals in the department quickly emerged. GPs and hospital doctors worked together to draw up this protocol, including recommendations for the management of Covid-19, adapting national doctrines to the local context, as well as a referral directory. This protocol enabled healthcare professionals to call their hospital colleagues if necessary, thus facilitating the management of a greater number of patients with Covid-19 by GPs rather than by hospitals. Infectiologists from all hospital centers have contributed to the project, as have representatives of community physicians. It also enabled hospital professionals to envisage GP patients returning home with medical follow-up. It is this double movement (from the GP to the hospital and from the hospital to the GP) that has led to this protocol being expressly named "GP–hospital–GP".

Following its drafting, the document was distributed widely in Seine-et-Marne by the *Ordre des médecins* and via the Maillage website, run by the DAC coordination support system, which publishes important information for healthcare professionals in the territory. A webinar was organized in December 2020 to present the protocol to general practitioners in Seine-et-Marne. Many healthcare professionals responded to the call from this working group. The group continued its work in early 2021 to update the protocol as recommendations evolved, and by organizing a collective medical reflection on Covid-19 vaccination. It also organized a second webinar in March 2021 to inform and raise awareness among local professionals, thereby facilitating the setup of vaccination centers in the department.

At the same time, the organizations set up by the group in the first wave have produced concrete results. For example, professionals have set up a home telemonitoring platform, *Terr-eSanté Melun*, using the *Terr-eSanté* Covid-19 regional digital information-sharing tool developed for remote monitoring of Covid-19 patients. It enables patients with Covid-19 in the acute phase to stay at home, while monitoring their vitals and having easy access to the platform and the *Samu* emergency medical service, in the event of worsening symptoms. The attending physician is also able to check the status of their patients through this tool. In conjunction with the platform, a "reserve" of independent nurses was set up to enable home visits to measure the vital signs of the most fragile patients, or those unable to use the digital tools themselves. These actions have helped to streamline hospital admissions and discharges. This organization made it easier to manage the strain generated by the various waves of the Covid-19 pandemic on the *Samu* emergency medical service and hospital intensive care services.

7.2.2.2. *Alliance Santé 77 mobilized to care for long Covid patients*

From April 2021 onward, despite the resurgence of the epidemic, the group continued its work, this time to raise awareness among professionals and improve knowledge of the prolonged symptoms of Covid-19 (long Covid) in order to facilitate early tracking, the identification of hospital referrers and early and adapted management of the patients concerned.

Alliance Santé 77 organized itself and replicated this experimental approach to manage the emerging problem of patients presenting prolonged symptoms linked to Covid-19. The actors involved proposed the organization of a graduated pathway for patients. The DAC coordination support systems communicated a call number to provide a gateway for professionals and patients seeking information and support. At the same time, follow-up by the SSR care and rehabilitation services specializing in Long Covid have been accredited and funded by the RHA. A sub-working group of *Alliance Santé 77* has drawn up a guide and a Long Covid diagnosis and referral form for general practitioners, including a directory of hospital resources that can be called upon, as well as referral criteria. Medical research and experimentation are in their infancy and are constantly evolving in an attempt to identify suitable care methods for these patients: the region cannot therefore claim to be "at the cutting edge", but the group is organizing itself to ensure a scientific and regulatory monitoring, and to facilitate its dissemination to all professionals.

An additional benefit of this organizational innovation is the sharing of a position between headquarters and the RHA delegation, enabling rapid capitalization and regional deployment of this work. In this way, the Seine-et-Marne tools were presented to the regional expert committee before summer 2021 and distributed laterally to the other RHA DDs and the DAC coordination support systems of the other *départements*, enabling rapid appropriation and use of similar tools to help diagnose Long Covid patients. A training session for all regional Long Covid/DAC coordination support systems was organized by members of *Alliance Santé 77* before they were set up. Finally, work has begun on deploying these Long Covid patient pathway tools in *Terr-eSanté eCovid*, so that all patients and professionals in the region will be able to record symptoms and coordinate and monitor treatment.

7.2.2.3. *Improved access to healthcare and support for public hospitals*

In addition, *Alliance Santé 77* has begun to roll out more structured field projects at the initiative of its members. These actions took place against a backdrop of general tension throughout the healthcare system in the wake of the pandemic: tension within the human resource departments of healthcare establishments, generated by the concomitant infectious diseases of children and adults during the winter months (bronchialitis, influenza, etc.) and the epidemic resurgence with the Omicron variant. An SAS healthcare access service pilot version has been deployed, providing local access to unscheduled general medical care. In addition, home telemonitoring facilitates early discharge from hospital, and the collective use of digital patient files containing relevant information enhances coordinated care by healthcare professionals.

From October 2021, the actors in *Alliance Santé 77* organized themselves to understand together and in a coordinated way the pressure on pediatric beds linked to the epidemic of infantile bronchiolitis, following the Covid-19 crisis. The organization of a pilot version for the SAS healthcare access service was strongly supported by a managerial commitment from the *Samu* emergency medical service department, which, on the one hand, protocolized the use of unscheduled appointments and, on the other, set up a system for systematic telephone calls to all doctors concerned by the booking of an unscheduled appointment. This system of trust between the actors involved helped to facilitate the de-scheduling of appointments. GPs were invited to take part in the regional crisis unit organized by the RHA with health establishments. They agreed to offer overbooked unscheduled care slots for children, so that the *Samu* emergency medical service could offer general medical appointments close to home within 24 hours, as an alternative to hospitalization. Using open-source software, the DAC coordination support systems and the RHA have created a scheduling tool tailored to the needs of GPs (who can declare their available slots online in a confidential manner) and the needs of the *Samu* emergency medical service (the *Samu* emergency medical service has access to a global view of availability and can also display a map showing the distance from the appointment location to the caller's home). The *Samu* emergency medical service has also organized its resources so that medical regulation assistants (MRAs) can book appointments for this experimental "pediatric SAS-like" healthcare access service, pending the recruitment of funded, unscheduled care operators. As a result, 92% of the pediatric patients concerned by SAS healthcare access services were able to find a consultation during the day – 104/112 patients in five weeks, three to four consultations a day – because of an effective partnership between the *Samu* emergency medical service and 30 volunteer GPs, enabling these children to avoid a trip to the emergency room.

The feedback was positive for 100% of those involved in the Seine-et-Marne CRRA 15 emergency medical call reception and control center and reinforced the feeling of the *Samu* emergency medical service regulators that they were doing a useful and personalized job. The number of calls is increasing and varies from day to day (from 0 to 11 per day). In addition, a remote home monitoring system has been set up at the Melun hospital to streamline hospital discharges and enable pediatric patients who are discharged early to remain at home. The system is based on discharge criteria and monitoring frequency, defined in collaboration between the pediatric departments and the ReS@M telephone platform (formerly *Terr-eSanté Melun*). This time, the *Terr-eSanté* digital tool is used to identify patients and share information between hospital departments and with the GP.

Building on these successes, local actors are currently testing the extension of the SAS healthcare access service to adult patients. In this way, without any resources, and because of the mobilization of actors motivated by improving healthcare pathways, patient services and collaboration between professionals, the region has succeeded in organizing a pilot version of the SAS healthcare access service. This kind of organization now needs to be professionalized and made sustainable through the funding and implementation of dedicated resources to enable the use of appropriate software, the recruitment of OSNP unscheduled care operators in the *Samu* emergency medical service/SAS healthcare access service front office dedicated to booking appointments, and the remuneration of GPs for the allocation of slots and consultations; nevertheless, the collaboration between actors is a solid foundation that has already been laid. This has been made possible by the sheer willingness of the actors involved to commit to an innovative organization. This common will, which was heard at the time by the RHA DD and supported by the deployment of operational tools, was only possible because good working practices had been established over the past year and a half, and the actors knew and trusted each other.

7.2.2.4. A catalyst for the deployment of shared digital tools to manage healthcare pathways

At the same time, there is a growing need for professionals to share information on patients who are cared for by healthcare professionals in the community, but who also spend time in hospital, and to work more closely as a team in order to organize their healthcare pathways, make the right decisions and use the right resources at the right time. For example, the CPTS local professional health community currently being set up in the *départements* have organized working groups for the delivery of unscheduled care and information sharing. At the same time, public hospitals are questioning their ability to send discharge reports more quickly to members of the patient's circle of care. The need to use common digital tools to enable professionals to identify patients in common and share information is growing. The actors in *Alliance Santé 77* are therefore keen to set up networks and a coordinated organization for the use of the *Terr-eSanté* regional digital sharing tool to complement the national tools currently being deployed with the *Ségur* digital system, the DMP (*dossier médical partagé*) shared medical record, a genuine digital patient health record and secure messaging, enabling information to be sent securely.

7.2.2.5. Increased dialogue between actors generates organizational innovations

Lastly, the fact that local actors have the opportunity to get to know each other and talk to each other more frequently within *Alliance Santé 77* is also a catalyst for the convergence and joint local projects that naturally emerge between certain members. For example, the *Samu de Seine-et-Marne* emergency medical service was quickly informed of the work undertaken by the Provins hospital and the region's EHPAD residential establishments for dependent elderly people to organize the geriatric care network, and benefits from this work: the EHPAD create *Terr-eSanté* accounts for their residents and publish the DLU (*Dossier de liaison d'urgence*) emergency liaison file, enabling the regulating or emergency doctor to access the useful information required for the safety and continuity of care in the event of a call to the emergency services. In another example, a natural convergence is taking place between the *Samu* emergency medical service and the North and South DAC coordination support systems, as the emergency services are able to identify at an early stage highly vulnerable patients who are frequently the subject of emergency calls, who could benefit from the reinforced support of a DAC coordination support system.

Therefore, beyond crisis management, *Alliance Santé 77* is a local catalyst for the overall improvement of the healthcare system, through the deployment of SAS healthcare access services; the joint use of *Terr-eSanté*, a regional tool for professionals to exchange information about their patients; the deployment of a departmental home tele-monitoring platform; and by acting as a catalyst for local projects initiated by certain members. In this way, it supports the RHA, which is better able to carry out its missions of regional coordination, adapting public health policies to local conditions and improving the healthcare system to create seamless healthcare pathways for patients. What is more, it is clear that such an organization, based on a network of closely linked actors, is highly responsive and resilient, able to withstand shocks and unforeseen events. It also boasts a high degree of innovative capacity, enabling it to develop professional practices and set up operational projects to respond to the difficulties encountered during crises.

7.2.3. *Barriers and mechanisms to the implementation of collaborative, innovative and resilient organizations*

The co-construction of public policies between institutions and healthcare professionals, the organization of healthcare pathways, the decompartmentalization of GPs and hospital services and the organization of professionals into patient-focused care teams have all been part of the recurring vocabulary of healthcare policy for at least two decades now. In reality, however, it is still in the early stages of being implemented at the local level. On the one hand, it still relies heavily on the goodwill of convinced and committed professional and institutional early adopters, ready to invest their unpaid time and to carry out voluntary action in the service of patients and the local community. On the other hand, there are still many obstacles to its implementation, and we are still far from being able to measure the impact that the Covid-19 pandemic will have on the French public healthcare system.

7.2.3.1. *Institutional obstacles to participative management in healthcare*

We have already mentioned the obstacles associated with the organization of the RHA itself, and more generally with the ways in which public health policy is organized in France. For example, the RHA's role as an administrative guardian and supervisory body means that it must be cautious in its dealings with partners. In addition, its organization reflects the fact that public health programs and policies are often deployed "in hubs", which does not facilitate the implementation of healthcare pathways and work partnerships between city, hospital and medical and social actors. What is more, the fragmentation of decision-making between different political and administrative levels and the time required to reach decisions on strategic guidelines in relation to the immediacy of operational expectations make it difficult to reconcile the guidelines of public policies implemented in different territories, and to make them coherent and sustainable. Finally, the deployment of identical systems in all regions to ensure equal access and service can sometimes be difficult to reconcile with the need to adapt to regional specificities, both in terms of socio-demographic situation and healthcare needs, and in terms of medical demography.

It should also be noted that the involvement of patients or patient representatives in innovative organizations such as *Alliance Santé 77* would, in fact, enable services to be better adapted to patients' needs. However, healthcare democracy at the local level is still hampered by the limited number of patients who are trained as representatives, peer helpers or professional trainers, who have a good grasp of the issues and the healthcare system, and who are therefore in a position to participate with professionals in these discussions. While the Covid-19 pandemic has challenged many of these obstacles, new challenges have emerged. For example, the increased role played by prefectures, town halls and regions in healthcare may lead to fragmentation and inconsistency in decision-making. In addition, it remains to be seen whether the new modes of operation that emerged during the crisis will be sustainable in the future.

7.2.3.2. *Organizational obstacles to collaboration between actors*

Innovative organizations such as *Alliance Santé 77* come up against other structural obstacles in the healthcare system: first and foremost, the presence of two distinct modes of medical practice – private practice and public hospital medicine – which give rise to ignorance, different professional attitudes and even competition. By way of example, the deployment of SAS healthcare access services raises questions and will undoubtedly lead to changes in long-established organizations such as the *Samu* emergency medical service's private dispatch service and the home emergency care provided by structures such as *SOS Médecins*. Drawing on their collective experience within *Alliance Santé 77*, the members of the group have considered how to overcome this obstacle by organizing the governance of the *SAS 77* healthcare access service in such a way as to break away from the traditional division between these two modes of practice, by proposing colleges representing the different professions, including a regulation college integrating both the *Samu* emergency medical service regulators with those from private practice.

Another major obstacle is the implementation of digital healthcare tools which, prior to the work undertaken in the wake of the *Ma santé 2022* roadmap and accelerated by the *Ségur du numérique en santé*, whose core aim is to digitize healthcare, were not the subject of coherent global architecture schemes across a territory, and whose appropriation and use by healthcare professionals and institutions remained limited. The practical effect of this is that healthcare professionals, especially doctors, have little access to the right information at the right time to inform their decision-making. For patients and their families, the appropriation of information is often limited, and the guarantee of the right to protection of personal data is uncertain. This issue has been clearly identified by *Alliance Santé 77*, which has made it one of its priorities, with the desire to structure itself around the appropriation of a common tool, *Terr-eSanté*, freeing itself from the constraints specific to each practice, so that professionals can truly identify and organize themselves as a circle of care around the patient, through a digital file shared throughout the territory.

7.2.3.3. *Adapting RHA's institutional positioning: a major mechanism for innovation*

In this context, adapting the positioning of the RHA and the department's healthcare actors was the determining factor in the formation of *Alliance Santé 77* and the implementation of concrete collective projects to serve the region. As for the Covid-19 pandemic, it was a context that accelerated the emergence of this atypical organization. Indeed, crisis management lateralized institutional decision-making within the RHA, giving the RHA DD greater autonomy and leverage to take action at its own level. In addition, the DD departmental delegations have benefited from temporary human resource reinforcements from the agency's head office. The creation of a shared post in this context, as well as the establishment of rapid decision-making circuits between head office and the delegation, acted as catalysts for the development of local projects, for their support by head office, for the identification of public policies into which they could fit, for the rapid release of temporary seed funding and for dissemination to other *départements*.

In addition, the crisis prompted the DD departmental delegations to set up, with the actors involved, decompartmentalized departmental crisis cells associating the *Samu* emergency medical service and hospital services, but also town health professionals and DAC coordination support systems, actors who were previously not in the habit of working together on a daily basis. Finally, it has accelerated the introduction and appropriation by healthcare professionals of digital tools enabling the organization of dematerialized meetings, which has made possible regular dialogue between actors who previously exchanged less with each other and with the RHA, due to geographical distance, and who did not work together on a daily basis, to resolve the same challenges. In addition, healthcare professionals became aware of their need to share more information, both among themselves and on patients shared by the city and the hospital, especially patients with Covid-19 in the acute phase at home. These factors were decisive in the emergence of *Alliance Santé 77* and the implementation of its projects in a *département* such as Seine-et-Marne, where distance is a limiting factor in organizing meetings and collective projects.

7.2.3.4. *Investing to reduce local inequalities: a decisive role for the RHA*

While the adaptation of the RHA's positioning was decisive in the emergence of *Alliance Santé 77*, its ability to mobilize additional human resources during the management of the Covid-19 pandemic in a medically deficient region such as Seine-et-Marne also made it possible to organize, lead and support the implementation of projects devised by the actors involved. A rebalancing of the human and financial resources available to supervisory bodies such as the RHA, as part of a policy to reduce local inequalities, is *sine qua non* for the long-term success of such projects. More generally, areas in difficulty such as Seine-et-Marne can be made more attractive to healthcare professionals when they have the opportunity to participate in partnership organizations of this kind, to be supported in the day-to-day exercise of their profession as well as in the implementation of the innovative projects they lead, and to participate with the RHA in the co-development of the area's healthcare policy.

7.2.3.5. *How Covid-19 paradoxically facilitated the medical deficit*

In addition to the Covid-19 pandemic, Seine-et-Marne's geographical particularities and, even more so, its medical demographics, provided a facilitating context for setting up *Alliance Santé 77*. Indeed, Seine-et-Marne is a semi-urban and rural *département*, very spread out with few healthcare actors. For example, the department has 6.55 doctors per 100,000 inhabitants, compared with 7.54 in the Ile-de-France region and a national average of 9. Due to their limited numbers, professionals have a greater interest in helping each other and in working together in a decompartmentalized way between the city and the hospital, by "population basins" around the major public hospitals. What is more, they are more likely to adopt a culture of collaborative work, where a larger number of professionals working in the same area can, on the contrary, generate competitive effects. For example, when *Alliance Santé 77* proposed to support crisis management in a neighboring department by using the Covid-19 remote monitoring platform, political obstacles quickly emerged, linked to the complexity of relationships between healthcare professionals in the neighboring *département*.

What is more, the limited number of professionals to be involved in projects in Seine-et-Marne makes communication more fluid and interpersonal relationships stronger. The scale on which projects are deployed is more modest, which facilitates their implementation and the effective use of even fairly simple tools and organizations. Most of the actors capable of supporting large-scale projects are already present within *Alliance Santé 77*, even though the plenary session brings together no more than 40 people.

Similarly, tools based on open-source software developed in-house for SAS healthcare access services needs have been sufficient to enable the system to function at the outset, and the involvement of 40 volunteer GPs has been sufficient to make available to patients a significant number of unscheduled care slots to cope with the increase in pediatric calls to the *Samu* emergency medical service in October 2021.

"The Covid crisis we are just coming through has shaken up our healthcare system profoundly: organizations, professionals and even patients. In emergency medicine, the terrible impact on teams, the number of patients, the seriousness of the situation, the number of deaths, etc. were all destabilizing factors that led us to innovate in order to continue fulfilling our mission of care. The *Samu* emergency medical service's objectives were to provide good patient care and protect the public hospital, which was under appalling strain. In our environment of Seine-et-Marne, where the healthcare service is one of the poorest in France, in terms of institutions as well as cities, the actors listened to each other, understood each other and decided to find organizations that would increase their efficiency. These organizations were coordinated with the help of the RHA. This work led to the formalization of a city-hospital collective: *Alliance Santé 77*. Homecare coordination and monitoring tools have been implemented. As a result, fewer people are being referred to emergency departments, more care is being provided in the local area, and there is real cooperation between the city and the hospital. All this has only been made possible thanks to an innovative vision on the part of the city and hospital actors, and the RHA at the departmental delegation level. The services provided exceed initial expectations. They are new tools for everyday life and crisis management. The actors are already working on developing this innovative organization to prepare for the future, because the stakes are high: quality of care, local care and the attractiveness of the region".

Box 7.1. *Testimony of Dr. François Dolveck, Director of Samu 77 and head of the emergency department at Melun hospital, medical advisor to GCS Sesan and medical director of the MRA AP-HP school*

7.2.3.6. *Leveraging DACs: an asset for local coordination of actors*

The third mechanism identified is the presence of two established DAC coordination support systems, "neutral" devices fulfilling a public service delegation to support local coordination between healthcare professionals, institutionalized by the law relating to the organization and transformation of the healthcare system of July 24, 2019, financed by the RHA, and covering the whole territory, without white zones, their close collaboration with the RHA DD and the good understanding between the DAC coordination support system management enabling joint projects.

Indeed, the North and South DAC coordination support systems of Seine-et-Marne already existed at the start of the Covid-19 pandemic: the South DAC coordination support system had been accredited since January 2020, and the North DAC coordination support system had already begun to respond to requests for support from healthcare professionals, regardless of the patient's age or pathology, even though it was only accredited later in January 2021. They were also based on long-standing healthcare networks in each territory, and DD 77 departmental delegation had made the choice from 2019 to legitimize them with partners and work on improving healthcare pathways in close collaboration with them. As a result, the two DAC coordination support systems were in a position to support the emergence of *Alliance Santé 77* from the outset: they were able to participate in leading the collective, organizing meetings, formalizing the deliverables to differ, providing it with tools for organizing video conferences, an experimental SAS healthcare access service tool and the *Maillage de territoire* network portal, and then more recently, jointly financing a permanent leadership position, currently being recruited.

The DAC coordination support systems' role was facilitated by the department's socio-demographic characteristics. It was easier for the DAC coordination support systems to play their role as "gateway" to provide knowledge and support for all healthcare actors in the area, since there were fewer of them than in other *départements*. They were also better able to play their role as "territory watchdog", objectifying health pathway disruptions and difficulties in the organization of healthcare, and informing the RHA of these observations, as the number of local partners was limited.

> "The *Alliance Santé 77* is a wonderful initiative born of people and motivated professionals, aware of needs and united around a single objective: the pandemic. While the lack of resources may have slowed things down, and the health context may have been confusing, *Alliance Santé 77* has demonstrated, through its very existence, that successful healthcare requires consultation and exchange, trust and mutual respect between all healthcare actors in the same area, without exclusion, so that an effective partnership can emerge to provide local solutions adapted to the circumstances, for the sole benefit of the population. *Alliance Santé 77* now needs to give itself the means to make this adventure a lasting example that can be adapted, why not, to each territory. For Seine-et-Marne, this is now a new mission that the *Ordre des médecins*, as the representative of the entire medical profession, present and driving force from the outset, wishes to continue".

Box 7.2. *Testimony of Dr. Claire Siret, President of the Seine-et-Marne Departmental Medical Council*

7.3. Lessons learned

An atypical organization such as *Alliance Santé 77* has been made possible by the strong and constant involvement of local healthcare actors and by the adaptation of their positioning to mirror that of the RHA. Like *e-Santé*, the deployment of digital tools and the use of metadata, it is a mechanism for innovation to improve the efficiency of the healthcare system and facilitates local appropriation by professionals. It has a tangible impact on local healthcare, as it enables public actions to be implemented that are more localized and better adapted to the needs of patients and professionals. By taking part, the RHA is innovating in the exercise of its role as a regional coordinator: it supports the actors, puts them in touch with each other, facilitates mutual understanding of each other's organizations and constraints, improves functional links to make the concept of a healthcare pathway effective, favors laterality and partnership in its relationships with healthcare professionals and makes a concrete contribution to the implementation of collective projects and innovative organizations in the region. Finally, it adopts an experimental approach, testing solutions as problems arise and adjusting its decisions and structures as they go along, rather than imposing new systems defined regionally or nationally and automatically deployed according to the same organizational modalities in all territories.

The Covid-19 pandemic contributed to the emergence of this new position. Medical demographics in Seine-et-Marne were a major facilitating factor. However, we maintain that the principles of an organization like *Alliance Santé 77* can be reproduced in other regions. By setting public policy objectives, relying on the energy and conviction of those involved in healthcare in a given area, focusing on what makes sense in the healthcare professions, leaving room for maneuver to professionals and organizing local collaborations rather than imposing one-size-fits-all models, an administration such as the RHA can help projects emerge that are adapted to local needs, difficulties and capacities.

What is more, the resilience of this type of organization depends essentially on the human time invested in it. The next crisis will not have exactly the same characteristics, and the operational preparations that may have been made in the wake of it (stocks of masks and medicines, relocation of part of production, etc.) will not be enough to respond, but the network of actors will be able to remobilize, innovate and respond rapidly. Indeed, this experience shows that it is partnership and mutual support that enable the system to withstand new challenges such as the Covid-19 pandemic.

Such organizations have neither the means nor, above all, the vocation to permanently offset the limitations of the French public health service, as highlighted by the Covid-19 pandemic. The pandemic showed that just-in-time operations left little margin for managing peaks in activity and highlighted severe strains on human resources, with salaries and working conditions that make recruitment difficult, alongside costly administrative and management burdens. What is more, funding models and public service management are not very collaborative and leave little room for maneuvering within territories, proving to be ill-adapted to supporting new practices and new challenges. Last but not least, healthcare democracy is still not sufficiently effective so as to enable patients to become involved at a very early stage in the deployment of services tailored to their needs and expectations. Such a turnaround requires in-depth structural measures. On the other hand, their deployment can complement and contribute to the concrete improvement of healthcare pathways at the local level. This requires strong political impetus to recognize the added value of managerial and organizational innovation for the healthcare system, in the same way as digital technology and data, and to remove the many regulatory, organizational and financial obstacles to their deployment that still exist.

The following mechanisms can be activated to facilitate their deployment and sustainability:

– fund and carry out action research to identify indicators for measuring the cost–benefit ratio and impact of such organizational innovations;

– dedicate human and financial resources within the RHA and at the local level to ensure the long-term viability of these organizations, which are largely based on voluntary work and the mobilization of a limited number of professionals at this stage, particularly in areas where medical desertification is significant;

– recognize the added value of managerial and organizational innovation in improving the healthcare system, in the same way as digital technology, the use of big data and so on;

– trust the actors and support collaborative schemes through innovative, long-term financing and contractual arrangements, for example by signing agreements based on collective objectives between the supervisory authority and several organizations, and CPOM (*Contrats pluriannuels d'objectifs et de moyens*) multi-year contracts for objectives and resources for local areas, and incentive remuneration for pathways and coordinated practice;

– dedicate funding to local innovation "outside the framework", as Article 51 is still rather rigid in its conditions of implementation;

– rebalance decision-making and financial capacity in the healthcare system in favor of the local and regional levels;

– organize experience-sharing forums for innovative healthcare organizations;

– support the training of patient representatives to facilitate healthcare democracy and enable constructive involvement of patients in local organizations.

7.4. Acknowledgments

We would like to thank all those who took the time to review this chapter and give it their critical appraisal and input, especially Delphine Caamano and Julien Marchal.

8

The Alliance Manager: A Key Actor in Healthcare Coordination Systems

Bringing together a number of healthcare coordination agencies and structures, DAC (*Dispositifs d'appui à la coordination*) coordination support systems are tasked with supporting the various professionals involved in managing the most complex situations, while helping to structure and improve care paths across the region. To achieve their objectives, the DAC coordination support systems will have to deploy partnership strategies that go far beyond simple relationships, but rather focus on establishing synergies with local actors, thereby creating genuine collective know-how.

In order to achieve this, these DAC coordination support systems will need to develop new managerial capabilities, in particular by strengthening their human resources skills, which are key to the success of local strategic alliances. Will the "alliance manager", the builder and pilot of partnerships, be the key actor in DAC coordination support systems? This chapter will therefore attempt to determine whether this function, recognized in other fields of intervention, can take root in these innovative coordination mechanisms.

8.1. Background context and questions

The author has been involved in setting up and managing healthcare coordination structures for almost 35 years. Over the course of various professional activities, the author has observed many factors contributing to success but also, at times, a

Chapter written by Laurent CENARD.

number of instances that challenged growth. By the term "coordination structures", we mean the health networks that have developed in various forms since the 1980s and their very recent transformation into coordination support units. Within these structures, the human resource's function, particularly through the mobilization and development of the right skills and the implementation of a range of management practices, does not always appear to be a top priority. Yet, it is an essential element in the creation, management and development of these innovative, constantly evolving healthcare organizations. The notion of an alliance, even if the term partnership is more often used, is intrinsically linked to these coordination mechanisms. It is based on the knowledge and mutual recognition of the various professionals involved, and their ability to work together to achieve the fundamental goal: to improve the quality-of-care services being offered to patients.

In this chapter, we will therefore attempt to highlight a key function in the creation of these structures: the alliance manager, who will be responsible for their construction and management, particularly in relation to external partners and public authorities. Essential to "big" trading companies, especially multinationals, the alliance expert plays an active role in their strategy. A newly emerging profession, alliance managers are currently being established in other types of companies, especially small and medium-sized enterprises (SMEs) and why not as part of the key innovative healthcare organizations of tomorrow. After setting out the framework of coordination mechanisms, in particular healthcare networks and their "descendants", the DAC coordination support systems, the alliance manager function will be explained, with regard to its current deployment, outside the scope of these healthcare coordination mechanisms. We will then attempt to build bridges with the DAC coordination support systems, highlighting the ways in which this function can help them to develop strategy and meet the challenges of coordination schemes, both internally and externally. To date, this function has been partially integrated into DAC coordination support systems; however, there is little awareness of it, and consequently it is not very structured or well-studied. To date, this relies essentially on the structure's director, who is often the actual alliance-maker for the system in question.

We will then look at the qualities and skills needed to be a successful alliance builder. Finally, we will try to interweave a few ideas to ensure that this function is fully integrated into current and future systems, particularly in the initial and/or ongoing leadership training. The aim of this chapter is to explore the role of the alliance leader within coordination systems, in particular, within DAC coordination support systems. From a methodological point of view, these elements are derived from readings adapted from management science, whose analyses were compared with participant observations. Indeed, the various professional experiences of the author have led to them participating in the construction, management and evaluation of several coordination systems. As an actor in the field, consultant and associate member of *Larequoi*, the author has conducted surveys, participated in research projects and written articles and notes on these health organizations. Far from proposing a definitive framework, this first draft of a reflection on strategic alliances in coordination arrangements merely draws attention to a key point in the success of DAC coordination support systems and their integration into the French healthcare system. This contribution lays the foundations for what will undoubtedly be a much broader reflection, with all the caution and limitations that such exploratory research requires. This reflection may merit becoming the pursuit of future academic work.

8.2. Case studies

8.2.1. *Coordination systems*

8.2.1.1. *The constitution*

The function of coordination in the healthcare field was established in the 1990s, with the creation of coordination structures between city and hospital professionals, constituting the first city-hospital networks. Initially perceived as "unnatural", this partnership was a response to the dysfunctional nature of the French healthcare system, unable to cope with the complexity of patient care. In the absence of a therapeutic solution, the emergence of the AIDS crisis led healthcare professionals, faced with frequent recourse to hospital care and the social difficulties associated with this pathology, to organize themselves with other healthcare actors, other patients, their families, supported by activist or militant associations. The aim of these convergences was to respond to a health emergency, and to:

> [...] the   expression of a break with the hospital – university development model [...] and a new call is gradually gaining momentum: medicine in search of a human complement. (Barré et al. 2005, p. 18, author's translation).

Various actors, not necessarily all from the healthcare field, have established collaborative arrangements in the spirit of co-construction, in order to respond to different challenges, particularly those linked to patient care. Assertiveness was key to the creation of these atypical organizations and, in 1991, they received mixed funding support from the French government and the French health insurance system[1], enabling the networks to be institutionalized for the first time. This

---

1 Circular DH/DGS of June 4, 1991 on setting up city-hospital networks for the prevention of infection and health and social care for people with HIV infection in France.

financial support empowered the structuring and professionalization of these networks, initially based on the creation of "coordinator jobs, veritable executives in the organization of urban care" (Patte 1998, p. 12, author's translation). Most of these new jobs were filled by nurses, making them the first managers of these innovative organizations. The Jupé/Barrot ordinances of April 1996[2] reinforced this formalization of existing city-hospital networks, enabling new networks to be set up around other pathologies and health themes (drug addiction, oncology, diabetology, palliative care, health-precarity, etc.), consolidating partnership dynamics on the ground. Cooperative approaches, however imperfect, have been one of the cornerstones of this process.

8.2.1.2. *The confirmation*

We had to wait until the reforms of 2002[3] to have a definition for these organizations, which stated that these health networks:

> [...] are designed to promote access to healthcare, coordination, the continuity and interdisciplinarity of healthcare services, particularly those specific to certain populations, pathologies, or healthcare activities. [...] They are made up of self-employed health professionals, occupational physicians, health establishments, health centers, social or medico-social institutions and health or social organizations, as well as user representatives. (Law No. 2002-303 of March 4, 2002, Article 84, author's translation).

This legislative framework has led to genuine institutional recognition, as well as establishing relationships between the various actors involved in coordination. Between 2001 and 2007, a succession of special funds was set aside for the development of networking, with the aim of improving the effectiveness of the healthcare coordination policy, and decompartmentalizing the healthcare system, all the while promoting partnerships. As the first lifecycle of healthcare networks drew to a close, these changes somewhat removed their innovative aims, but in so doing laid down the foundations for their organization and the beginnings of a human resources (HR) framework. Over the last 15 years or so, these spontaneous coordination structures have been transformed – at the instigation of the public

---

2 French Ordinance No. 96-345 of April 24, 1996 regarding the medical control of healthcare expenditure; French Ordinance No. 96-346 of April 24, 1996, concerning the reform of public and private hospitalization.

3 French Law No. 2002-303 of March 4, 2002, regarding patients' rights and the quality of the healthcare system and French Law No. 2001-1246 of December 21, 2001, concerning the financing of social security for 2002.

authorities, but above all because of the activism of their initiators, the true "founding fathers" – into more orderly organizations with employees whose mission is to "perform the music for the project". The leaders of these structures, not always "equipped" with strategic and managerial skills, have nonetheless succeeded in arranging their partnership relations around common visions, and the sharing of knowledge and skills, with great dynamism. The health networks have developed an organizational learning process, which evolves as a function of the mistakes they make or the context in which they operate.

8.2.1.3. *Institutionalization*

In 2012, some 700 networks were financed by the FIQCS (*Fonds d'intervention pour la qualité et la coordination des soins*) intervention fund for the quality and coordination of care. Public authorities point to contrasting results, in particular "a high degree of heterogeneity in the activity of health networks" and "variable efficiency", without necessarily questioning their practices in supporting health networks. The human resources of these networks have evolved considerably, and now most often rely on a director or coordinator, assisted by an administrative manager and/or an administrative secretary. In addition, there is a healthcare coordination team, made up of doctors, nurses, psychologists, social workers and so on, depending on the theme and maturity of the network. Sometimes, depending on local dynamics and experimentation, one or more project managers are integrated into these systems.

As a result, these health networks have moved from an "initiator", sometimes "founder", "employee activist" approach to a structured, more formalized organization made up of several multi-professional employees. The current aim of this new framework, as of 2012, is to refocus health networks on their mission of supporting multi-skilled local coordination, to be at the service of GPs and local teams in order to handle complex situations. This has enabled single-issue networks to become multi-purpose, bringing together, for example, oncology, palliative care and gerontology in a single "all-ages, all-pathologies" system. These "new 3-in-1" networks will now interface "from birth to death".

However, a number of mergers, not always deliberate, have led to the breakdown of existing partnerships. In 2016, as part of the French law on the modernization of our healthcare system, the public authorities set up the PTA (*Plateformes territoriales d'appui*) local support platforms to support primary healthcare providers in complex situations, regardless of age or pathology. In light of these developments, some healthcare networks have seized on these mechanisms to strengthen their action, while attempting to bring together the various existing coordination structures in the same territory. Indeed, as early as 2011, the public authorities, in a logic that is not always easy to understand, organized or encouraged the development of new coordination structures, such as MAIA, whose public health aims are not open to debate, but which have nevertheless drawn attention to the sheer number of coordination structures. As a result, in 2019, the French healthcare system had no fewer than seven coordination mechanisms, all of which were intertwined and, furthermore, were competing with each other, creating difficulties, when they should be working toward making healthcare paths more fluid and simpler, in order to reduce... complexity!

Network	Abbreviation	Year of constitution
Healthcare networks	–	1996
Support program for returning home after hospitalization	PRADO	2011
Local information and coordination center	CLIC	2011
Action method for integrating care and assistance services in the field of autonomy	MAIA	2011
Local support coordination	CTA	2013
Program for elderly people at risk of losing their autonomy	PAERPA	2013
Local support platforms	PTA	2016

Table 8.1. *Description of the different systems in 2019 before the introduction of DAC coordination support systems*

Therefore, with a view to "simplifying and converging local coordination support systems", the DAC coordination support systems are being deployed under the aegis of the Regional Health Agencies (RHAs), which are responsible for this convergence with a deadline of July 2022. Ultimately, the DAC coordination support systems are to be the sole point of contact for healthcare, social and medico-social professionals, with the following missions:

– information and referral to appropriate local resources for healthcare, social and medico-social professionals, patients and their families, at the suggestion of a professional;

– support for the structuring and local improvement of healthcare pathways;

– contributing to a shared diagnosis of local healthcare needs and supply;

– leading or taking part in local forums for consultation between professionals and so on.

When we take a closer look at these missions, it becomes clear that partnerships are at the heart of their development. Over the past 2 years, these various structures and coordination networks have been converging toward a new model, between creation or constructive merger/absorption, sometimes forced and therefore deleterious for relations between local actors. To paraphrase Courie-Lemeur in her book *Les réseaux de santé, les enjeux de la pérennité*, healthcare coordination arrangements are a "perpetual construction site" (Courie-Lemeur 2018, p. 53).

8.2.2. The strategic alliance, a new partnership vision for DACs

As we saw in the previous chapter, partnership appears, at all levels, to be an intrinsic component of coordination arrangements, even if each manager does not always define it in the same way. The words "cooperation", "collaboration" and "contractualization" used by the heads of these organizations cover disparate realities. Partnership is the "central core" of DAC coordination support systems. In fact, as mentioned above, these networks were created from existing structures, supplemented by various local organizations that had institutional and/or healthcare organization clout. This new assembly forms their strategic core, with a consensus on a common vision within the framework of the various bodies, boards of directors or steering committees, linked to the associative status, the dominant model for DAC support.

The history of coordination structures also highlights the ongoing re-composition of their own strategies in order to better respond to their healthcare missions, but more often than not, this reorganization is linked to an injunction from the public authorities. The introduction of DAC coordination support systems fully confirms this new logic of pooling, under prescription, which modifies the relationship between the operator and the public authorities. This leads the leaders of this new system to:

> [...] rethink the internal organizational architecture of their structures, so as to identify the resources and skills that operate within them and rearticulate them in a logic of greater transversality, to carry out actions beyond the sector's compartmentalization, and to be able to respond in a personalized way to increasingly complex requests for intervention. (Grenier and Guitton-Philippe 2011, p. 108, author's translation).

Therefore, to respond to the new framework, these new organizations will have to rediscover the ancestral instincts of the pioneers, more specifically in the co-construction of their relationships with actors who have not been integrated into their organization, but also with the supervisory authorities. These DAC coordination support systems will need to implement a new logic in order to build their partnership strategy, based in particular on their legitimacy to coordinate the various actors and systems in a given territory, within which there will obviously be areas of convergence, but also strong divergences. It is also pointed out that these new structures do not always have natural credibility and legitimacy, especially when they have been recomposed and the former leaders have not been retained to support the DAC coordination support system. A strong partnership is needed, involving professionals with no hierarchical links between them. The strategic alliance that is to be established cannot be based on an imposed approach, but rather on a negotiated one, which leaves plenty of room for consultation when setting up the framework and the objectives. The DAC coordination support systems, as the promoter of this dynamic, will have to commit to an approach that consists of:

> [...] having the ability to obtain a coalition of interest, to bring together a growing number of allies that make promoters increasingly legitimate and that, in a recursive way, allows actors' mentalities to change as structures change. (Minvielle and Constandriopoulos 2004, p. 47, author's translation).

Should we not be talking about strategic alliances rather than partnerships now? A number of management theorists have distinguished alliances from partnerships, pointing out that the latter term was reserved in the "market" sector for a "commercial" relationship between at least two competing structures. The term "alliance", on the other hand, is based on a logic of working "with" others, thereby encouraging more elaborate solutions. There are many articles that define what a strategic alliance might be, intended for companies within the production industry, which nevertheless could be applied, with adaptations, to DAC coordination support systems. Particular noteworthy is the work by Hennart (1988), who evokes, among other things, "complementarity" cooperations, oriented towards accessing new markets or resources and/or skills that the company does not (yet) possess. This initial classification could be supplemented with the work of Ingham (2015), who highlights the role of organizational learning as a source of motivation for bringing structures together. Zouabi Ouadrani and Smida (2019) identify the motivations for strategic alliances in the healthcare field, admittedly focused on healthcare institutions, but which are partly applicable to DAC coordination support systems. Elements concerning *rapprochement* are highlighted as "a means of coping with institutional constraints (legal and political, cultural and social) in order to ensure social legitimacy and absorption of uncertainty" (Zouabi Ouadrani and Slmiuda 2019, p. 537, author's translation).

These elements make sense in light of the effort to structure coordination mechanisms, set in motion in 2019, notably as a result of the public authorities' injunction to bring them together. It is therefore a strategic "command" partnership, not necessarily desired by the structures, that has been demonstrated in the DAC coordination support system setups. It should also be pointed out that, during this conciliation phase, the setup is not always based on "confraternal" trust. For some of the actors, when setting up these new arrangements, their very survival was at stake. On the other hand, once the DAC coordination support systems have been set up, the alliances that need to be strengthened and/or built are in response to the need to perpetuate these nascent systems, but above all to ensure their performance. In this situation, cooperation can be conceived as a complementary resource between partners with distinct skills based on a convergence of interests and long-term commitment.

In this way, we could attempt to define the notion of a strategic alliance for DAC coordination support systems: this could refer to the links to be established with and between the various partners in the territory, who decide to pool human and methodological resources, technical skills and practices, within the framework of co-constructed strategies, in order to meet the objectives entrusted to them by the State. The dynamics required to reach the objectives set by the State will commit these systems over longer periods and will require their managers to put in place genuine pacts with medium- and long-term visions. We are fully committed to a "win-win" logic, which is a way of contracting between partners, sometimes very heterogeneous, based on non-hierarchical and, above all, non-centralized relationships.

This initial framework, which needs to be studied in greater detail, cannot be universal. Indeed, depending on the history of each DAC coordination support system, its leaders and local partners, specific alliances may be forged. To date, there is certainly a model promulgated by the public authorities, but observation shows that, depending on various parameters, these structures differ in terms of their organization, in the objectives to be achieved, and thus create new innovation dynamics. Operators take ownership of the approach.

8.2.3. *Which alliances for DACs?*

Drawing up an exhaustive list of partners with whom the DAC coordination support systems should establish alliances would be too tedious and, in any case, incomplete, as the mobilization of professionals to be called upon depends on the missions of these structures, but above all on their concrete existence within the territory. Therefore, the notion of alliance will be found in all the DAC mission statements to ensure that the person under care can have a pathway that is best suited to their situation. When studying four texts[4] highlighting the primary mission statements of a DAC coordination support system, it is easy to confirm that alliances are at the center.

Support for professionals refers to those working in the healthcare field, whether on a self-employed or salaried basis, in healthcare, social and medico-social establishments and services. All of these professionals must be able to benefit from DAC coordination support system services. As part of the development of local facilitation, which is a fully fledged public service mission, DAC coordination support systems are expected to help "establish a virtuous dynamic with local actors". In the same text, there are elements that clearly lay down the foundations for an example contractual framework of a strategic alliance:

> [...] DACs do not take the place of local actors in implementing their projects and missions [...] To this end, the DACs know and recognize the missions, possibilities and limits to the intervention of each of the actors in the territory. (Cadre national d'orientation 2020, p. 1, author's translation).

As part of the partnerships to be established, the DAC coordination support systems will also have to step up their actions with patient representatives and, perhaps incongruously, with institutional partners, notably the RHA. Even if the latter steer, finance and control the system, a new coherent model is being established based on co-construction with local actors. This change in attitude on the part of the supervisory authorities has seen them evolve from a role of regulation and control to one of help and support for actors in the field, or even partnership.

To succeed in its mission, the DAC coordination support system will have to develop partnerships with existing or potential actors and bring the created coalition to life, with or without a formal agreement. This will be based on an essential initial strategic component, the main tasks of which will be:

– to identify the partner and analyze the context;

---

4 Decree No. 2021-295 of March 18, 2021 relating to complex healthcare pathway coordination support devices and specific regional devices. Ile-de-France DAC mission and organizational guidelines. ARS Ile-de-France. *Guide de déploiements*. November 2019. Cadre national d'orientation. Unification des Dispositifs d'appui à la coordination des parcours complexes. Ministère des Solidarités et de la Santé, Caisse nationale de solidarité pour l'autonomie, Caisse nationale de l'assurance maladie, June 2020. Dispositif d'appui à la coordination ; boîte à outils, ministère des Solidarités et de la Santé, Caisse nationale de solidarité pour l'autonomie, January 2021.

– to define and negotiate the alliance strategy;

– to manage and coordinate actions;

– to support and monitor the alliance;

– to enhance its value and, of course, evaluate it, etc.

This dynamic could be set in motion, certainly in a dual relationship with a partner, but above all in a more systemic logic of local event facilitation, enabling the development of a network of alliances.

8.2.4. Human resources: the key to a successful strategic alliance

Is human resource management not one of the most overlooked aspects of coordination schemes? Behind this somewhat provocative statement, observation toward the evolution of these organizations over several years has revealed a lack of interest on the part of the initiators of these schemes, public authorities and even researchers. It is as if the focus over all these years of deployment has been essentially on the construction process, on integration into the organization of the healthcare system, and also on the coordination function, without necessarily looking at the management of these systems. The DAC coordination support system guidance framework does, of course, highlight methodological elements such as the coordination of collaborative work, project management, change management strategy and quality approach, communication strategy and so on, but there is little qualitative information on the human resources required, the expectations of public authorities in terms of skills to be mobilized or adapted, and the development of new professions. Management of the DAC coordination support system is reserved for the "jack-of-all-trades" director, tasked with a range of missions, which include:

– participating in the association's strategic thinking in conjunction with the administrators;

– proposing and implementing changes;

– managing a multi-professional team;

– drawing up budgets and funding applications, negotiating and ensuring their implementation and follow-up;

– initiating and strengthening relations with various partners, public authorities and institutional bodies.

Even if the task of developing and "bringing to life" the alliances is and will be the responsibility of many other DAC coordination support system employees, the role of the director is essential. They will need to mobilize their talents for mediation and co-construction in order to establish the cooperative dynamics that are vital to the success of these new arrangements. To date, the job descriptions of current DAC coordination support system managers, and recruitment advertisements, only mention very general partnership objectives, even though they represent a significant, if not perhaps the most important dimension for the success of these organizations.

8.2.5. *The alliance manager, a key DAC professional?*

The proliferation, diversity and complexity of partnerships in commercial companies has, over the past 15 years or so, led to the emergence of a new profession: the alliance manager. The academic literature and that produced by professional associations are *prolix* in terms of both Anglo-Saxon and French definitions (Blavet 2018): manager, partnerships or alliances director, alliances and partnerships manager, alliance-maker, *allianceur*, alliance manager, strategic alliance manager, alliance account manager, global director for strategic alliances, or strategic partenerships manager and so on. However, despite its rapid growth, this recent profession is encountering difficulties in structuring itself, due to the diversity of statuses, positioning within companies and confirmed mission goals. On the other hand, many authors have highlighted two key elements:

– alliances and partnerships create value for the company;

– the role of the alliance manager is essential to this creation of value, which is sometimes difficult to quantify.

When applied to DAC coordination support systems, which are organizations with a public service mission, these elements may question, or even provoke, certain managers. Behind this notion of value, we need to perceive a logic that is not simply focused on profit, but rather on the establishment of shared synergies, creating genuine collective know-how, enabling us to achieve our objectives efficiently. The establishment of an interface culture creates collective values for DAC coordination support systems, as it does for companies with commercial objectives. For this reason, it is clear that:

> The alliance manager is not a manager like any other, given [their] interface position. [They are] a builder and a pilot facing specific challenges, who must break away from traditional approaches. (Blanchot 2006, p. 1, author's translation).

In this way, the builder's function is based on forming and building partnerships with the "right" actors. In the context of DAC coordination support systems, these partnerships, as we saw earlier, are often existing or new local actors, with whom it will be necessary, at some point, to cooperate in order to respond to local public health issues. Unlike "commercial" companies, one does not necessarily have to search for and select a partner. On the other hand, given the multitude of actors involved, prioritization will certainly be necessary. What is more, the role of "builder" will require those in charge of these coordination structures to negotiate the initial terms of collaboration and to define, together, the objectives to be achieved. To date, few structures in charge of coordinating healthcare and coordinating regional initiatives have been able to define such precise partnership arrangements.

The steering function makes it possible to:

– monitor, maintain and even enhance the quality of the partnership;

– evaluate results;

– modify the initial objectives and/or adjust the actions taken to achieve them in light of these results.

Within the DAC coordination support systems – even though in many areas they are still in the process of being constructed – the steering of partnerships still appears perfunctory, as it is not based on any real strategy or programming. Depending on the company's sector, size and so on, the literature sometimes separates the mission of "builder" from that of "pilot". In DAC coordination support systems, these missions are inseparable. More often than not, in commercial companies, the alliance manager is one of the company's resources, attached to a department and leading a development team. In view of the scope of DAC coordination support systems, this mission reports directly to the manager, who must mobilize their various collaborators, most of whom will be involved in creating and maintaining partnerships with various healthcare actors. They must also collaborate with institutional actors, whether or not they fund the DAC coordination support system's actions. It is up to this actor to determine the framework for local cooperation and to govern it. They are accountable to their governing bodies, and to the funders, for adherence and the objectives pursued, and are also responsible for managing any conflicts that may arise.

To draw a parallel, the symbol of the coxswain in rowing is illustrative. The coxswain must manage the direction of the boat in order to achieve the set objectives and must advise and coach the crew in order to determine the pace, but also to make adjustments according to events happening in real-time. They are the tactician during the race, but also beforehand, in the preparation of the objectives with their staff, like the DAC coordination support system director is for their authorities. In this way, we find construction, piloting and, sometimes, constitution, as even some coxswains participate in the design and adaptation of their boats. "Know-how" appears to be essential to this profession, which is consistent with the need to create collective value. To "steer their boat well", the coxswain will have to deal with conflicts and obstacles, both internally and with partners.

DAC coordination support systems are the assembly, sometimes not always chosen, of existing actors who have their own activities, autonomy and leaders. This means they have to cope with organizational and cultural resistance, particularly during the setup phase, when a lack of trust can combine with managerial, relational and communication difficulties, accentuated by the uncertainty of the environment. Early identification of these obstacles is essential so that a new equilibrium can be renegotiated through mediation or arbitration, possibly in conjunction with the supervisory authorities.

On the other hand, certain steps can be taken to establish a framework, notably through a partnership agreement, setting out the rights and duties of each party. A "structure for dialogue at the top" (Guth 1998) must also be put in place to reinforce trust. Returning to the DAC coordination support system, we must not lose sight of the fact that in most partnerships, unlike commercial ventures, conflicts are unavoidable, as highlighted above. In fact, in the territory in which it operates, networks of actors are obliged to collaborate. There is therefore an obligation to build and manage alliances.

8.3. Lessons learned

After such analysis, the following question must be asked: is alliance-building a job to be formalized in the future for DAC coordination support systems? It already seems appropriate to rethink the place of partnership, which is not simply the desire or obligation to collaborate, within the framework of DAC coordination support systems. Certainly, other professions linked to coordination need to be professionalized, but we must not forget the management and managerial functions, as has all too often been neglected by those in charge of these schemes, and also by the public authorities. Partnerships are an important issue for these structures, and a major mechanism for implementing strategy. As such, they need to explore and decipher their environment, while taking a closer look at each other's challenges and complementarities, in order to "situate" themselves and then develop, through co-construction, an effective alliance. To achieve this, DAC coordination support system managers will have to rethink the way they work together, in order to forge links that will enable more fluid and effective relations. Although all DAC coordination support system employees and administrators can and should be involved in local alliances, the task of alliance-builder falls to the DAC coordination support system director. In future, if the structures that develop their missions are entrusted with others and permitted to innovate, they will take on a different scope than those of today, perhaps necessitating, in time, the creation of a specific position to take charge of this dynamic.

Although the role of alliance manager is still in its infancy and tends to originate in the commercial sector, a number of studies have highlighted the qualities and skills that can be integrated into other sectors of activity, notably healthcare. On the other hand, it is important to point out that in view of their knowledge and experience, DAC coordination support system managers already mobilize high-quality interpersonal skills and know-how specific to this alliance-building function. As we have already mentioned, the establishment of a strategic alliance between several actors is based on a number of successive phases. Subsequently, it is worth asking which skills need to be mobilized as the partnership evolves. Indeed, when a DAC coordination support system is set up, partnership relationships exist, even if these are sometimes strained because they have been imposed. The role of the DAC coordination support system manager, possibly supported by their governing bodies, will be to set out a genuine vision for the partnerships to be initiated, developed or strengthened: the strategic alliance is launched.

To carry out their mission successfully, the head of the DAC coordination support system must take on the role of ambassador, setting the framework while representing the interests that they must represent in cooperation with the other partners. They must be able to convince, while establishing a co-construction process. Their negotiating skills will be fully solicited, especially if areas of opposition arise. Last but not least, they will need to have or mobilize legal skills, so that the contract signed with the establishments stipulates "in black and white" the respective obligations of each party. In the implementation phase, they will need to convey the objectives of the partnership, without losing sight of them. They can also act as a facilitator and "networker", helping to build a common project. As part of the project management process, they will need to mobilize skills to avoid potential conflicts, while ensuring the quality of relationships. Above all, they must not forget that "the greatest political virtue is not to lose the sense of the whole" (Mounier 2014, author's translation).

In his article exploring what makes an alliance manager, *"Qu'est-ce qu'un manager d'alliances"*, Blanchot (2006) highlights the results of several studies defining skills for building sustainable relationships, managing through influence and negotiation, managing complexity and interdependencies, and managing roles, responsibilities and motivations. Taking some of these elements and comparing them with the framework faced by a DAC coordination support system manager, and simulating these tasks to completion, it is possible to highlight the key competencies and skills given in Table 8.2.

Knowledge	Know-how	Intrapersonal skills
– Identification of actors, their strategy, objectives, operations and interdependence, as well as knowledge and understanding of local informal systems. These elements form the basis of the strategic alliance, enabling a mapping of partners and a configuration of roles and responsibilities – Expertise in the organization's operations and its own challenges, both internally and externally – Have a precise vision of the partnership strategy, as the "network head", and share it with all the associated actors through dynamic, appropriate communication – Establish precise, achievable and measurable objectives to evaluate the partnership – Monitor developments, trends and experiments carried out by local partners and public authorities, to "stay one step ahead" – Legal knowledge to establish or rely on to determine the terms of the partnership, stating the framework with flexibility	– Ability to mobilize local resources, including the skills of various partners, to create synergies – Manage in a consultative, co-constructing and co-managing way – Create the conditions for developing a common culture – Ability to synthesize and analyze data – Oral expression, public speaking – Negotiation and contractualization – Writing skills – Lobbying techniques	– Leadership, interpersonal skills, ability to listen and motivate – Demonstrate diplomacy, agility, flexibility and open-mindedness – Ability to negotiate and persuade convincingly – Ability to establish principles of transparency and openness in relationships between partners – Ability to communicate, listen and understand – Empathy, conflict resolution, etc. – Ability to develop trust – Anticipation and initiative – Renunciation of hierarchy with partners – Strength of conviction – And, of course, discretion and respect for confidentiality

Table 8.2. *Skills and competencies of an alliance manager of DAC coordination support systems*

This list is by no means exhaustive. It provides an initial framework, which could be followed up with a further study of DAC coordination support system managers to determine a more precise "profile". Following various observations, it appears that for some DAC coordination support system leaders, some skills can be acquired, but there also some abilities that are innate, such as being optimistic, determined, creative and pragmatic, but also adapting in the face of adversity, which are part and parcel of their professional heritage. To date, however, it is difficult to discern from job descriptions or advertisements some of these skills, which are undoubtedly essential to the success, constitution, construction and management of DAC coordination support systems, while at the same time starting to consider, in the medium term, possible adaptations to this system.

The alliance between local actors is the central foundation upon which these systems will be built, not only in terms of local coordination, but also on a day-to-day basis, in the management of complex situations involving healthcare professionals, patients and their families. This chapter does not take into account the alliance with the patient on their overall healthcare, whereas the notion of patient partner will surely be a strong component of the performance of the French healthcare system, based on cooperation between professionals and the patient "through dialogue, the complementarity of their knowledge that enables co-learning and the co-construction of a personalized care project" (Laloux et al. 2019, p. 16, author's translation).

When recruiting, knowledge and know-how will be essential; the director will have to propose and drive the strategy of the association that supports the DAC coordination support system, manage the latter administratively and financially, steer and monitor the actions undertaken, while managing the administrative team and the multi-disciplinary team. In addition, we need to add missions linked to partnerships. As we have already shown, interpersonal skills are a key factor in the success of the alliance-maker. The recruiter will also need to identify personality-related elements. When you put all these elements together, it becomes clear that this is a complex search: you might well be searching in vain for "a five-legged sheep".

Professional management experience of around 10 years in a complex organization with a significant amount of alliance content, coupled with a master's degree in management science or a related field, could be an interesting approach. The creation of a specific training program, "under the supervision of the supervisory authorities", to train these future managers, does not necessarily appear to be a relevant initiative. Indeed, a range of profiles can only be an asset when it comes to thinking about strategy in a global, cross-functional way. Currently, complementary training courses are appearing for DAC coordination support system actors; learning about partnership is present, but often in a descriptive logic, without any genuine invitation for input by the alliances needing leadership, and above all ways to acquire the intrapersonal skills. While natural abilities are certainly necessary to make a "good" alliance builder, learning-on-the-job is always a possible avenue. To date, few specific training courses on alliance development have been created, and when they do exist, they are geared exclusively to commercial logic, which has little or nothing to do with the building of DAC coordination support systems. If government funding is available, it would be preferable to allocate it to training courses that focus more on management through cross-functional approaches, such as change management, interpersonal communication, personal development, crisis management and so on. The objectives of such an approach are to ensure that the alliances are developed in the best possible way, to provide keys to better understanding and to offer toolkits to enable managers of emerging DAC coordination support systems to acquire and/or consolidate relational skills. It would perhaps be worthwhile studying existing training courses offered by universities or training institutes that lead to the acquisition of these skills and setting up alliances (yes, that is right) to create training courses adapted to the field of intervention of DAC coordination support systems. Other innovations could result, in particular, by integrating support logics for DAC coordination support system teams, a collective know-how to facilitate relationships with the various partner actors could be established. The creation of forums for exchanges and meetings could also be considered. In light of these few perspectives, there is a real challenge for DAC coordination support system managers, who will likely have to get out of their comfort zone in order to build and manage alliances in complex environments.

8.4. References

Barré, S., Evin, C., Fouré, P.Y. (2005). *Traité pratique des réseaux de santé*. Éditions Berger-Levrault, Boulogne Billancourt.

Blanchot, F. (2006). Qu'est-ce qu'un manager d'alliances ? [Online]. Available at: https://basepub.dauphine.fr/handle/123456789/805.

Blavet, L. (2018). Le profil de l'Alliance Manager. Report, MOOC Management des alliances et partenariats, Institut Montpellier Management.

Courie-Lemeur, A. (2018). *Les réseaux de santé : les enjeux de la pérennité*. ISTE Editions, London.

Grenier, C. and Guitton-Philippe, S. (2011). La question des regroupements/mutualisations dans le champ sanitaire et social : l'institutionnalisation d'un mouvement stratégique ? *Management et avenir*, 47, 98–113.

Guth, J.P. (1998). *Batisseurs d'Alliance*. Eyrolles, Paris.

Hennart, J.F. (1988). A transaction costs theory of equity joint-ventures. *Strategic Management Journal*, 9(4), 361–374.

Ingham, M. (2015). L'apprentissage organisationnel dans les coopérations. *Revue française de gestion*, 41, 55–81.

Laloux, M., Néron, A., Lecocq, D. (2019). Le partenariat patient : une pratique collaborative innovante incluant le patient partenaire. *Santé conjuguée*, 88, 14–18.

Minvielle, E. and Contandriopoulos, A.P. (2004). La conduite du changement, quelles leçons tirer de la restructuration hospitalière ? *Revue française de gestion*, 150, 29–53.

Mounier, E. (2014). *Le personnalisme*. Cairn, Paris.

Patte, D. (1998). Les enjeux de la coordination. *ADSP*, 24, 16–17.

Zouabi Ouadrani, B. and Slmiuda, A. (2019). Quels besoins à l'origine d'une alliance stratégique entre organisations sanitaires. *Journal de gestion et d'économie de la santé*, 6, 532–557.

PART 3

Innovation and Resilience of Healthcare Organizations

Introduction to Part 3

This section looks at the dynamic relationship between the innovation and resilience of healthcare organizations through the lens of various perspectives, from researchers to practitioners to healthcare institutions. Organizational innovations resulting from experiments under Article 51 of the French Social Security Financing Act are analyzed by researchers and by institutions, with findings that intersect, diverge, reinforce and, above all, complement each other. Innovations in the practices of hospital healthcare staff, whether social, organizational or technological, are accompanied by common issues, as shown by the analyses of university researchers and of a hospital researcher-practitioner.

In Chapter 9, Jihane Sebai and Bérangère L. Szostak focus on the creativity of hospital healthcare providers to ensure continuity of patient care and to remedy disruptions in healthcare pathways despite differing material and human constraints, particularly in times of crisis. They are particularly interested in social innovation through design and see it as a way of breaking with the bureaucratic practices entrenched in the French hospital system. They propose three factors deemed necessary for the deployment of successful social innovations in the hospital environment, with a view to fostering its resilience. They call attention to the challenge this represents, particularly in view of "pernicious problems" that can wear down and discourage the actors involved in this innovation process, and encourage the production of solutions to the irritants of everyday hospital life, using a co-creation and co-design approach in a process of "reflection in action".

In Chapter 10, Cécile Dezest, Isabelle Franchisteguy-Couloume and Emmanuelle Cargnello-Charles look at innovative experiments linked to the creation of innovative spaces in a locality, stemming from Article 51 of the French Social Security Financing Act 2018, as well as the role of the patient in these innovations.

Introduction written by Aline COURIE-LEMEUR.

They stress the importance of involving all actors within the healthcare system, overhauling the principles of healthcare organization in France, as well as including the patient as a stakeholder within the scheme, for the successful deployment of organizational, technological and social innovations akin to innovation spaces to improve patient healthcare. They identify points to watch out for and mechanisms for success in building such spaces, with regard to the patient's role.

In Chapter 11, Marianne Sarazin questions the implications of the use of new digital technologies in medical practices, which she describes as a revolution. In particular, she draws attention to the professional skills of healthcare professionals, who are adapting resiliently to this invasion, which calls into question the meaning they give to some of their tasks. She develops two case studies based on experiments in integrating new technologies into the practices of certain healthcare professionals and warns that the transformation of roles they provoke calls into question the entire conception of each type of profession. She concludes by stressing the importance of not forgetting that the object of change is life itself, which calls for extra precautions and that the "sick" object takes on a whole new meaning through the prism of a technology that interferes in human relationships.

In Chapter 12, Sophie Bataille, Élise Bléry, Charlotte Roudier-Daval and Michel Marty take a step back to present two case studies on innovative working methods deployed within the Ile-de-France RHA: one is linked to the experiments resulting from Article 51, and the other is linked to local coordination within the framework of the Chronic Heart Failure pathway. These case studies illustrate the evolution of the institutional position of the RHA and the *Assurance maladie* from a top-down approach to a lateral one, where the supervisory authorities become companions, co-constructors, local facilitators and partners, enabling the development of collective intelligence. They point out that such intelligence is essential if we are to meet the challenges of socio-demographic and epidemiological change and improve the management of increasingly prevalent chronic diseases. They warn of the complexity of these transformations, which calls for in-depth support. The main challenges are to succeed in making mutual trust a common objective, to involve users at every project stage, and to pursue the transformation of institutions toward a service-oriented outlook.

Social Innovation through Design in Hospitals: Challenges and Proposals for Conditions of Success

The health context of Covid-19 has put the spotlight on the creativity of care and healthcare actors in terms of alternatives and solutions to ensure continuity of care and to remedy the breakdown of healthcare pathways, despite the various material and human constraints. While this is nothing new in itself, it does underline the need to break with the bureaucratic practices already entrenched in the French hospital system to enable these actors to devise original solutions to their problems in the day-to-day exercise of their duties. How can this be achieved? This chapter examines this question, drawing on work in the fields of design and healthcare facility management, and puts forward three proposed success factors. In particular, it considers: (i) the appropriation of social innovation through design by the hospital's general management; (ii) the legitimization and defense of social innovation through design by actors; and (iii) the need for democratic consultation between the actors and the adaptability of the design to the hospital context.

9.1. Background context and questions

Protocols in healthcare systems fluctuate continually between the application of specific standards and procedures (healthcare pathways, evaluation of practices, recommendations, evidence-based medicine, best practices, etc.) and the development of artisanal practices resulting from experimentation, adjustments, initiative and improvisation by those working in the field, which may subsequently give rise to new standards and procedures (Tassaux et al. 2010). This

Chapter written by Jihane SEBAI and Bérangère L. SZOSTAK.

is understandable insofar as variability and unforeseen events very often appear the norm in healthcare systems for which there are many complexities. Indeed, the object of work itself, in this case carried out by the human being, is extremely complex in nature and needs to be better understood and specified (Xiao 1994; Amalberti and Hourlier 2007). Therefore, given the lack of knowledge of numerous parameters, efforts to standardize protocols seem insufficient and leave room for uncertainty in the diagnoses and treatments proposed (Cuvelier 2013). Added to this is the constant need to renew the skills and know-how required to deploy innovative techniques and manage new pathologies. One of the major challenges for healthcare system protocols is to ensure the compatibility of these two modes of action: standardized, procedural medicine and traditional medicine.

In short, it can be summarized by the term organizational resilience, that is, the process, ability or result of adapting to a shock despite circumstances, challenges or threats external to the entity under study. Put another way, for healthcare systems, it is a question of their ability to ensure the compatibility of these two consubstantial modes of action, so that protocols are effective in dealing with the full range of complexities inherent to healthcare. The question then is how to foster the resilience of healthcare systems and thus support their ability to better articulate the two modalities (Morel et al. 2009; Cuvelier et al. 2011) and improve the ways in which systems develop and continue to function despite disruptions and disturbances (Cuvelier 2013).

While it is fair to say that the last 2 years (2020–2021) appear rich in answers to this question, notably through the development of artisanal practices linked to current standards and procedures, openness to experimentation with a view to encourage the development of innovative responses in the public sector (Sørensen and Torfing 2012; Gagnon and Côté 2016; Côté et al. 2017) long predates the pandemic crisis. Indeed, healthcare organizations, such as other public sector structures (Gagnon and Côté 2016; Côté et al. 2017), are increasingly open to innovation (Damart 2013). They use participative approaches and creativity tools such as design thinking (Pellerin and Coirié 2017; Grosjean et al. 2019). This echoes, in short, what service organizations have been doing for the past 15 years, interacting with many different actors. The greater the number of actors involved, and the more diverse and varied users' expectations, the more urgent the need for participatory innovation, for both actors and users. This openness to innovation in healthcare organizations is underpinned by the competitive spirit in which the public sector in general and the care and healthcare sector in particular increasingly find themselves when faced with private-sector services, particularly clinics. This is prompting them to renew the meaning and values of public service, by encouraging a process of modernization and service transformation to focus more on the individual.

In this way, healthcare organizations are developing what contemporary authors call social innovation through design (Le Bœuf 2015; Catoir-Brisson and Royer 2017)[1]. Put another way, with tools and methods specific to the discipline of design, organizations are developing original responses to complex problems of a social nature (Laville et al. 2014; Pellerin and Coirié 2017).

On the other hand, the literature shows that the integration of design into an innovation strategy is not a straightforward undertaking because this discipline often calls into question many choices of a strategic nature, and conditions must be met to achieve this (Borja de Mozota 2002; Gay and Szostak 2019). This seems all the more difficult for public-sector organizations, given that design tools and methods, and especially design thinking, were conceived and developed by and for private companies, such as Apple, IBM, 3M and IDEO (Brown 2009). In addition to the coexistence of standardized, procedural medicine and artisanal medicine, the particularity of healthcare organizations, defined by their dual structure (administrative structure and medical structure, made up of experts such as doctors), seems a second difficulty, since design calls for all points of view to be considered on the same level, whether the person is a healthcare executive, secretary, orderly, nurse or surgeon. The question that then arises is to determine the success factors for developing social innovation through design in healthcare establishments, such as a public hospital. The broader aim is also to contribute to a better understanding of how to support the resilience of these establishments, which are now facing disruptions and new challenges.

To answer this question, this chapter draws on work in design and healthcare facility management and puts forward proposals for conditions of success. In particular, it highlights the importance of ensuring that design is appropriated by the organization's general management and that this creative tool is legitimized and defended by the actors involved in social innovation through design, while bearing in mind the need for democratic consultation between actors, from all groups, and adapting designs to the hospital context. The final part of the chapter sets out potential managerial recommendations for healthcare organizations, as well as suggesting research perspectives on social innovation through design within hospitals.

9.2. Conceptual framework

Following the Second World War in England, design became an asset of social and economic policy, and a stimulator and catalyst for the development of

---

1 See also "Social innovation through design". Available at: https://projekt.unimes.fr/innovation-sociale-design/.

innovation in healthcare (Lucie-Smith 1983; De Noblet 1988; Guidot 2000). This was the case in the 1950s in particular, during the nursing shortage crisis, when the King's Fund was introduced in all British hospitals. Although the standardization of beds was originally part of an economic reform of hospitals (Lawrence 2001), improved patient comfort was highlighted as the social dimension underpinning the project's deployment and supported its legitimacy. We therefore consider innovation to be social in the field of healthcare design, when it goes beyond the logic of use (user-centered design)[2] to address social issues (human-centered design) (Tromp et al. 2011), and to change the behavior of all the actors involved in these issues by mobilizing tools that enable such changes, such as design thinking.

To support this statement, we reveal the conceptual framework in three stages. First, we clarify what is meant by social innovation through design, and second, we consider it in the case of hospitals, in order to, third, set out a framework for the appropriation of design as a management tool. We then propose success factors for the development of social innovation by design in public hospitals.

9.2.1. Social innovation through design

According to Catoir-Brisson and Royer (2017), the current resurgence of social innovation is strongly correlated with the social changes of the contemporary world, engendered by the various crises that run through us. For Laville et al., social innovation refers to a process and:

> [...] an intervention initiated by social actors, to respond to an aspiration, meet a need, provide a solution or take advantage of an opportunity for action in order to modify social relations, transform a framework for action or propose new cultural orientations. (Laville et al. 2014, p. 11, author's translation).

With the individual and their needs and aspirations at the heart of its concerns, and with growth and sharing its foundation, social innovation encompasses all observable transformations. It also concerns organizational changes in relations between public policies and citizens and engenders renewed cooperation by including and linking actors in the process of societal change (Özdirlik and Pallez 2017). It involves rethinking traditional project management methods, integrating new actors, notably through participatory methods. For Manzini (2007), social innovation by design rests on four fundamental pillars that offer relevant avenues for carrying out design projects that can be meaningful for everyone involved: creative

---

2 This refers to industrial design.

communities, collaborative networks, the multilocal society and new management tools.

For our part and in this chapter – and knowing that, according to Mulgan (2014), social innovation through design in public services requires the use of varied design methods while adapting them to the specific context of public policies and services, and that this also implies learning from both users-citizens and decision-makers (Catoir-Brisson et al. 2016) – we view social innovation as a project discipline based on a creative culture with its own "epistemological originality" (Findeli 2003, p. 168), which makes design and the tools associated with this discipline more appropriate. Social innovation through design is thus linked to user-centered design, co-design, public policy design and, more generally, service design (Özdirlik and Pallez 2017). It also concerns other design specialties, insofar as they question the relationship between devices and their users, and projects are based on five central practices: (1) practicing observation and immersion in user experience, (2) favoring participatory methods, (3) approaching the problem from a systemic vision, (4) practicing ideation and consultation, and (5) experimenting with ideas in co-design workshops based on prototypes (Catoir-Brisson and Royer 2017). As such, design is a methodology that encourages the uptake of these practices, increasingly being introduced within hospitals in France.

9.2.2. *Hospital design in France*

Innovations in equipment, materials and medical techniques no longer seem sufficient in a context that makes clinical effectiveness, patient safety and patient experience the core pillars of healthcare (Damart 2013). In addition to the challenges posed by their complex governance and institutional functioning, increased staff workloads and financial constraints, hospitals are increasingly faced with the challenge of reshaping standards and personalizing care. Design, particularly design thinking, a pragmatic method for designing products, services and experiences that are desirable to consumers, has proven to be an effective way of meeting these new needs.

This so-called user-centered method (Verizer and Borja de Mozota 2005; Verganti 2006, 2008) includes practices emblematic of design, when it comes to developing innovations that are not disruptive. It values holistic approaches to problems (Manceau and Morand 2014) and emphasizes the collective as the appropriate level for solving problems (Celaschi et al. 2011). It has the virtue of presenting actors resistant to creativity and innovation with an easy-to-understand method, broken down into clear steps. With reference to Tim Brown, we have identified three of them:

– discovering customer or user needs: this involves understanding the problem and, in particular, the irritants encountered during the experiment;

– emergence of ideas in line with the criteria defined by the actors: this involves letting go of one's own perceptions and understandings, which is facilitated by dialogue with all the actors concerned by the problem;

– iterative testing of the ideas retained: this is carried out using storyboards, rough prototypes and small-scale experiments in real-life situations, known as proof-of-concept (POC).

In the course of these stages, the actors are encouraged to develop their curiosity to fully grasp, feel and experience the needs and irritants experienced by the user. This calls for empathy, with the aim of understanding this user's point of view on a cognitive and emotional level, whether from verbatim accounts (and interviews) or ethnographic surveys, observation, immersion in users' living and working environments (Liedtka 2011, 2018; Carlgren et al. 2016).

Adopting these different innovation and creativity practices is not as easy. Indeed, design implies successful appropriation by all the actors involved.

9.2.3. *Social innovation through design in hospitals: a question of appropriating management tools*

By the term 'management tool', and with reference to David (1998, p. 44), we mean "any formalized device enabling organized action" (author's translation). The scientific discourse claims both the material and immaterial properties of the variables relating to "reasoning pattern" (Moisdon 1997, p. 7) that lead to an understanding of the tool as being transformed by its interactions with the actors. It is then a matter of constructing meaning with actors to invent models of collective action (Ségrestin 2004) and accepting that management tools bear the imprint of their designers (Szostak et al. 2018).

It is in this logic that the issue of management tool appropriation appears to be significant, especially in a sector recognized for its ethics, respect for values and the non-market social dimension that sets it apart. To understand the appropriation of tools, de Vaujany (2005, 2006) puts forward three perspectives of "joint comprehension" of appropriation, acceptance and use of the management tool:

– The rational perspective sees the tool as a vehicle for rationalization, as a working tool. In this case, appropriation is "instantaneous", leaving no room for interpretation. Designers often have effectiveness and efficiency as their primary objectives; they seek to optimize and correct a situation defined as unsuitable. They create the tool and then distribute it to the actors.

– The socio-political perspective sees the management tool as a tool for rhetorical valorization by means of "argument", or as a tool to exert influence. Its appropriation is collective and long-term. It represents a social act. Actors are called upon to make the management tool fit for use, which imposes on them a relationship to the tool, its handling and learning, which can sometimes be difficult. The actor is led to reinterpret the tool.

– The psychocognitive perspective sees the management tool as a learning tool for the individual and/or the group, an affective object or an information-processing object. Appropriation necessarily takes place over the medium and long term. It is believed that the management tool can either hinder or, on the contrary, serve the interests of the actor, provided they are willing and able to learn.

These three perspectives provide a better understanding of how to successfully appropriate management tools in an organization. Complementing de Vaujany's analysis (2005, 2006), Szostak et al. (2018), in their meta-analysis of articles on the subject, as it applies to social economy organizations (SEO), propose four conditions for the appropriation of management tools:

– Democratic consultation and appropriation of the management tool: whether or not the tools are indispensable to the organization, collective reflection remains essential so that everyone can express their views and adhere to the tool, despite possible discussions and disagreements.

– Legitimization of the management tool and its appropriation: this refers to the fact that certain tools are suggested, or even imposed, by entities outside the organization. This is particularly true of technical tools for practicing a trade, or for reassuring third parties and securing subsidies.

– Adaptability of the management tool and its appropriation: the subject is to understand to what extent the management tool is malleable, to the point of integrating new dimensions and new uses, particularly when the tool has been proposed, as is very often the case, by people from the profit-making world, i.e. the private sector.

– The social manager's commitment to the management tool: they are the guarantor of the values defended and the definition of the organization's political objectives. This calls for managers who are defined as much by their values as by their skills.

We use these four conditions to build proposals for success factors in the development of social innovation through design in healthcare establishments such as public hospitals. Although they certainly emerge from work specific to SSE organizations, two arguments lead us to this choice of analytical framework. First, the authors point out that the first three conditions are ultimately specific to all organizations. Second, SSE and public-sector organizations share common characteristics and values, such as a dual structure, the pursuit of social impact and limited profitability.

9.3. Case studies

The success of social innovation through design depends on a number of factors that actors need to become more aware of. We therefore propose three factors conducive to success. While these are proposals, they are the result, on the one hand, of the observation of situations where social innovation has been developed through design in healthcare establishments and, on the other hand, from interviews and exchanges with experts in the sector, whether they are designers, caregivers or managers[3].

9.3.1. *The appropriation of social innovation through design by hospital management*

Design is not instantly adopted due to the complexity of the object under consideration (healthcare), even if it has to be said that, on the whole, those involved in healthcare establishments do not appear to be removed from the various practices, such as interviews, observations, personas, prototyping and so on that have been adopted. Nevertheless, while the hospital environment is very open to medical research per se, it is less enthusiastic when it comes to social and managerial innovation. However, the recurrence of organizational difficulties, in particular those highlighted by the Covid-19 crisis, is prompting hospitals to imagine ways of renewing themselves, supporting innovation, change and intrapreneurship. This could be done, for example, by launching calls for projects[4] in which design is exploited. This type of call would fully legitimize the development of new ideas through design.

This would be aligned, moreover, with what the French state is seeking to do, by equipping itself with a platform called *"Comment faire"*[5] ("How To"), run by the

---

3 The authors of this chapter have been investigating the integration of design and change within healthcare establishments, including hospitals, for over 15 years. They have likewise been involved in associated training programs.

4 This is the case, for example, of the *Assistance publique-Hôpitaux de Paris*, which, following the Covid-19 crisis, launched appeals via the *APRES* Fund (*Appui aux projets pour le renforcement du sens*); June 2020 (7.5 million euros) and July 2021 (1.5 million euros).

5 Available at: http://comment-faire.modernisation.gouv.fr.

DITP (*Direction interministérielle de la transformation publique*)[6]. It presents itself as "The toolbox for public innovation", and design thinking is presented as the heart of the approach. Guides are provided to help staff integrate design and its methods, such as design thinking, into their practices (persona, running a creativity session, user pathways, idea pitching, identifying actors using ecosystem approaches, etc.).

Several projects are currently underway in healthcare establishments, some of which have been running for several years. For example, design thinking has been adopted by the Hôpitaux universitaires de Strasbourg (HUS), which since 2008 has had an internal structure staffed by designers who support a large number of internal projects. The experience has led to the creation of a collaborative platform between HUS and numerous partners, named *"la Fabrique de l'hospitalité"* around the same objectives of improving spaces and time spent in hospital[7]. Since 2016, the Paris Psychiatry and Neurosciences University Hospital Group has been home to *lab-ah*, the laboratory for cultural innovation through design[8]. The aim is to design mediation and implement operational and research-action projects, drawing on design to give shape and form to these projects, and on the cultural development specific to the hospital (heritage, practices). As part of its "reinventing user reception"[9] project, the Simone-Veil Hospital in Eaubonne launched a design thinking approach in 2018 with 80 participants. This is in line with the Baureals project launched in 2017 by *Lyon Sud Hospital, Hospices civils de Lyon*: 180 medical and non-medical professionals rethink the hospital with the participation of patients[10]. The underlying idea is to involve those who experience hospital activities, whether they are orderlies, nurses, stretcher-bearers, doctors, secretaries and so on.

However, design practices will certainly influence the relationships between actors, especially those just mentioned, as they will have to get in touch with each other, and in particular with patients, which is not as common a practice as one might think. For them, it is more of an apprenticeship, an opportunity to develop new skills and knowledge. This, however, presupposes the involvement and commitment of these actors, so that they understand the process and master the various stages of design, which will be made possible by the construction of meaning within the framework of creating models for collective action (Ségrestin 2004). With this in mind, it might be useful to think about the choice of words and the qualification of practices in a vocabulary that is familiar and close to that generally used in hospitals.

---

6 Brought about by Law No. 2015-1165 of September 21, 2015.

7 Available at: https://www.lafabriquedelhospitalite.org/.

8 Available at: https://www.ghu-paris.fr/fr/le-lab-ah.

9 Available at: http://www.klap.io/comment-lhopital-simone-veil-a-reinvente-laccueil-des-usagers-grace-au-design- thinking/.

10 Available at: https://www.chu-lyon.fr/lhopital-lyon-sud-reinvente-lhopital.

9.3.2. *Legitimization and defense of social innovation through design by actors*

In view of the complicated situation of hospitals, it seems that all tools to stimulate innovation, creativity and intrapreneurship are welcome (see DITP and the "*Comment faire*" platform). It is essential to encourage healthcare professionals to express their needs to enable them to find a co-created solution: by taking them out of their daily routine this is likely to generate a sense of freedom and enjoyment. It is no longer a question of following protocols or instructions, but of thinking and reflecting on alternatives to overcome redundant day-to-day problems, via a bottom-up process.

Design to develop social innovation would become a space for dialogue, for actors who perhaps do not work in the same care unit, do not have the same status or are not within the same category (Grenier and Denis 2018). This would make it possible to counter the specificity of the healthcare environment, which is structured by specialties, whereas the subjects to be investigated are generally viewed as a whole: a holistic approach is far better suited to addressing a particular problem, which in many ways is the goal of the project, but also favors the design thinking tool.

Moreover, the practice of design fosters commitment on the part of actors, whether during ideation, prototyping or implementation sessions, and this supports the main drivers of these actors' engagement (Pihkala and Karasti 2016) in a process of "reflection in action" (Luck 2018). This reflexivity, nurtured by the cross-views and complementary points of view of the actors, enables them, in particular, to make explicit the irritants of the challenge they have decided to tackle, irritants that everyday practice tends to dissolve and make implicit (Grosjean et al. 2019). This enables the co-construction of an acceptable and accepted solution.

All of this is only possible, however, if we ensure that managers are engaged (Szostak et al. 2018). Due to their professional trajectory, their skills and their training, they must be in a position to defend the essential values of the hospital and the healthcare environment, while being able to take into account the skills and work habits of the actors. They are the guarantors for the respect toward the hospital, its values and for the work carried out according to the specific characteristics of the facility (Table 9.1).

AP-HP (Paris Public Hospitals) comprises 39 hospitals, which receive over 10 million patients a year. It is the largest employer in the Paris region, with almost 100,000 staff (doctors, researchers, paramedical staff, administrative, technical and blue-collar personnel). Research is an important facet of this healthcare establishment (innovation HUB, 650 active patent portfolios, 600 innovative projects, 60 start-ups and five innovation labs). Numerous medical breakthroughs have made this a preeminent center. However, with the Covid-19 crisis, hospitals were put under even greater pressure, even though there were already a number of irritants and *pain points*. Calls for projects were then launched to try to resolve these difficulties, notably through the APRES fund (*Appui aux projets pour le renforcement du sens*), which rolled out in June 2020 (7.5 million euros) and again in July 2021 (1.5 million euros).

Remaining within the framework of this call, the Hospital at Home (HaH) program launched a call for expressions of general interest, called the "*Carte blanche aux équipes*" (*carte blanches* to teams) in May 2021. It was initiated and supported by the *Innovation* mission, whose management is composed of two fully suitable people. The first is Inès Gravey (Chief Innovation Officer for *Hospitalisation à domicile*, "hospitalization at home"), who previously headed up a hospital in France and spent a year immersed in design at Kaiser Permanente, a healthcare provider in the United States that integrates design at all project levels. The second is Dr. Adrienne Reix, medical coordinator of the *Innovation* mission: she has also worked in an emergency department and in an EHPAD. She completed her master's degree in management and wrote her dissertation on design as a mechanism for adapting hospitals to current changes. By the end of 2021, they had surrounded themselves with a designer. The call urges teams to investigate irritants by experimenting with essential design practices (observations, interviews, personas, co-design and prototyping).

Box 9.1. *The "Carte blanche project" case study at HaH/AP-HP*

9.3.3. *The need for democratic consultation between actors and the adaptability of design to the hospital context*

If social innovation through design seems possible in hospitals, two other conditions need to be met. Democratic consultation means involving all actors: carers, caregivers and patients. The design process must be an opportunity to think collectively about social practices, but also a process of mutual learning. One way of achieving this is to use creative methods that combine, for example, the three modalities of design (Brandt et al. 2012, p. 165, translated by the author): telling, making and enacting. The aim would be to encourage actors to talk about their practices, highlighting the challenges and issues at stake, but also capturing the differences from one care unit to another. Through this technique, professionals benefit from a space of mutual learning, aimed at a shared understanding of the issues at stake, which facilitates their participation in the process of co-construction and the materialization of knowledge (Barrett 2010). Differing points of view and perceptions of certain alternatives are resources in the participatory design process. In fact, it is this heterogeneity of viewpoints that is sought in the design process, so that they can be confronted and a common solution to the different problematic visions can emerge. All of this amounts to a democratic consultation.

On the other hand, the point on which we need to be vigilant is the actual involvement of all actors within the hospital, which remains very hierarchical. Hospital administrative staff is composed of several categories, with different hierarchical levels (A, B, C), where category A is the most highly placed. Category C staff may therefore be more discreet and less willing to express their ideas in front of a doctor, for example.

In addition, it is important to work on the adaptability of the design to the context of appropriation, in this case the public health sector, the hospital. Taking into account actors' knowledge and considering them experts in their daily lives (in the case of patients) or in their clinical or administrative practices (in the case of professionals) are at the heart of the promises of approaches that claim to be social innovation through design (Bason 2014; Manzini 2015). It is necessary, first, to engage both healthcare professionals (doctors, nurses and care assistants) and design experts (experienced designers) in these approaches and, second, to consider these professionals not solely as mere users, but as "engineers of everyday life"[11] (Bélanger et al. 2012).

However, while it is true that the basic tools of design thinking (personas, empathy, POC, ethnographic observations, etc.) are sufficiently generic to be adapted to this sector, the question seems different when it comes to the criteria for validating an idea. In this case, the criteria are desirability to the consumer (user in our case), technical (or service) feasibility and the suitability of the idea to the business model. This last criterion calls into question the very definition of the public sector, that which is shared, without focusing solely on economic profitability. Given the injunction often given to hospitals to develop projects with constant resources, and if the social innovation thus developed through design deserves to last, the question of the economic model should give rise to significant discussions at the governance level for hospitals engaged in social innovation through design.

9.4. Lessons learned

The aim of this chapter was to propose success factors for the development of social innovation through design within hospitals. After proposing a conceptual framework demonstrating the importance of investigating this issue through reflections on management tools, we developed three proposed success factors, summarized in Table 9.1.

This work further highlights how the implementation and deployment of successful innovations in hospitals remains a significant challenge, to be met with a

---

11 Expression borrowed from Hubert and Vinck (2014).

view to fostering resilience in the organizations involved (Grenier and Denis 2018). Moreover, positioning social innovation through design potentially highlights "struggles" between actors to solve everyday problems in a sustainable way (Catoir-Brisson et al. 2016). These are "pernicious problems", which require regular, iterative work, likely, on the other hand, to wear out and discourage actors engaged in training others in coping strategies, to include those leading the project. Given the current level of fatigue among hospital staff, we need to question the sustainability of using a method based on iteration, trial-and-error, or at least a methodological approach to limit wear and tear and discouragement.

Proposed success factors	Definitions
Success factor 1: hospital management's ownership of social innovation through design	Management can free up material resources (dedicated space, design toolbox), human resources (position, professional training) and financial resources (money dedicated to the innovative project) to develop innovation through design.
Success factor 2: legitimization and defense of social innovation through design by the actors involved	The structure of the project in which the social innovation is developed is recognized by everyone, as are all the practices and tools used (teamwork, collective reflexivity and empowerment of actors).
	The project leaders are legitimate in their actions and have design skills through training, experience, passion and so on.
Success factor 3: the need for democratic consultation between actors and the adaptability of design to the hospital context	All actors (caregivers, administrative staff and patients, carers) are involved in the problems being investigated.
	Without ignoring profitability, the indicators for assessing the performance of social innovation through design take into account the "public service" nature of the hospital.

Table 9.1. *Summary of success factors*

That said, social innovation through design enables actors to "(re)discover the power of collaboration" and "new forms of organization" (Manzini 2015, p. 3) centered on "users". It also encourages the production of artifacts and solutions to the problems and irritants of everyday hospital life, using a co-creation and co-design approach to engender a process of "reflection in action".

It seems to us that it is essential to dig deeper into these results, so that the hospital manages to better articulate standardized, procedural medicine and artisanal medicine, in order to continue to function despite disruptions and shocks, such as those induced by the Covid-19 crisis (Cuvelier 2013). This ability is proving to be a genuine resilience factor, and this work shows just how much design thinking can strengthen it.

9.5. References

Amalberti, R. and Hourlier, S. (2007). Human error reduction strategies in health care. In *Handbook of Human Factors and Ergonomics in Health Care and Patient Safety*, Carayon, P. (ed.). Lawrence Erlbaum Associates, Hillsdale.

Barrett, M. (2010). Boundary object use in cross-cultural software development teams. *Human Relations*, 63(8), 1199–1221.

Bason, C. (2014). *Design for Policy*. Gower Publishing, Farnham.

Bélanger, E., Bartlett, G., Dawes, M., Rodriguez, C., Hasson-Gidoni, I. (2012). Examining the evidence of the impact of health information technology in primary care: An argument for participatory research with health professionals and patients. *International Journal of Medical Informatics*, 81(10), 654–661.

Borja de Mozota, B. (2002). *Design Management*. Éditions d'Organisation, Paris.

Brandt, E., Binder, T., Sanders, E.B.N. (2012). *Tools and Techniques: Ways to Engage Telling, Making and Enacting*. Routledge, New York.

Brown, T. (2009). *Design Thinking*. Pearson, Paris.

Carlgren, L., Rauth, I., Elmquis, M. (2016). Framing design thinking: The concept in idea and enactment. *Creativity and Innovation Management*, 25(1), 38–57.

Catoir-Brisson, M.J. and Royer, M. (2017). L'innovation sociale par le design en santé. *Sciences du Design*, 2(6), 65–79.

Catoir-Brisson, M.J., Vial, S., Deni, M., Watkin, T. (2016). From the specificity of the project in design to social innovation by design: A contribution. *Proceedings of the Design Research Society Conference 2016*, Brighton and Hove.

Celaschi, F., Celi, M., Garcia, L. (2011). The extended value of design: An advanced design perspective. *Design Management Institute Review*, 6(1), 6–15.

Cote, V., Belanger, L., Gagnon, C. (2017). Le design au service de l'expérience patient. *Sciences du Design*, 2(6), 54–64.

Cuvelier, L. (2013). L'ingénierie de la résilience : un nouveau modèle pour améliorer la sécurité des patients ? L'exemple de l'anesthésie. *Santé Publique*, 4(25), 475–482.

Cuvelier, L., Granry, J.C., Orliaguet, G., Moll, M.C., Baugnon, T., Falzon, P. (2011). Resilience's resources in pediatric anesthesia. *Proceedings of the 3rd International Conference on Healthcare Systems, Ergonomics and Patient Safety (HEPS)*, Oviedo.

Damart, S. (2013). *Innovations managériales en établissements de santé*. EMS, Caen.

David, A. (1998). Outils de gestion et dynamique du changement. *Revue française de gestion*, 120, 44–59.

De Noblet, J. (1988). *DESIGN : Le Geste et le Compas*. Aimery Somogy, Paris.

Findeli, A. (2003). Design et complexité : un projet scientifique et pédagogique à visée transdisciplinaire. *L'Autre Forum*, 7(3), 10–18.

Gagnon, C. and Côté, V. (2016). Public design and social innovation: Learning from applied research. *Proceedings of the Design Research Society 50th Anniversary Conference*, Brighton.

Gay, C. and Szostak, B. (2019). *Innovation and Creativity in SMEs: Challenges, Evolutions and Prospects*. ISTE Ltd, London, and John Wiley & Sons, New York.

Grenier, C. and Denis, J.L. (2018). S'organiser pour innover : espaces d'innovation et transformation des organisations et du champ de l'intervention publique. *Revue politiques et management public*, 34(3/4), 191–206.

Grosjean, S., Bonneville, L., Marrast, P.H. (2019). Innovation en santé conduite par les médecins et infirmières : l'approche du design participatif à l'hôpital. *Innovations*, 3(60), 69–92.

Guidot, R. (2000). *L'histoire du design 1940-2000*. Hazan, Paris.

Laville, J.L., Klein, J.L., Moulaert, F. (2014). *L'innovation sociale*. Erès, Toulouse.

Le Bœuf, J. (2015). Histoires du design : questionnement critique. *Sciences du Design*, 1, 76–85.

Liedtka, J. (2011). Learning to use design thinking tools for successful innovation. *Strategy & Leadership*, 39(5), 13–19.

Liedtka, J. (2018). Why design thinking works. *Harvard Business Review*, 96(5), 72–79.

Lucie-Smith, E. (1983). *A History of Industrial Design*. Phaidon, Oxford.

Luck, R. (2018). What is it that makes participation in design participatory design? *Design Studies*, 59, 1–8.

Manceau, D. and Morand, P. (2014). A few arguments in favor of a holistic approach to innovation in economics and management. *Journal of Innovation Economics & Management*, 15(3), 101–115.

Manzini, E. (2007). Design research for sustainable social innovation. In *Concevoir recherche maintenant : essais et projets sélectionnés*, Michel, R. (ed.). Verlag, Berlin.

Manzini, E. (2015). *Le design, quand tout le monde conçoit, une introduction au design pour l'innovation sociale*. MIT Press, Cambridge.

Morel, G., Amalberti, R., Chauvin, C. (2009). How good micro/macro ergonomics may improve resilience, but not necessarily safety. *Safety Science*, 47(2), 285–294.

Mulgan, G. (2014). *Design in Public and Social Innovation. What Works and What Could Work Better*. Nesta, London.

Özdirlik, B. and Pallez, F. (2017). Au nom de l'usager : co-concevoir la relation au public dans une mairie. *Sciences du Design*, 1(5), 69–84.

Pellerin, D. and Coirie, M. (2017). Design et hospitalité : quand le lieu donne leur valeur aux soins de santé. *Sciences du Design*, 2(6), 40–53.

Pihkala, S. and Karasti, H. (2016). Reflexive engagement: Enacting reflexivity in design and for participation in plural. *Proceedings of the 14th Participatory Design Conference*, Aarhus.

Ségrestin, D. (2004). *Les chantiers du manager*. Armand Colin, Paris.

Sørensen, E. and Torfing, J. (2012). Introduction: Collaborative innovation in the public sector. *The Innovation Journal: The Public Sector Innovation Journal*, 17(1), 1–14.

Szostak, B.L., Boughzala, Y., Dine, S., Yahiaoui, S. (2018). La dynamique d'appropriation des outils de gestion dans le champ de l'ESS : est-elle spécifique ? *Management & Avenir*, 2(100), 111–133.

Tassaux, D., Cottet, P., Paries, J. (2010). Résilience aux soins intensifs. *Revue médicale suisse*, 275(45), 2401–2404.

Tromp, N., Hekkert, P., Verbeek, P.P. (2011). Design for socially responsible behavior: A classification of influence based on intended user experience. *Design Issues*, 27(3), 3–19.

de Vaujany, F.X. (2006). Pour une théorie de l'appropriation des outils de gestion : vers un dépassement de l'opposition conception-usage. *Management & Avenir*, 9(3), 109–126.

Verganti, R. (2006). Innovating through design. *Harvard Business Review*, 84(12), 114–122.

Verganti, R. (2008). Design, meanings, and radical innovation: A metamodel and a research agenda. *The Journal of Product Innovation Management*, 25(5), 436–456.

Veryzer, R.W. and Borja de Mozota, B. (2005). The impact of user-oriented design on new product development: An examination of fundamental relationships. *Journal of Product Innovation Management*, 22(2), 128–143.

Xiao, Y. (1994). Interacting with complex work environments: A field study and a planning model. PhD thesis, University of Toronto, Toronto.

10

Article 51: Innovative Experiments to Help the French Healthcare System?

Article 51 of the French Social Security Financing Act 2018 authorizes the deployment of experiments aimed at proposing organizational innovations within a territory, which will be followed in a second phase by an allocation for where to conduct these experiments. The aim of this chapter is to study how Article 51 constitutes a space for innovation, as well as the role of the patient in this scheme. Drawing on the study of the *Ange gardien* (Guardian Angel) project in Nouvelle-Aquitaine, from a non-participant observation approach, we will see that the experiments possible under Article 51 correspond to modalities similar to those of innovation spaces. These allow us to envisage new frontiers and recognition of spaces for action, discussion engineering and an alignment of interests between actors. The inclusion of the patient as a stakeholder also enhances the effectiveness of the innovation process.

10.1. Background context and questions

In France, current events are a sad reminder that the public hospital system, despite having adopted numerous reforms aimed at improving its performance, is still suffering in the face of growing healthcare needs inherent to chronic pathologies and an aging population. The malaise that gripped hospital departments in the wake of the Covid-19 pandemic underscores the challenges facing the French healthcare system.

Chapter written by Cécile DEZEST, Isabelle FRANCHISTEGUY-COULOUME and Emmanuelle CARGNELLO-CHARLES.

Reforms carried out over the last 30 years or so have focused on improving the performance of healthcare entities within their organizational boundaries (certification of healthcare activities, creation of clusters and activity-based pricing), or at best by networking these entities or bringing them closer together (healthcare networks, health cooperation groups and regional hospital groups). However, the need for coordination to manage patients throughout their healthcare pathway means that new forms of cooperation and coordination must be envisaged (Bloch et al. 2014). An in-depth overhaul of the healthcare system must be envisaged; however, innovation can no longer be incremental and must become radical (Christensen 2003) in a healthcare sector on the verge of paralysis. Against this backdrop, the French healthcare system continues to deploy technological innovations but is also beginning to propose organizational and social innovations. In particular, the experiments being rolled out across the country under Article 51 show that new ways of organizing patient care are possible and will benefit from being rolled out across the country when their relevance is demonstrated.

Moreover, innovation is rife in today's economic sector: coworking spaces, living labs, fab labs and other platforms offer new ways of creating knowledge that are conducive to innovation. The notion of an innovation space, when viewed as "the deliberate implementation of a form of organization to compensate for or to extricate oneself from the limitations of existing structures and rules" (Grenier et al. 2017, p. 201, author's translation), can provide responses to the changing needs of the healthcare system. Article 51 offers the possibility of experimenting with new healthcare organizations based on novel financing methods. The aim is to test new organizations by derogating from many common law financing rules, applicable to the city as well as in hospital or medico-social establishments.

The aim of this chapter is to highlight how Article 51 constitutes a space for innovation, but also to describe what the patient's role is in this scheme.

In order to provide answers to these two questions, we will draw upon a single case study and a non-participant observation approach, in the context of the deployment of the *Ange gardien* project within the Nouvelle-Aquitaine region after considering whether or not Article 51 constituted a space for innovation.

10.2. Conceptual framework

In this first part, we introduce the notion of innovation space and consider the place given to the patient in this environment. We then define the general framework of Article 51 in order to better understand how experimentations can constitute a space for innovation that ensures a place for the patient.

10.2.1. *Innovation spaces: a concept that brings innovation to healthcare?*

The work of Brown and Duguid in 1991, and that of Wenger in 1998, highlighted the importance of proximity in the innovation process. This need for proximity and relationships between individuals can be approached through the notion of innovation space, which is defined as an organized arrangement of expertise, relationships and interests, deliberately constructed to foster the emergence of new ideas and practices (Westley et al. 2014).

There is a wide variety of innovation spaces: fab labs, living labs, design labs, opens labs, coworking spaces, makerspaces, hackerspaces or platforms, for example. All have the same objective: to develop collaborative and iterative processes conducive to creation, whether material or virtual (Aubouin et al. 2019).

They can be physical spaces, such as fab labs or platforms, or virtual spaces based on digital and computer exchanges. In all cases, the purpose of these spaces is to encourage the sharing of ideas and experiences, with a view to imagining or deploying innovations. These spaces serve to organize exchanges at different levels, whether cognitive, social, relational or political. They seek to bring people together, in the way that they think, design and gather. Capdevila (2016) speaks of these spaces as "transmitters" or nodes that can connect ideas or people with a common goal.

This way of working encourages collaboration and the decompartmentalization of exchanges, which distinguishes these spaces from more conventional organizations, constrained by their mode of governance and decision-making (Arhne and Brunson 2008). Boundaries are more permeable and structures are less conventional. In this sense, these spaces are described as open (Chesbrough 2003; Chesbrough et al. 2006), offering free access to resources, in the spirit of collaboration and sharing of knowledge, skills and tools. With these characteristics, these spaces are conducive to creativity and experimentation.

Their specific features depend on the objective of the innovation process. For example, fab labs focus on improving participants' creative abilities, using adapted tools such as design thinking (Brown 2008) or creative problem solving (Parnes 1967), whereas living labs focus on improving or developing new products through the exchange of knowledge within and outside the company (Chesbrough et al. 2006).

The advantages and disadvantages of these approaches also differ according to the form of the space chosen. Capdevilla (2016) presents an analysis of these characteristics and the motivations of these open spaces, enabling a typology to be drawn up. The study is continued by Aubouin and Capdevila (2019) who show that each type of space corresponds to a specific motivation, whether economic, utilitarian or altruistic.

10.2.2. *From participatory design to living lab*

The patient is often in an asymmetrical information relationship with the doctor or carer who has the competence and expertise in the healthcare being provided. In recent years, however, the patient's status in the organization of healthcare activities has evolved.

As early as 2007, HAS (*Haute Autorité de santé*), the French National Health Authority recommended involving patients individually or in association with the design, implementation and evaluation phases of a program specific to activities for those with chronic conditions. Chronically ill patients regularly interact with healthcare professionals in the context of their own healthcare.

In this way, the patient is included in the overall dynamic and invited to share their experience, being the only one, or one of the only ones, to have a comprehensive view of their journey.

Right from the design phase, the patient becomes a stakeholder for innovation. Innovation is no longer the work of experts alone but stems from collaboration between different actors. It emerges from the confrontation of different points of view concerning the organization of care, a confrontation necessary to the knowledge creation cycle, as identified by Nonaka and Takeuchi in 1997. This heterogeneity of viewpoints is also sought in participatory design approaches (Grosjean et al. 2019).

Patient involvement was analyzed by Castro et al. (2016), who surveyed over 5,000 publications. By highlighting varying degrees of patient involvement, patients will, in the context of personalized medicine (Gross 2017), be invited to weigh in on therapeutic choices, the mode of care and the fight against their disease.

The participatory design approach requires a strong commitment to democratic values, the creation of a space for dialogue and the expression of divergences, which are seen as resources in the participatory design process (Gregory 2003). In this sense, the patient is not questioned about the relevance and ergonomics of this or that tool. The innovation process does not follow a precise, let alone pre-established, framework; it is more a matter of devising solutions and solving problems as and when they arise, and networking (Offner 2000) through adaptation, and trial and error (Salhin and Wedlin 2008).

The concept of the living lab extends this opening up of the innovation process to users, but also includes a dimension of disseminating scientific culture (Morabito 2014) by anchoring it in a territory. The concept of the living lab enables authors to be involved right from the start of the innovation process but also to experiment in real-life contexts, providing a structure and governance for stakeholder participation in the innovation process.

The deployment of these spaces in the context of healthcare activities positions the user as an actor responsible for their health (Picard and Poilpot 2011, p. 5), but the organizational conditions of their implementation influence the type of involvement and participation of patients, as well as the results achieved (Kletz and Marcellin 2019). When we talk about integrating patients into the innovation process, we are not talking about soliciting them at the end of the process, but rather "placing them in an organization" (Kletz and Marcellin 2019, authors' translation).

Therefore, the main purpose of the living lab is to review traditional organizations and, above all, to create spaces in which professionals confront users. This implies specific arrangements (social, relational, political, cognitive, for example) conducive to innovation, such as experimental platforms (Cartel 2013) and experimental spaces (Ziestma and Lawrence 2010).

Living labs thus make it possible to draw on new resources (cognitive, material, etc.) that foster new capacities for action (Aggeri and Labatut 2010), beyond the routines of everyday life. They also imply a renewal of forms of governance (more collaborative and less compartmentalized) in work organizations.

10.2.3. *Article 51, a space for innovation?*

The deployment of Article 51 opens the door to new forms of cooperation, enabling partnerships between healthcare structures (Sebai 2016) or new cooperation between city and hospital. These new forms of cooperation seem particularly well suited to the healthcare sector (Contandriopoulos et al. 2001).

The aim of Article 51 is to improve the patient pathway by facilitating access to healthcare (hospital, medico-social or outpatient). In other words, the aim is to improve the quality of patient care, always with a view to equity of access to healthcare. A *coordinated healthcare pathway* is the watchword of this article, which looks at both an organizational dimension as well as a financial one, due to the possibility of derogations from financing rules, applicable to both city and hospital or medico-social establishments.

Local or regional, and national or interregional experiments are encouraged by Article 51. As part of nationwide experiments, three expressions of interest were launched in May 2018, including the IPEP (*Incitation à une prise en charge partagée*) "incentives for shared care" project, which introduces the notion of profit-sharing, the *PEPS* (*Paiement en équipe des professionnels de santé*) "payment for professional healthcare teams" project, which favors remuneration and an episodic view of the healthcare being provided.

The Article 51 system is clearly organized and managed. At the head of the system is a strategic council charged with innovation in healthcare, which formulates innovative proposals and monitors experiments with a view to their potential generalization. This strategic council brings together, around the same table, a large number of actors from across the healthcare ecosystem. These include healthcare professionals, representatives of regional and national public authorities, and patient representatives. The patient is integrated into the Article 51 mechanism at the highest level and is consulted on the direction to be taken and, in particular, on project evaluation methodologies. In other words, the patient is physically present in the innovation space. The strategic council is a forum for discussion and sharing between all the representatives of the system's stakeholders on the changes to be made to the healthcare system. It will bring together the various actors twice a year but will allow for an incremental approach that leaves room for construction as we go along, where every contribution counts. The health innovation technical committee, the Regional Health Agencies (RHAs), and the general *rapporteur* complete the setup of the system's organization.

The term "stakeholder community" is used several times in reports from the strategic advisory board. In reality, it is a network organization in which each of the representatives is made legitimate. In addition to the strategic council, workshops are organized to discuss doctrinal points and topical issues; the heterogeneity of actor status leads to a wealth of conclusions within these physical spaces, which are conducive to innovation.

In addition to these physical spaces, there are digital spaces available to actors allocated by the Article 51 scheme. First, there is the operational project submission platform, which encourages and enables anyone to post an innovative project. This digital tool removes the barrier of geographical distance or the administrative burden of paper files. The tool is a catalyst for innovation and facilitates exchanges between the various bodies involved. This platform brings together project sponsors and application processors at every stage of the selection process for innovative projects.

An information platform completes the operational platform. It enables the authorization of remunerations to developing organizations.

Article 51 is in line with the prerogatives of *Ma santé 2022*, a strategic plan that aims to propose responses to reduce health inequalities and enable professionals to better cooperate with each other. The plan emphasizes the need for patients to become real actors for their own health and have access to information. The patient is recognized as an extremely rich source of information to determine the quality of the healthcare required, and the need to involve them in all health-related actions from the outset is acknowledged.

While the *Ma santé 2022* plan includes the patient in the assessment of the healthcare professional's human and interpersonal skills and gives a training role to expert patients in a medical studies curriculum, Article 51 associates the patient with its highest body, the strategic council.

10.3. Case studies

In this section, we present the context in which the project was born, its implementation within a territory and the results obtained.

10.3.1. *Project context and implementation*

The PAG (*Projet Ange Guardien*) "guardian angel" project is an experiment currently underway in the Landes region of France. It is an organizational innovation in the management of chronic inflammatory diseases such as chronic obstructive pulmonary disease, asthma, inflammatory rheumatism, diabetes and Raynaud's phenomenon.

As part of a doctoral project, we were able to gain an insight into the workings of the PAG project through a phase of non-participant observation of project presentations and evaluation meetings. The aim here was to highlight actual activities, rather than those reported by the actors observed. In order to complete this work, we conducted semi-directive interviews with the project leaders and the project manager. These interviews, lasting around 1.5 hours each, were transcribed. The aim was to clarify and test the concepts identified in our field of investigation. This work is part of a qualitative approach insofar as the elements observed are difficult to measure but are more conducive to precise, detailed descriptions, which contribute to a holistic understanding.

This study is based on the interpretivist paradigm, which considers that reality is the fruit of the researcher's mental interpretation. In this framework, the aim of research is "to apprehend a phenomenon from the perspective of the individuals involved in its creation, according to their own language, representations, motivation and intentions" (Hudson and Ozanne 1998, authors' translation). The subject and the observed object are interdependent. Interpretivism is particularly well suited to the qualitative research method. The material derived from interpretivist studies tends to be descriptive in nature. Observing innovative experiments requires a clear understanding of situations, events, the regulatory and institutional context in which these innovations take place, and the behavior and motivations of those involved. The abductive approach was the guiding principle of this exploratory work, with a back-and-forth between the theoretical framework and field reality.

The PAG project introduces collaborative practices between general practitioners (GPs), specialists, hospital doctors, pharmacists and PTA (*Plateformes Territoriales d'Appui*) – local support networks. In fact, the whole point of this system is to streamline the healthcare pathway in the management of a chronic inflammatory disease. The idea is to link all the medical and social actors involved in patient care. The aim is to bring together primary care physicians with hospital specialists and the PTA. The latter was born out of the "digital care territory" (*Territoire de soins numériques*) program that arose from the January 26, 2016 French Law on the modernization of the healthcare system. The PTA is made up of eight coordinators, a nurse in charge of coordination, a part-time doctor and a person in charge of relations with partners within the territory. Links between private practitioners and hospital staff are strengthened, that is, between those involved in home care and those involved in hospital care. The PTA is the central body for this coordination, where each healthcare provider involved in the healthcare of the same patient can have discussions with their colleagues, retrieve information on the patient (such as the date of their last appointment with the GP, the person in charge of care, the medical prescription, etc.) and organize medical appointments with the appropriate professional at a specific point in the healthcare process. The aim is to break down the traditional boundaries between the hospital sector, private practitioners and medical/social professionals, consistently striving toward optimum patient care.

Sixty-seven general practitioners and 19 specialists are taking part in this project, along with pharmacists. They are all working on an innovation with a triple dimension: human (collaborative work), digital (creation of the *PAACO-Globule* software for PTAs) and social (seeking to keep patients in their family and professional context). The software is developed in partnership with the RHA, and medical data are hosted by the RHA. Digital innovation is the key factor in this coordination, facilitating and securing exchanges between professionals. For example, because of *PAACO-Globule*, outpatient healthcare professionals can access a patient's hospital records and consultation reports. As for hospital doctors, this digital tool enables them to communicate with private practitioners. So, when we speak of exchanges between healthcare professionals, we are actually talking about the circulation of sensitive data, subject to medical secrecy. The digital interface guarantees the confidentiality of exchanges. In addition to medical professionals, professionals such as pharmacists and social workers are integrated into this collaborative dynamic, to ensure optimum, comprehensive patient care.

Subsequently, we have medical and paramedical professionals interacting with each other, hospital and independent professionals in constant exchange.

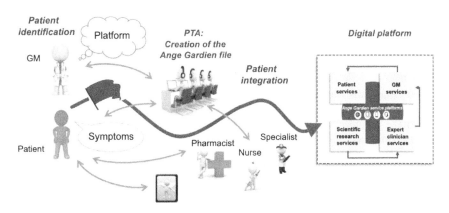

Figure 10.1. *The relationship between the patient, healthcare and the PTA–PAG. For a color version of this figure, see www.iste.co.uk/courielemeur/innovation.zip*

The other aspect of this innovation is social. In fact, the project was born out of a very important social need: to keep patients independent for as long as possible. Chronic inflammatory diseases have the particularity of generating a large number of work stoppages, and excessive use of analgesics and corticoids. This all adds up to significant costs and distress at work and, by extension, throughout society. Early management of these chronic pathologies helps to avoid the dual penalty of deteriorating health and job loss. The *Ange Gardien* project is a response to this social need: treatment at the right time means effective treatment and limited socio-professional repercussions.

Furthermore, one of the major points justifying experimentation is to test new remuneration modalities such as the IPEP (incentives for shared care) project. The IPEP project is an experimental approach proposed by Article 51, modeled on the USA's Accountable Care Organizations (ACO). This remuneration allows for collective profit-sharing in addition to standard pricing on the basis of pre-established quality objectives and compliance with a de-spending target. The main aim of the IPEP project is to encourage cooperation between healthcare professionals to improve the health of populations, the quality of care and the efficiency of allocated resources.

After 18 months of experimentation in the Landes region, some 1,000 patients have been taken on and integrated into this scheme.

To clarify the proposed system, let us take the example of the *Ange Gardien* program of an asthmatic child (Box 10.1).

---

1) GPs participating in the *Ange Gardien* project have been made aware of the symptoms of the pathologies treated by the *Ange Gardien* project. Indeed, specialists have drawn up a list of symptoms to be considered and made available to GPs who are on the front line. GPs suspect or diagnose asthma in their young patients during a standard consultation at their doctor's office.

2) The GP then suggests to the parents that their asthmatic child join the *Ange Gardien* project. The parents accept and are informed by the GP that they will be contacted by the PTA.

3) The GP notifies the PTA via *PAACO-Globule* (a platform for secure exchanges between healthcare professionals and the coordination center) that there is a patient to be integrated into the *Ange Gardien* program, and the GP then provides the contact details of the patient's parents.

4) A PTA coordinating nurse contacts the parents of the asthmatic child to confirm their decision to join the *Ange Gardien* project. The parents confirm.

5) Following this call, PTA staff create a file in the child's name with the parents' contact details, the name of the attending physician and the physician's diagnosis.

6) Digital tools are then made available to the staff who will be intervening and to the patient (phone application).

---

7) The PTA organizes the child's spirometry test and transmits the results via *PAACO-Globule*.

8) The attending physician is then informed and takes note of the assessment via *PAACO-Globule*. In consultation with the specialist, they draw up a treatment plan for the asthmatic child.

9) Therapeutic education, a medical diary, prescription relay and crisis management are all available on the patient's application.

Here, the patient and the attending physician form the central pair.

12) The patient's medical file is enriched by the various health or medico-social professionals who will be caring for the patient. The coordinating nurses also help to enrich the file as the telephone exchanges with the patient progress.

Box 10.1. *An example of an asthmatic child's Ange Gardien pathway*

10.3.2. *Results of the* Ange Gardien *project*

In concrete terms, because of the implementation of the *Ange Gardien* project, there are fewer appointments with doctors, greater peace of mind in the management of pathologies, and easier communication with specialists. Patients are guided and warned at times when their condition is considered critical. Specialist referrals and appointments for check-ups are initiated by the coordinating nurses, greatly relieving the patient of these formalities.

The project's initiators, four professors from Bordeaux University Hospital (CHU), speak of a successful experiment in the Landes region, because of the resources allocated and committed, and the people involved in the *Ange Gardien* consortium (CHU doctors, engineers and consultants from the IT services company that developed the application, university researchers), people from the PTA and Nouvelle-Aquitaine RHA and private practitioners (URPS and *Maison de santé*). The project manager, who belongs to the Bordeaux University Hospital, organizes meetings with the project leaders and other stakeholders. She is also responsible for involving the URPS physicians (key actors in the project) in this project, who are part of a hospital team.

The project's promoters have invested a great deal of time and effort in communicating their ambitions for this experiment in order to get as many healthcare professionals on board as possible. Project presentation meetings were organized by the project leaders to explain their approach and encourage participation among professionals.

Since February 2017 when the *Ange Gardien* project was set up, we have come to the conclusion that the gains for patients cared for under the *Ange Gardien* project are significant. Indeed, because of this free service, the patient avoids disruptions in their healthcare pathway, and staying at home is encouraged. Any hospitalizations are organized by the PTA, giving the patient peace of mind; likewise, social professionals are mobilized by the PTA. All of these elements add fluidity to the patient's healthcare pathway, making the process much faster and less disruptive.

It should also be pointed out that without the *Ange Gardien* system, the patient would not necessarily have had recourse to social and peripheral healthcare professionals, such as psychological counselling and prevention programs. Nor would they have benefited from the increased vigilance afforded by PTA and the use of a digital application, which plays a central role in care. *PAACO-Globule* enables information to be shared between the hospital and the various doctors, making examinations easier for the patient, who no longer has to go to the hospital, but simply to the doctor's office.

The innovative digital tool reduces the distances between hospitals and country towns, and even more so for those living in more remote rural areas. Access to healthcare is becoming increasingly equitable and the socio-professional repercussions of illness are limited. Patients no longer have to block off their day for an examination. They can simply make an appointment with their GP or a nurse. As a result, absenteeism is reduced, and illness has less impact on working life.

With this coordinated approach, patients are more likely to have their chronic pathology detected at an early stage, thus limiting the risk of deterioration in their state of health. For example, a general practitioner in Mont-de-Marsan, involved in the *Ange Gardien* project, detected a case of Raynaud's phenomenon early on, resulting in appropriate treatment and avoiding late, emergency treatment, when there are fewer satisfactory therapeutic options available. The doctor–patient relationship is thus strengthened, and recommendations are perfectly personalized. Indeed, the attending physician is at the heart of the *Ange Gardien* system and thus becomes the patient's dedicated contact. The doctor is aware, in real-time, of their patients' progress. Their bond becomes even closer. As for medical recommendations, these are completely personalized as a result of the comprehensive care provided. Here, GPs and specialists work together to respond to the patient's therapeutic needs, taking a global view of their healthcare. The attending physician can explain to the specialist the constraints of the patient's daily life, and the specialist can give an informed opinion on the diagnosis. This ongoing exchange means that treatment can be highly responsive, providing the right answer at the right time, without having to wait several weeks for a medical appointment.

GPs, for their part, report that they feel more confident in the exercise of their profession because of this collective work. They can draw on the lists of key symptoms for which they have a whole network of knowledge and know-how upon which to rely. Ultimately, it constitutes a reassuring sharing of skillsets that the healthcare professional can draw upon.

Specialist doctors always rely on their generalist partners to be called upon at the right time. This is a major challenge for them, since the earlier a chronic pathology is detected, the greater their means of action. Specialist physicians can thus achieve better results.

For healthcare establishments, the *Ange Gardien* project in the Landes region has also been a success since it has been a driving force in tele-expertise. As a result, there have been fewer hospitalizations and less use of emergency departments.

Lastly, research teams report that their work is enhanced by the *Ange Gardien* project as there are more early cases to study.

An important factor attributed to the success of the *Ange Gardien* project in the Landes region is that the system facilitates exchanges between GPs and specialists, saving time and improving the patient care process. It also enables the integration and participation of the various parties involved throughout the healthcare process.

10.3.3. *Discussion*

Following this description of the *Ange Gardien* project currently underway in the Landes region of France, two important questions arise. Is the *Ange Gardien* project a space for innovation as typically defined? What role does the patient play throughout this experiment?

10.3.3.1. *The Ange Gardien project, a space for innovation?*

Article 51 of the *Ange Gardien* project stipulates that the scheme should encourage innovative experiments in healthcare. In this context, the IPEP project is particularly relevant as it aims to promote the coordination of healthcare for chronic inflammatory diseases. The project aims to create forums for exchange between the Nouvelle-Aquitaine RHA, doctors, professionals and patient representatives, with the stated aim of encouraging patients to enter the treatment process at an early stage. In this sense, this points to social innovation as it has the aim of enabling patients to remain autonomous for as long as possible.

The notion of space implies proximity between actors (Brown and Duguid 1991; Wenger 1998). In the case of the *Ange Gardien* project, a divide appears between certain profiles, in particular between doctors, dominated by strong professional logics (Lehoux et al. 2014). Hospital doctors and private practitioners have not had the same career paths and take care of patients with different profiles. They therefore assess patient care differently, which sometimes leads to heated confrontation. Nevertheless, an important element of *rapprochement* is that the GP is at the center of the *Ange Gardien* project. In this sense, doctors have common ground, the GP being valued because they have important responsibilities in terms of patient orientation, and the hospital doctor because they will devote themselves to the most severe cases, only at specific stages along the patient's healthcare pathway. The space represented by the *Ange Gardien* project thus reinforces professional identities and reputations between peers (Gandini 2015; Merkel 2018).

In all cases, these moments of exchange help to bring together the key actors of the healthcare process. They appear indispensable, even if certain tensions are perceptible. It is because of these encounters, which reduce the boundaries between communities (of private practitioners, hospital staff, RHA, patient representatives), that trust can be built up, enabling the production of new knowledge essential to the implementation of the project (Amin and Cohendet 2004).

Capdevilla (2016) points out that space plays a role in the organization of exchanges and can be seen as a "transmitter" or node that connects people with a common goal. The *Ange Gardien* project meetings were organized in a relatively formal and constrained way from the outset, as participants did not yet know each other and found it difficult to position themselves in relation to one another. A certain caution was palpable during the preliminary exchanges. As the meetings progressed, exchanges became more open as participants got to know each other better. In this way, the *Ange Gardien* project can be seen as a space for sociability, teaching private practitioners and hospital doctors to communicate and work together. One facilitating factor was that the exchanges were organized by a meeting facilitator, in this case the project manager, who always tried to make sure that everyone was able to give the same level of input.

As Grenier and Denis (2017) point out, the *Ange Gardien* project can be defined as a space for innovation by three of its characteristics: its boundaries, space for discussion and legitimacy. The *Ange Gardien* project's boundaries can be understood at different levels, including geographical, political and social.

The *Ange Gardien* project is located in the Landes *département*, a rural area with a large surface area and no major cities; Mont-de-Marsan, the *département*'s prefecture and most populous town, has a population of 30,000. The political characteristic of the project is that the experiment is supported by the Nouvelle-Aquitaine RHA, with a strong desire on the part of hospital doctors for the project to develop. The social dimension is reflected in the very aim of the project, which is to improve healthcare for certain chronic inflammatory diseases. The discussion engineering required that the aligned interests and communication on the goals of the *Ange Gardien* project were well established by the project's promoters, helping the various actors to understand their place and the significance of their participation. As for the project's legitimacy, there is no doubt either internally or externally. The value of the *Ange Gardien* project is understood, and its legitimacy is unquestioned.

The *Ange Gardien* project is in fact a living lab, insofar as it is a space for innovation rooted in contextual reality (heterogeneous status of stakeholders and doctors' practice structure, with all the resistance this implies), as well as in local specificities (poor local network where rural patients are sometimes inadequately integrated into digital technology). The exchanges described above undoubtedly made a major contribution to the roll-out of the project, particularly as a result of the confrontation between professionals and users.

In concrete terms, the *Ange Gardien* project has given rise to new practices, facilitating coordination around the management of chronic inflammatory diseases. The creation of a dedicated platform, combined with the development of an IT tool (*PAACO-Globule*), has improved the organization of healthcare. Innovation is clearly present and considered an undeniable step forward by all those involved.

The *Ange Gardien* project has all the operating characteristics of an innovation space.

10.3.3.2. *The Ange Gardien project and the role of the patient*

The HAS (2007), the French National Health Authority, emphasizes the need to involve patients, or their representatives through associations, throughout the processes of design, implementation and evaluation of a program specific to a chronic disease. This view holds that the patient has a legitimate role to take part in exchanges with professionals and doctors because of their experiential knowledge (Charpak 2017). Knowledge would no longer be limited to the scientific knowledge of doctors but would be complemented by knowledge that comes from the field, that of patients and their loved ones.

This logically leads us to question the place of the patient in the *Ange Gardien* project, which is integrated into this specific framework of chronic disease management.

Initially, the *Ange Gardien* project did not integrate the patient. It is worth recalling the difficulties at the start of the *Ange Gardien* project, where the divide between private practitioners and hospital doctors was very pronounced. The weight of hospital doctors was significant, and the guidelines for exchanges was very hospital centric (Domin 2013). The explanation lies in the genesis of the project, which was initiated by a team from the CHU, and whose originators were hospital doctors. The priority of the first meetings was to bring together hospital doctors and private practitioners, and no consideration was given to other actors for as long as these integration challenges continued. As tensions diminished, the patient was approached. Gradually, the discussion space became less compartmentalized, leaving more room for other actors who were not doctors, in particular patients (Cartier et al. 2012; Bloch and Hénaut 2014). This did not come about without its own set of challenges. Questions arose as to which associations should be included. At what point in the process? For what specific questions? Not to mention the lack of availability of patient representatives, the additional organizational difficulties associated with integrating these additional actors, and a fear from doctors that their medical authority was being called into question and undermined (Jouet 2014; Mougeot et al. 2017).

With hindsight, we realize that the patient played a role, particularly during the design and implementation of the *PAACO-Globule* digital tool, which represents the exchange platform between healthcare professionals and the coordination center. The *Ange Gardien* project is in line with the current trend toward digital healthcare and telemedicine (Dumez et al. 2015; Buthion 2016). In this sense, the digital tool has taken on a central role in coordinating actions between doctors, pharmacists, professionals and patients. Consideration for the patient has quite logically emerged as an important factor in the organization of healthcare on this platform. Experiential knowledge of the patient has proven to be essential and necessary for the definition of healthcare processes. Exchanges with patient representatives were particularly re-recognized as legitimate by the various stakeholders, be they doctors, RHA representatives or other healthcare professionals (Kletz and Marcellin 2019). Patients and their loved ones, finally seen as holding relevant knowledge useful to experts and professionals, have thus become an essential stakeholder in the definition of new healthcare policies (Gross 2017). On a more general level, the integration of patient associations has, in the case of the *Ange Gardien* project, enabled the constitution of "innovation communities" (Von Hippel 2005). In this way, the involvement of all stakeholders in the patient's lifecycle was essential to the definition of innovative healthcare methods. The patient was also an integral part of the *Ange Gardien* process.

10.4. Lessons learned

Although public hospitals have demonstrated their ability to improve their performance and organization, the issue of resource allocation and funding alone cannot explain the profound crisis that has recently been spreading throughout the

French hospital system. The explosion in chronic diseases and an aging population are contributing to a worsening situation that can be felt by all those involved in the healthcare system.

The stakes involved in the evolution of the healthcare system are enormous. However, rather than a one-off, localized adjustment to improve the performance of healthcare systems, the deployment of organizational, technological and social innovations in patient care requires the involvement of all actors in the healthcare system and a complete overhaul of the principles underpinning existing healthcare organization in France.

	Lessons learned/ mechanisms to use	Points to watch out for
Constructing spaces for innovation	– Interaction between casuals, hospitals and supervisory bodies – Coordination is in the *Ange Gardien* project's DNA: proximity, in the broadest sense of the term, is essential between actors – A dedicated physical space where everyone's voice counts – Alignment of interests strengthens the *Ange Gardien* project's legitimacy	– Be aware of the tensions that may persist between casuals and hospital staff.
Dynamics of the patient's role	– Patient representatives, actors on the Article 51 Strategic Council – Incremental approach – Digital tools: a way for patients to express themselves – In line with the strategic plan for Article 51 and *Ma santé 2022*: patients are to be involved from the start of the project	– The difficulties encountered at the start of the *Ange Gardien* project, linked to the divisions between the casual and hospital sectors, have put the actual role of patients on the back burner – Care must be taken not to alter the priorities initially established because of conflicts. This has a lot to do with people management and project management

Table 10.1. *Points to watch and mechanisms to use in building innovation spaces and the role of the patient*

The experiments conducted under Article 51 offer the opportunity to deploy innovations in ways that are similar to the ways in which innovation spaces operate. By offering a new context favorable to the deployment of new exchanges, an alignment of interests between actors and recognition of the space to act, these innovation spaces propose a new framework for innovation. Nevertheless, we can identify points to watch out for and mechanisms to employ in the construction of innovation spaces and in defining the role of the patient. These are summarized in Table 10.1.

Provided they take into account patients, their families and patient associations, the actors in the French healthcare system now have the opportunity to propose full-scale experiments to test the development of new ways of providing care. Healthcare pathways can be used to mobilize skills and resources in order to improve the management of rapidly expanding chronic diseases.

10.5. References

Aggeri, F. and Labatut, J. (2010). La gestion au prisme de ses instruments. Une analyse généalogique des approches théoriques fondées sur les instruments de gestion. *Revue finance contrôle stratégie*, 13(3), 5–37.

Amin, A. and Cohendet, P. (2004). *Architechtures of Knowledge: Firms, Capabilities, and Communities*. Oxford University Press, Oxford.

Arhne, G. and Brunson, N. (2008). *Meta-Organizations*. Edward Elgar Publishing, London.

Aubouin, N. and Capdevilla, I. (2019). La gestion des communautés de connaissances au sein des espaces de créativité et innovation : une variété de logiques de collaboration. *Innovations*, 58, 105–134.

Bloch, M.A. and Henaut, L. (2014). *Coordination et parcours : la dynamique du monde sanitaire, social et médico-social*. Dunod, Paris.

Brown, T. (2008). Design thinking. *Harvard Business Review*, 86(6), 84–92.

Brown, J.S. and Duguid, P. (1991). Organizational learning and communities-of-practice: Toward a unified view of working, learning and innovation. *Organization Science*, 2(1), 40–57.

Buthion, A. (2016). Marché unique européen du numérique et politique française de santé. *Annales des Mines. Réalités industrielles*, 3, 61–65.

Capdevilla, I. (2016). Une typologie d'espaces ouverts d'innovation basée sur les différents modes d'innovation et motivations à la participation. *Gestion 2000*, 33(4), 93–116.

Cartel, M. (2013). La fabrique de l'innovation institutionnelle : les marchés du carbone comme champs d'expérimentations managériales. PhD thesis, École Nationale Supérieure des Mines de Paris, Paris.

Cartier, T., Mercier, A., de Pourvourville, N., Huas, C., Ruelle, Y., Zerbib, Y., Renard, V. (2012). Constats sur l'organisation des soins primaires en France. *Exercer*, 101, 65–71.

Castro, E.M., Van Regenmortel, T., Vanhaecht, K., Sermeus, W., Van Hecke, A. (2016). Patient empowerment, patient participation and patient-centeredness in hospital care: A concept analysis based on a literature review. *Patient Education and Counseling*, 99(12), 1923–1939.

Charpak, Y. (2017). La participation des citoyens à la décision en matière de santé et sur leur propre santé : enjeux, pièges, risques et innovations. *Réalités industrielles*, 2, 60–63.

Chesbrough, H.W. (2003). *Open Innovation: The New Imperative for Creating and Profiting from Technology.* Harvard Business School Press, Boston.

Chesbrough, H.W., West, J., Vanhaverbeke, W. (2006). *Open Innovation: Researching a New Paradigm.* Oxford University Press, Oxford.

Christensen, C. (2003). *The Innovator's Solution.* Harvard Business School Press, Boston.

Contandriopoulos, A.P., Denis, J.L., Touati, N., Rodriguez, R. (2001). Intégration des soins : dimension et mise en œuvre. *Ruptures – Revue transdisciplinaire en santé*, 8(2), 38–52.

Domin, J.P. (2013). *Une histoire économique de l'hôpital (XIXe-XXe siècles). Une analyse rétrospective du développement hospitalier.* La Documentation française, Paris.

Dumez, H., Minvielle, E., Marrauld, L. (2015). États des lieux de l'innovation en santé numérique. Working Paper, Fondation Pour l'Avenir.

Gandini, A. (2015). The rise of coworking spaces: A literature review. *Ephemera Theory & Politics in Organization*, 1(1), 193–205.

Gregory, J. (2003). Scandinavian approaches to participatory design. *International Journal of Engineering Education*, 19(1), 62–74.

Grenier, C. and Denis, J.L. (2017). S'organiser pour innover : espaces d'innovation et de transformation des organisations et du champ de l'intervention publique. *Revue politiques et management public*, 34(3), 191–206.

Grosjean, S., Bonneville, L., Marrast, P. (2019). Innovation en santé conduite par les médecins et infirmières : l'approche du design participatif à l'hôpital. *Innovations*, 60, 69–92.

Gross, O. (2017). *L'engagement des patients au service du système de santé.* Doin, Paris.

HAS (2007). Guide méthodologique structuration d'un programme d'éducation thérapeutique du patient dans le champ des maladies chroniques. Report, Haute Autorité de Santé, Saint-Denis.

Hudson, L.A. and Ozanne, J.L. (1988). Alternative ways of seeking knowledge in consumer research. *Journal of Consumer Research*, 14, 508–521.

Jaeger, M. (2010). L'actualité et les enjeux de la coordination des actions et des dispositifs. *Vie Sociale*, 1, 13–23.

Jouet, E. (2014). La recherche en santé et les patients : de l'utilisation des corps à la contribution active. In *Nouvelles coopérations réflexives en santé : de l'expérience des malades et des professionnels aux partenariats de soins, de formation et de recherche*, Jouet, E., Las Vergnas, O., Noël-Hureaux, E. (eds). Archives contemporaines, Paris.

Kletz, F. and Marcellin, O. (2019). L'innovation avec le patient : un renouvellement par le design organisationnel. *Innovations*, 60, 93–120.

Lehoux, P., Daudelin, G., Hivon, M., Miller, F.A., Denis, J.L. (2014). How do values shape technology design? An exploration of what makes the pursuit of health and wealth legitimate in academic spin-offs. *Sociology of Health and Illness*, 20(20), 1–18.

Merkel, J. (2018). Freelance isn't free. Coworking as a critical urban practice to cope with informality in creative labour markets. *Urban Studies*, 56(3), 526–547.

Morabito, M. (2014). *Recherche et innovation : quelles stratégies politiques ?* Presses de Sciences Po, Paris.

Mougeot, F., Robelet, M., Rambaud, C., Occelli, P., Buchet-Poyau, K., Touzet, S., Michel, P. (2018). L'émergence du patient-acteur dans la sécurité des soins en France : une revue narrative de la littérature entre sciences sociales et santé publique. *Santé Publique*, 30(1), 73–81.

Nonaka, I. and Takeuchi, P. (1997). *La connaissance créatrice.* De Boeck Université, Brussels.

Offner, J.M. (2000). L'action publique urbaine innovante. In *Repenser le territoire. Un dictionnaire critique*, Wachter, S., Bourdin, A., Lévy, J. (eds). Éditions de l'Aube, La Tour d'Aigues.

Parnes, S.J. (1967). *Creative Behaviour Guidebook.* Scribner, New York.

Picard, R. and Poilpot, L. (2011). Pertinence et valeur du concept de "Laboratoire vivant" (Living Lab) en santé et autonomie. Report, Conseil Général de l'Industrie de l'Énergie et des Technologies, Ministère de l'Économie des Finances et de l'Industrie.

Salhin, K. and Wedlin, L. (2008). *Circulating Ideas: Imitation, Translation and Editing. The Sage Handbook of Organizational Institutionalism.* Sage, Newcastle upon Tyne.

Sebai, J. (2016). Une analyse théorique de la coordination dans le domaine des soins : application aux systèmes de soins coordonnés. *Santé Publique*, 28(2), 223–234.

Von Hippel, E. (2005). *Democratizing Innovation.* MIT Press, Cambridge.

Wenger, E. (1998). *Communities of Practice. Learning, Meaning, and Identity.* Cambridge University Press, Cambridge.

Westley, F., Andatze, N., Riddell, I., Robinson, K., Geobey, S. (2014). Five configurations for scaling up social innovation: Case examples of nonprofit organizations from Canada. *The Journal of Applied Behavioral Science*, 50(3), 260–324.

Ziestma, C. and Lawrence, T. (2010). Institutional work in the transformation of an organizational field: The interplay of boundary work and practice work. *Administrative Science Quaterly*, 55(2), 189–221.

Innovation and Training for Healthcare Professionals: Impact on the Structural Resilience of Organizations

New digital technologies have invaded the world, turning social behavior on its head in both the private and professional spheres. This is not without consequences for the organization of life in general, leading to a significant reconsideration of the meaning given to certain tasks. The healthcare sector is also experiencing this revolution. Whether happily or unhappily, it is adapting to this invasion with a more or less constrained resilience, leading us to reflect on our professional skills. This chapter presents a few examples of how these new technologies are being integrated into the day-to-day lives of certain healthcare professionals, based on experiments carried out by *Aesio*, the mutual insurance group.

11.1. Background context and questions

Science and innovation have coexisted and even been assimilated into each other in an ongoing dance that moves and twirls with the times. The printing press revolutionized navigation; steam, train travel; electricity, energy sources and the microprocessor; information. Whether they are the mature fruits of profound knowledge or the pure inventions of an unbridled brain, it would be impertinent to say! The fact remains that the man-centered world of the Tautavel cave has changed a great deal on its way to becoming the Burj Khalifa Tower. Mankind whirls in the midst of all these changes, motivated by an enduring quest for survival, seeking ways to fend off predators and ways to overcome other obstacles. With the dinosaurs

---

Chapter written by Marianne SARAZIN.

gone and the Bengal tigers haunting India's dwindling nature reserves, man remains his own predator.

Whether this is a small or big revolution depends on the elected representative's point of view and their ability to grasp the "innovation". "Ability" can underlie "heredity": give a lion some grass and it will not eat it because all of its ancestral filiation and phylogenesis would take a hit; "will": ask a blind man if he wants to see; "perception": ask the great Vasarely about his conception of a circle, and you will be amazed by his three-dimensional vision.

Apprehending novelty is therefore a very complicated matter and depends on ancestral, cultural and emotional factors which, at an individual scale, are of no importance, but at a group scale can have greater epidermal, organizational and political consequences. Then, there is the question as to the meaning of innovation and collective interest, which is always very difficult to dissociate from the individual when it comes to talking about health.

That's right! Because for many decades now, the health sector has been no exception to the evolutionary phenomenon. Pasteur, with a stroke of his stylus, like a genius fencer, was able to hit the nail on the head that "jump started" our understanding of many different types of bacteria, which saw the treatability of tetanus, tuberculosis, measles, rubella and more recently, Covid-19. Innovation can therefore be a source of individual and collective well-being. Nevertheless, there are examples to the contrary, tempering the benefits of innovation and the forced march of healthcare systems, taking advantage of the digital invasion of all areas of healthcare and imposing a complete reorganization of the "care" paradigm!

Evolution and revolution: here are two experiments set up by *Aesio*, the mutual insurance group, one based on the use of robotics and the other on information technologies, both marching in the same direction, highlighting the reflections generated by this technology on both the organizational and professional changes induced. Implemented in the emergency of the Covid-19 pandemic, these raise the question as to whether they should be made permanent, and question what *real* contribution they can actually make to better healthcare.

These experiments are a good illustration of the principles of the multiple case study approach adopted by Yin (2003), adapted to the study of contemporary phenomena in their real-world context.

11.2. Illustrations

We mobilize the principles of the multiple case study approach according to Yin (2003), adapted to the study of contemporary phenomena in their real-world context, and explore the case studies of the Pepper robot and telemedicine.

11.2.1. *The Pepper robot*

The use of the Pepper robot (Ondras 2021), envisaged as a substitute or complement for tasks that can be performed by humans, is gradually taking root in people's minds.

This petite, friendly-looking robot celebrated its 10th birthday in 2022 and has toured the world in search of a place among humans. Even if Softbank has decided to halt its deployment, either because of insufficient interest or because more elaborate forms are coming onto the market, this robot concept still marks the entry of artificially designed actors with terribly human aspects and behaviors into everyday life!

Profoundly questioning the meaning of life, calling into question billions of years of cellular elaboration, and even the mighty Creator, God!

11.2.1.1. *Objects of fantasy*

Who has not had nightmares about *Frankenstein*, the robot uprisings of Isaac Asimov or Philip K. Dick? Twentieth-century literature broadly anticipated today's realities, portrayed by a no less prolific cinema, which resulted in *C-3PO* becoming as famous as the main heroes of *Star Wars*, or a *Robocop* more present in people's minds than *Sergeant Murphy*.

But what is it about robots that fascinates us so much? The fruits of our creativity, they often bear witness to a split personality: deformed constructions of metallic design, they are nonetheless imagined and conceived more often than not as a human doppelgänger. And even when the conceptualization is pushed toward fewer humanoid structures, such as Theodore Sturgeon's "dreaming crystal" or Tolkien's *Sauron*, they nonetheless remain very close to us in their sensory, reactionary and active behaviors. They are therefore adversaries or allies who can be understood and therefore mastered.

In effect, rapid progress in computer science and information retrieval has led to the notion of artificial intelligence, which holds the promise of even more sophisticated robots in the future. And this notion, beyond its extraordinary power of analysis, was perhaps not called "intelligence" by chance. It underpins the idea that it would be possible to conceive of an "object" capable of thinking and reasoning like humans, with complete independence, with a unique personality and character, able to make decisions that may even elude the usual structuring of human thought. This is where the fascination comes in: is it possible to duplicate human beings, to design "objects" that are not only capable of replacing them in all the usual tasks of life, but also able to approach life differently, with their own independent social structuring?

A challenge to any ego, no matter how well-developed!

11.2.1.2. *Testing the Pepper robot in institutions catering for the elderly*

Innovation in healthcare has never been so popular as with the advent of so-called "new" technologies, such as connected sensors, micro-processors, the Internet and so on. In 2020, the *Aesio* mutualist group developed a research and innovation group, drawing on skills already available in its various healthcare centers: clinics in particular, but also rehabilitation centers and establishments for the elderly. The aim is to take advantage of these technological opportunities to optimize care and healthcare management.

The introduction of the Pepper robot in elderly care homes is one of the programs chosen by the Group to alleviate a growing staff shortage, which since the Covid-19 pandemic has grown considerably. The primary aim of this experiment is to supplement existing staff with monitoring tasks and assistance with certain tasks, such as dispensing medicaments or other regular care. The other objective is to enable personalized remote contact with families without the intervention of nursing staff, and to encourage interactive development for patients suffering from confusion or established dementia.

This current experiment is interesting on several levels. It effectively calls into question an entire hierarchical care process that is still very humanized. Unlike other structures in which work is organized according to an industrial concept, around an inert object (a uniform, a hammer, a computer, software, etc.), in healthcare, the object of work organization is a human being, or even a group (e.g. the family around the sick individual), and most often, focused on easing suffering.

As a result, the worker–worked object relationship cannot be the same, nor can the qualifications and process(es) leading to the solution be the same.

The installation of the Pepper robot in this context has raised a number of questions:

– Technological: contrary to what science-fiction or the various global advertisers say, and as social networks and others imply, these robots remain a technological problem to be associated with a Wi-Fi network, ground-based recognition strips, design software to be maintained, sensors to be installed and storage premises. They also need to be installed on the premises themselves so that they can be adapted to their traffic patterns, and may need to be redesigned if they are to be deployed over the long term.

– Social: what is the robot's place in a healthcare team? How do we position it in a work hierarchy wherein a manager directs nurses, who in turn direct care assistants, all within a care process where the doctor consistently intervenes to ensure everything happens with respect to the diagnosis? Does it have to fit into this task progression? Or is it just another tool, such as specialized beds, patient carriers and wheelchairs? A survey was carried out among nursing staff to get a clearer idea of the robot's place within this type of organization. For the time being, the responses are still being processed, and it is too early to draw any conclusions. However, it is clear from the few interviews and discussions that have already taken place that the role of the robot remains very difficult to establish. Unlike the other care tools mentioned above, the robot's function as a substitute for certain relational tasks raises questions among caregivers about their own role and function. The image of the nurse as a "consoling mother", with the added qualification of being able to soothe the sick, is replaced by that of a "care technician", whose maternal function is transferred to a robot. The result is a reflection on the value of the profession in this context and therefore, in the longer or shorter term, on the selection profile of future caregivers.

– Functional: this involves transferring tasks to another member of staff, either on a permanent basis, which means redesigning the overall organization of a team, or on a one-off basis to temporarily offset a need. The robot installation project came at a critical time during the Covid-19 pandemic, when team disorganization was at its height. So, whether a robot could continue to perform certain tasks was genuinely questioned. The return to a more normal situation called into question all thoughts on working around the robot, with the sensations of a time of crisis quickly taken over by a historical routine that is hard to change. Questions are still being asked, and it has been decided to set up the robot on a trial basis, to consider its positioning within a team situation.

The installation of a robot is not as simple as the designers' imagination or the various fantasies might have led us to believe, which is perhaps why SoftBank has abandoned its manufacture. Unless, of course, it is because other, more elaborate robots are planned to replace humans!

And what about the patient? Various experiments around the world on elderly people suffering from dementia seem to show a certain effect on the cognitive functions of robots (Tanioka 2019). The question remains, however, whether a "real person" would not be just as useful, and whether robotization might not be concealing a trend toward the complete industrialization of care for economic ends, dragging social organizations further in their wake toward disengagement and unbridled egoism! A topic for continued debate...

11.2.2. *Telemedicine*

Telemedicine is another recent example of technology taking charge of health. From *Nounours* and *L'Île aux enfants* to *Le Grand Échiquier* and *Apostrophes*, who has not gazed in amazement at a television set, its vivid images replacing an imagination that's harder to fulfil? And now, patients will be able to see their doctor on a screen and forget about the white cabinet on the second floor of the building!

11.2.2.1. *The role of television in health*

Inaugurated with great fanfare by the coronation of Elizabeth II, RTF (*Radio-diffusion-télévision française*) changed the face of France forever with the introduction of thousands of television sets into homes across the country. A cultural revolution! Information invaded the daily lives of millions of French people, bringing modernity to lives that were still very rural and focused on their own environment. The world opened up to them, with its share of disrupters and enticements of all kinds. The farm and the village became very small, fading into the background as New York towers, Malibu beaches and Madagascan rainforests flashed across the screens, and seductive *femme fatales* and *mister muscles* were offered up as fantasies to housewives all over the country.

Since then, television has become part of our lives, evolving into an even more instantaneous form of communication via WhatsApp, Zoom and other interactive image carriers, allowing for life outside of real-life. Undoubtedly beneficial in certain situations! Let us not just mention the coronavirus and its attendant confinements: the remoteness, speed of action, time and money saved for certain exchanges are all qualities attributable to this new means of exchange.

Healthcare has not escaped this revolution, spurred on by the 2020 pandemic. From now on, you can take care of a patient remotely, check their auscultation and even operate on them, all from the comfort of your sofa, sipping a juice box or some unmentionable spirits in a Hawaiian shirt.

Nevertheless, the simplicity of this relatively costly situation should not overshadow the organizational and conceptual changes it brought with it, which are raising a host of questions about the place of everyone involved in this technology. The big "healthcare" machine, which involves numerous players within a well-established hierarchy of tasks, is no exception to this trend.

And the patient! What about the patient? Forgotten in the great debates, even if they regularly come to the forefront with all the ethical considerations linked to the transfer of personal data, what do they think? If the virtualization of exchanges has no impact on the dress being fabricated 10,000 km from its designer, the same cannot be said of the patient, who will be dissected by a medical team that will decide their fate, without them having had the chance to shake hands with his benefactor!

11.2.2.2. *Implementation at the* Clinique Mutualiste de Saint-Étienne

The pandemic saw a number of innovations using this technology, further identifying the possibilities of this approach.

One of these was the care, during the pandemic, of patients suffering from dementia via a cable car (Bartz 2016).

Confinement was a time of great suffering for patients with dementia and their families. It interrupted a life stabilized by habits and led to aggravation and significant behavioral changes in patients, and consequently great exhaustion in their families. As a result, the pandemic limited the number of care facilities available, and additional solutions had to be found to deal with situations that had become urgent. The clinic's geriatricians decided to use a cable car to care for patients and their families. The cable car had the advantage of enabling both a medical examination and a visual exchange with patient and family.

But what does this kind of care entail? As with the Pepper robot, technology brings with it structural change:

– Equipment: to carry out a remote examination, one needs to understand how important it is to have the right equipment. Live perceptions have to be transcribed via an electronic channel. As a result, "consultation booths" have been developed to report blood pressure, heart sounds, dermatological images or ultrasound images, all uploaded to a remote computer server to enable remote order-type data exchange, via secure channels specific to the transfer of health data. These cabins are located in specially-adapted premises that can accommodate patients and their attendants.

– Qualified personnel: indeed, the basis of a good examination is the ability to use the instruments available for the purpose in the correct manner. An ultrasound probe, for example, needs to be oriented at an angle that optimizes blood flow; likewise, a blood pressure monitor needs to be positioned correctly. On the other hand, immediate care such as wound dressing or general examinations cannot be carried out on a screen as this does not allow for a complete view of the patient. Finally, the patient's installation for the examination reinforces the need for qualified personnel to be present in order to carry out the examination.

A four-way relationship ensues: the patient, the nurse, the doctor and the screen. A delicate marriage, requiring a relationship of trust that is harder to establish, and calling into question everyone's role, like when the Pepper robot was introduced into an organization.

In contrast to the previous experiment, where the nurse lost their prerogative at the expense of a "heap of bolts and wires", in this configuration, standing beside the patient, they predominantly take on the role of experienced observer whose intuition, based on professional experience, asks that they fathom the unfathomable. This is usually the role of the doctor, who is removed from the diagnosis and instead takes on the role of technician, interpreting what the nurse and telemedicine tools tell them. This change in professional approach refocuses on a more technological approach to learning, leaving the nurse in the role of observer, which is usually only assigned to them during precise clinical examinations. This calls into question the qualification and skills of the nurse, who will thus be in the role of examiner, with all the deferral of responsibility that this implies. This also has implications for the nurse's approach to their job. Taking on responsibility, especially when it may have consequences for others, is a learning process but also a skill in itself.

For the time being, telemedicine remains an ancillary tool, but its continued use, as with that of the Pepper robot, also raises the question of how to modify professional teaching.

As for the patient, in this particular case of dementia, they rather appreciated this distance from the doctor. They clung more to the soothing aspect of the nurse, a professional intermediary who can adapt to the medical discourse and soften its contours.

11.3. Lessons learned

Innovation is a fertile ground that has driven civilizations toward a permanent transformation of their environment. Beneficial or harmful? The answer to this question is often schizophrenic. Change is not for everyone, and we need to approach it with full knowledge of the facts. Innovations in healthcare are no exception to this rule, but we must not forget that the subject of change is life itself, which means that extra care must be taken. The situations considered in this chapter clearly illustrate this complexity, where the "sick" object takes on a whole new meaning through the prism of a technology that interferes with human relationships. Up until now, technology has served only as a support for diagnosis and treatment. Today, it is even used to transmit the message between the protagonists, thus removing the subliminal element conferred by an attitude, an intonation, an aspect of the healthcare professional or the patient that can contribute to making it easier to interpret and less worrisome in the context of an illness. On the other hand, the transformation of roles it provokes calls into question the complete conception of each and every profession. Should we requalify nurses and entrust them with patient diagnoses? Is it possible to conceive of a super-expert doctor who would support nurses in their care, waltzing from one patient to the next, contributing their insights in the same manner as a strategy consultant? There are many questions that cannot be answered at present, given the speed of technological change, but which will require precise assessment to ensure that healthcare is not altered to the detriment of patients.

11.4. References

Bartz, C.C. (2016). Nursing care in telemedicine and telehealth across the world. *Soins*, 61(810), 57–59.

Ondras, J., Celiktutan, O., Bremner, P., Gunes, H. (2021). Audio-driven robot upper-body motion synthesis. *IEEE Transactions on Cybernetics*, 51(11), 5445–5454.

Tanioka, T. (2019). Nursing and rehabilitative care of the elderly using humanoid robots. *The Journal of Medical Investigation*, 66(1/2), 19–23.

Analysis of Two Innovative Working Methods at the Ile-de-France RHA

In order to better respond to the dual challenge of epidemiological and population aging, on the one hand, and improving the working conditions of healthcare professionals and the individuals' lives, on the other, public authorities need to transform themselves.

Developments inspired by innovation methods are currently being trialed, illustrated by the implementation of the provisions of Article 51 of the French Social Security Financing Act 2018 and local "chronic heart failure pathway" events. While these dynamics are demonstrating their effectiveness, real change management remains necessary, particularly within institutions.

12.1. Background context and questions

Improved quality of care for acute pathologies is leading to increased patient survival and an aging population with chronic illnesses.

In addition, economic constraints are having an impact on the entire healthcare system, leading to a reduction in the capacity of healthcare establishments. Medical and paramedical demographics are fragile. Outpatient care and the links between general practitioner (GP) and hospital are in the process of being set up.

The challenge for the healthcare system is to respond to these changes by improving the management of chronic illnesses in the community, enhancing

Chapter written by Sophie BATAILLE, Élise BLÉRY, Charlotte ROUDIER-DAVAL and Michel MARTY.

patients' quality of life, reducing (re)hospitalization and mortality and improving the quality of working life for healthcare professionals by meeting their needs.

To speed up the adaptation of the healthcare system to these challenges, public authorities are mobilizing and implementing new methods.

On a national level, Article 51 is an innovative tool that enables healthcare professionals to experiment with new organizational and financing models. The first case study concerns the feedback from Article 51 supported by the Ile-de-France Regional Health Agency (IDF RHA).

At the regional level, since 2016, IDF RHA has been committed to improving a chronic disease pathway, developing an innovative method for identifying actions adapted to each locality that relies on a local event approach. This is the second case study to be presented.

12.2. Case Studies

12.2.1. *Article 51 and the mobilization of collective intelligence*

"Article 51 [of the French Social Security Financing Act 2018] is intended to better support professionals in the initiatives that they have been expecting from us for years now". That is how Olivier Véran described Article 51 in November 2017, during the debates preceding its adoption. Article 51 is therefore a promise to pave the way for reforming our regulatory models in order to encourage innovative healthcare modalities.

It is a regulatory mechanism for experimentation in the healthcare field. The Article 51 project must be innovative, feasible, efficient and reproducible. It has been designed to be a powerful mechanism for transforming healthcare provision and its financing methods to improve the relevance and quality of care. To achieve this, it enables healthcare actors to derogate from legal rules. The aim is to better respond to needs by testing projects that emerge from the actors involved, but also to select projects that can be reproduced at a national scale.

12.2.1.1. *Innovation, collective intelligence and health*

Article 51 is more than just a possibility to derogate, and it implies a real change in the approach to transforming the healthcare system. It overhauls the historical methods used to design models, which until now had been mainly conceived by the public authorities followed by consultation with healthcare actors via their representatives. Healthcare professionals then had to appropriate and integrate their practices within a regulatory framework drawn up by legislators and regulators.

Today, the aim is to move away from this top-down approach and encourage initiatives from the field. Professionals in the healthcare system are being asked to play a key role in overhauling this framework. They must be daring, and propose new organizations by embarking on a path that does not necessarily guarantee success.

The regulator must agree to relax the focus on technical or administrative constraints, in favor of the fundamental interest of the projects. It must be in a position to provide support and service to experimenters and ensure that innovation tools are made available to them. This implies a change in position toward one that favors a collaborative, partnership-based working method.

Article 51 is therefore, fundamentally, an innovation tool, not only in its very essence – the possibility of derogation – but moreover in the techniques used to achieve it.

12.2.1.2. Collective intelligence methods used

The maturity of the projects proposed by our partners varies greatly. Very often, they need to be worked on collectively in order to create a model that can be applied in the field, and be adopted by all stakeholders, in line with their respective challenges and the framework of Article 51.

The need for reinforced and adapted support for project leaders was therefore quickly recognized and has been adapted as and when issues have been flagged, at every stage: design, development and its start-up in the field.

This concerns both the process (excessively long appraisal times, too many iterations with the promoter) and technical points (financing model, target audience, governance, etc.).

In response, a range of tools are available, based on the co-development of projects by all stakeholders and on collective intelligence. Many of these tools are derived from innovation methods combining co-construction with a user-based approach, process agility, a participative approach and event facilitation.

Article 51 is governed by an original structure that guarantees a high degree of transversality, with strong involvement from central management and the health insurance industry.

This structure brings together all the directors of the central administration of the Ministry of Health, its Secretary General, a Director General of an RHA and the Director of UNCAM (*l'Union nationale des caisses d'assurance maladie*), the national union of health insurance funds. This technical committee collectively analyzes the experimental projects, monitors them and issues an opinion on their generalization.

A strategic council, consisting of 62 members from different parts of the healthcare system, monitors the progress of experiments and their evaluation at different stages and receives the opinions of the technical committee and ultimately decides whether to authorize a project's implementation or not. A general *rapporteur* is responsible for project appraisals and evaluations.

At the national level, a team of operational referents is made up of representatives from each of the central departments and the CNAM (*Caisse nationale d'assurance maladie*), France's national health insurance fund. They liaise with the business experts in their organizations. The expertise of other national institutions and missions is also involved: HAS (*Haute Autorité de santé*) France's health authority, ANAP (*Agence nationale de l'appui à la performance*) France's national agency for support to the performance of health and medico-social facilities, ATIH (*Agence technique de l'information sur l'hospitalisation*) France's technical agency for information on hospitalization and DREES (*Direction de la recherche, des études, de l'évaluation et des statistiques*) France's research, studies, evaluation and statistics department.

At the regional level, RHA or DCGDR (*Directions de la co-ordination de la gestion du risque* – "risk management coordination department"), referents carry out the same type of mission, as well as facilitating events for their respective local networks.

Regular exchanges take place between everyone involved. These enable opportunities to meet the objective of identifying and supporting projects, with the support of a team at every stage, including decision-making.

A range of tools are also used to support the process.

The method is based on working in project mode. Governance with a clearly identified project manager supporting the healthcare team has proven to be a factor for success.

A detailed roadmap is enriched by iterative exchanges with institutions and the evaluation team. It can be drawn up and implemented with the help of a whole range of collaborative tools that evolve as needs and requirements change.

Guides are available based on feedback from other experiments and working groups on issues common to several project teams.

In order to improve the support provided to eligible developers, the mobilization of third-party experts to assist with the general formalization of projects, the development of the business and financing model or the formalization of the authorized project implementation method is made possible by a "framework agreement" public procurement contract, a joint initiative of nine RHAs.

The accelerator, a national structure inspired by project incubators, is the most emblematic mechanism in this toolbox. This service combines a multi-disciplinary team, project leaders and experts from public authorities, with collaborative design. Key points of validated projects are worked on collaboratively (project leaders and institutions) during workshops led by a team of designers in a neutral position. This "facilitation" makes it possible to share issues, obstacles and mechanisms and compare proposals with the reality of the actors likely to implement the experiments, whatever their mission. Recommendations, clear, targeted and concrete actions, and next milestones are shared by all at the end of the workshop.

This meeting of two worlds, the elimination of barriers and direct access to the technical and regulatory expertise available to project developers, greatly accelerates the advancement of projects.

Initially offered on an experimental basis during the appraisal phase, the acceleration sessions were applauded by all participants. In the midst of the Covid-19 crisis, they have been maintained in a dematerialized version and are now offered at every stage of the project. Regional accelerators are also being set up.

The desire to encourage the sharing of experience between actors and the creation of alliances around common issues or the resolution of bottlenecks has motivated the organization of best-practice communities. The idea is to capitalize on the know-how of authorized project leaders in the health and medico-social sectors in solving real-world problems.

ANAP, France's national agency for support to the performance of health and medico-social facilities, organizes thematic exchanges (e.g. information systems and first billing) in conjunction with relevant national experts, as well as "project leader coffee dates" on open topics. It manages the platform made available to the community (event viewing, document exchange, discussions, directory, etc.). At the initiative of the actors, sub-groups have been formed around questions such as "the elderly", "telemedicine" and so on, and, on the strength of this experience, some members have created their own community. A larger scale annual event is devoted to showcasing the trials underway and the methods employed. This "project leaders' day" consists of around 50 workshops aimed at a very broad audience of initiative leaders.

In each of these dynamics, by moving away from the bilateral relationship between project leaders and public authorities, a balance is sought between answering questions and problem-solving autonomy. From the point of view of the actors, who declare themselves to be over 85% satisfied, the strengths of this approach are simple answers to simple operational problems, *"à la carte"* participation that adapts to their needs and availability, informal and direct interaction with the participants, anticipation of key points based on *retex* and the possibility of contacting someone in the event of difficulty: rituals such as the "project leader coffee dates", sharing understanding, feedback, exchanges with public authorities, the exchange and provision of resources between project leaders and the thematic approach. There remains a need for logistical and methodological support for self-supporting approaches, more specifically in working groups with production objectives, where there have been major discrepancies between experiments, different self-supporting experiences and low levels of platform uptake.

Co-construction also takes place at the project evaluation stage, between the external evaluation team, project sponsors and institutional partners. Evaluation indicators are co-defined at a very early stage in order to validate their relevance and ensure that they are easy to construct, collect and analyze, as well as to encourage their appropriation.

At the regional level, the project mode has strengthened the links between the various areas of expertise of the business units. More matrix-based organizations have proved their worth. The IDF RHA is going to capitalize on this method by organizing an innovative project space, within which collegiality and the mobilization of a range of tools derived from innovation will be mobilized to support pathway projects.

12.2.1.3. *Meeting objectives*

By the end of 2021, 103 projects had been authorized, of which more than 60 have been started, with more than a million patients involved, 460 million euros have been allocated to the FISS (*Fonds pour l'innovation du système de santé –* "healthcare innovation fund") and 15 million euros on the FIR (*Fonds d'intervention régionaux –* "regional intervention fund") since the scheme began.

Experiments under Article 51 focus first and foremost on chronic diseases (vascular, joint and ophthalmic pathologies, etc.), followed by cancer, mental health and post-trauma surgery. All populations are concerned, with a large proportion of projects devoted to the elderly.

While the main objective is to improve healthcare pathways, and, in particular, coordination around them, the second concern of project sponsors is linked to accessing healthcare, with the desire to improve the use of new services for certain pathologies (psychologists, dieticians, indoor environment medical advisors, adapted physical activity educators, etc.).

Project leaders have a wide range of statuses: the majority are within healthcare establishments or groups of actors (URPS, France's regional union of healthcare professionals, federations, unions, etc.), but there are also medico-social establishments and homecare actors, city-based actors, individuals, manufacturers and so on. The majority (80%) of deployment sectors are within urban areas.

This enthusiasm for Article 51 as a response to needs was confirmed at the height of the Covid-19 crisis. While schedule adjustments were often imposed, the number of patients included in some projects increased. Some projects also arose directly from issues that emerged during the crisis. More generally, the themes addressed during the crisis and those of the experiments were found to be in line with each other, and new avenues of work were confirmed (e.g. information systems). Support and engineering based on a collective commitment, reinforced during this period, helped to maintain the dynamic and confirm the value of Article 51.

12.2.1.4. Converging objectives

The *Stratégie nationale de santé* (2017) ("national health strategy"), the 2018 STSS (*Stratégie de transformation du système de santé* – "health system transformation strategy") *Ma santé 2022* (2019) and finally the *Ségur de la santé* (2020) converge, in terms of objectives and methods to encourage willingness to change, with those of Article 51.

Article 51 has made it possible to test organizations that meet the objectives of quality, relevance, development of prevention, decompartmentalization of hospital and outpatient care, better coordination of actors, experimentation with new skills, enhancement of local resources, improved access to healthcare, putting the patient at the center of the system and so on.

It has made existing systems legible by giving them a place in organizations. It has enabled them to be appropriated, developed and used.

It has also enabled the joint construction of new economic and financing models, powerful mechanisms of transformation clearly identified and required by public authorities and stakeholders. It also accelerates the legal and fiscal changes required to keep organizations running.

Collaborative approaches, as close as possible to the actors and localities involved, are used to develop national intervention frameworks. For example, for the

2018 STSS, work was carried out using an "active consultation" approach, one of the key principles of which was to bring together, around the same table, healthcare professionals from GPs to hospital staff, medico-social actors, the public and private sectors, as well as user representatives. These stakeholders were included in the discussions and decision-making. For the *Ségur*, the idea was to deploy a method and a view of society based on co-construction, decompartmentalization, the desire to redraw the lines, to decentralize and to demonstrate confidence in healthcare actors.

The nature of Article 51 projects is at the very heart of the ambition to transform the system, supported by the public authorities. The most horizontal and collaborative method is also promoted at the highest level. Following on from the impetus of previous approaches, collective intelligence, at the core of Article 51, is proving its effectiveness in achieving shared objectives.

Particularly insightful at a time of health crisis, Article 51 is an excellent indicator of the problems inherent to France's healthcare system. It highlights the importance of supporting change in the implementation of reforms and public policies.

Involving users in trials can take different forms.

A large proportion of projects promote patient empowerment. The patient partner and the peer helper can act as trainers, moderators and interveners, both in the management and in the development of tools, as well as contributing their experience, for the design of educational programs and indicators. The latter will then be validated and standardized before distribution. These are based on the measurement for the quality of life (PROMS), the healthcare experience and the patient experience (PREMS). It is important to note that PREMS are not simply measures of patient satisfaction but are designed to objectify the patient's point of view through factual questions.

12.2.1.5. *The profound transformation of public administrations*

The continuity of financial support also illustrates the legislator's renewed interest in this scheme: the FISS health system innovation fund has been allocated a budget of 102 million euros in 2021, up from 30 million in 2019. The next step will be to bring proven derogations under common law.

Today, the public authorities are convinced on the value of this dynamic and are applying it to a wide range of fields and systems. One example is the State start up system: *betagouv*, part of the work being carried out by the inter-ministry directorate for public transformation.

12.2.2. *Local coordination: a case study on the Chronic Heart Failure pathway*

The second case study presents a method that mobilizes collective intelligence to identify action plans adapted to each locality, and for which the supervisory authority assumes the innovative role of local facilitator and collects the locality's ideas. The change here comes from the evolution in the position of the institutions (Ile-de-France RHA and *Assurance maladie*), where they no longer position themselves as funders or experts but as partners. Each actor in the Chronic Heart Failure (CHF) pathway is positioned at the same level, learning from the other.

12.2.2.1. *The context for setting up the CHF pathway's local events*

Chronic heart failure is a public health priority due to the ever-increasing prevalence of the condition as the population ages. By bringing together all healthcare actors (prevention, health, medico-social, social), patients and institutions, it will be possible to improve the management of chronic ambulatory diseases, patient quality of life and reduce (re)hospitalization and mortality.

For this reason, the IDF RHA, *Assurance maladie* and the various localities involved have organized local events throughout 2019–2020 in 14 IDF localities. These local events were part of the pertinence component of the first CAQES (*Contrat d'amélioration de la qualité et de l'efficience des soins* – "contract to improve the quality and efficiency of care").

Under the terms of this tripartite contract between the French *Assurance maladie*/RHA/healthcare facilities, two events were to be held in each of the signatory healthcare facilities' sub-regions, a year apart, bringing together all the healthcare professionals in the area concerned with this pathology (hospital cardiologists, emergency physicians, geriatricians, private cardiologists, general practitioners, private nurses, healthcare networks, local health professionals, patients' associations, hospital and pharmacy pharmacists, etc.), with the goal of improving this healthcare pathway.

The IDF is a region with significant socio-local inequalities in healthcare, and each locality faces different problems depending on its socio-demographic context, urban or rural environment, epidemiological context, size and supply of healthcare facilities, medical and paramedical demographics and so on.

The aim of these local initiatives is to identify the actions to be implemented, adapted to the specific characteristics of each locality.

The challenge facing the entire healthcare ecosystem is to successfully organize the management of chronic diseases on an outpatient basis, against a complex backdrop of poor medical demographics, growing economic constraints and inconsistent regional organization.

12.2.2.2. *Organizing local CHF events*

The aim of the first regional event was to produce a shared diagnosis that would enable us to identify the region's maturity and the pragmatic, locally-adapted actions to be implemented. The aim of the second regional event was to take stock of the actions previously identified, monitor the Health Insurance indicators (rate of rehospitalization within 6 months of returning home, rate of emergency room visits in the event of (re)hospitalization, etc.) and identify further actions. Unfortunately, the health crisis made it impossible to hold the second events in each locality.

These events brought together all local healthcare professionals involved in the management of this chronic disease, as well as patients and institutions. All were invited to share their views, challenges and solutions. These events were organized either in the city (amphitheatre, auditorium, town hall, etc.) or at the healthcare facility. The evening events were divided into several parts:

– a buffet reception to introduce, meet and greet, and get to know one another;

– a presentation by the RHA on the regional strategy for improving the CHF pathway, and of the local diagnosis (context of the locality, population demographics, epidemiology, medical and paramedical demographics, description of the healthcare offer);

– a presentation by the *Assurance Maladie* of the PRADO CHF system in terms of referrals by the healthcare facilities compared with regional referrals, and indicators of the healthcare pathway for patients with CHF in the locality (in the city and in the healthcare facility), in line with HAS, France's national health authority, recommendations, through analysis of SNDS (*Système national des données de santé* – "national health system databases");

– a presentation by the hospital (intervention by the cardiologist and/or geriatrician) on their difficulties in managing CHF patients, the structures in place and the obstacles and mechanisms already in place in the locality from the hospital's point of view;

– a presentation by a local general practitioner (or a network) on their challenges in managing CHF patients, the structures in place and the obstacles and mechanisms already in place in the locality from their point of view;

– a discussion with the audience (healthcare professionals, patients and their families, health insurance, RHA) to identify the challenges, maturity of the locality and the actions to be implemented in the locality;

– a conclusion to validate the actions to be implemented.

Although the framework of the local CHF events was the same, they all differed in terms of the issues raised, the maturity of the localities and the solutions proposed.

12.2.2.3. Results of the local CHF events

The results of the local events quickly revealed that each locality had a different level of maturity with regard to the CHF pathway and that the actions to be implemented needed to be adapted to each locality.

Some mature localities had adopted the existing CHF pathways and set up innovative systems.

Under the terms of Article 51, five university hospital groups (GHU) of the AP-HP (*Assistance publique-Hôpitaux de Paris* – "Paris Public Hospitals Assistance") have been experimenting since 2020 with an innovative set-up called CECICS (*Cellule d'expertise et de coordination des insuffisants cardiaques sévères en sortie d'hospitalisation* – "expertise and coordination unit for severe heart failure patients discharged from hospital"), which relies on state-registered nurses (SRNs) trained in the CHF cooperation protocol "telesupervision, titration consultation and unscheduled consultation, with or without telemedicine, of patients treated for heart insufficiency by a nurse" (Decree of December 27, 2019, translated by the authors). Some cardiologists are experimenting with cardiac rehabilitation in private practice by multi-professional teams (light private practice structure). Other teams are experimenting with cardiac telerehabilitation in patients' homes.

Some localities are already involved in task delegation, with advanced practice registered nurses (APRNs) or SRN nurses trained in the CHF cooperation protocol, and are deploying remote monitoring of CHF patients using connected devices.

On the other hand, some localities know little about existing mechanisms for improving the CHF pathway and face challenges in forging links between the GP and healthcare facilities.

Therefore, to improve the CHF pathway, the responses provided need to be adapted to each locality, depending on its maturity. The CHF pathway can be broken down into three phases: discharge of CHF patients from hospital, care in the community and (re)hospitalization. The aim is to progressively improve these three phases by mobilizing different systems:

– access to follow-up and rehabilitation care versus inclusion in PRADO CHF upon discharge from hospital;

– systematization of therapeutic optimization to ensure patients receive basic treatment quickly;

– systematization of therapeutic patient education (TPE) in the community;

– development of remote monitoring of CHF patients using connected devices;

– organization of semi-emergency access to cardiological expertise in the event of incipient cardiac decompensation;

– organization of direct (re)hospitalization in cardiology, geriatrics and hospitalization at home (HaH) if required;

– development of task delegation (APRN and SRN trained in CHF cooperation protocol);

– development of tele-expertise, for example, in EHPAD;

– decompartmentalization and coordination of healthcare professionals;

– improving the readability of the CHF pathway in the locality.

Although the "local events" method was ultimately traditional (meet and greet to exchange ideas directly, identify common objectives and agree on solutions), it gave rise to collective intelligence and became an innovative method for creating action plans adapted to each locality. The meetings created informal partnerships, with each actor accessible and open to change, questioning their own practices and listening to the constraints experienced by other actors. This collective intelligence enabled everyone to develop their skills and commit themselves, at the regional level, to a collective strategy for improving the CHF healthcare pathway.

The RHA and the *Assurance maladie* have questioned themselves, in particular with regard to non-operational systems that were too complicated to set up or still poorly valued, with regard to indicators that were still considered "too confidential" and as a result not sufficiently disseminated among healthcare professionals:

– numerous systems exist but are poorly known by healthcare professionals and therefore under-utilized: the challenge is to communicate on these systems to make them known and deploy them to develop their use;

– existing systems are dysfunctional: the challenge is to hear these dysfunctions and improve them to make them operational;

– healthcare provision in local areas is sometimes illegible: the challenge is to provide a comprehensive, exhaustive and up-to-date overview of local healthcare provision;

– indicators on the CHF pathway are too confidential: the challenge is to make these indicators accessible so that healthcare professionals can assess how their region is functioning and evaluate the impact of local actions implemented to improve the CHF pathway;

– systems and organizations better adapted to current requirements that need to be invented and put in place: the challenge is to support them, for example Article 51 experiments on CHF.

We have observed a need for everyone (healthcare professionals, institutions, patients) to meet to exchange points of view, practices and difficulties, to decompartmentalize, co-construct systems to improve care and set up coordinated care. There are few opportunities to re-group around a given issue in a given region and to broaden the circle of care used on a day-to-day basis.

12.2.2.4. Perspectives

The 14th and final local event on CHF pathway improvement took place in January 2020. The health crisis halted the momentum, and the second event in each locality could not be carried out.

However, as the Deming Wheel (Figure 12.1) shows, to achieve the objective, these events are only the first step in a dynamic strategy that involves support, monitoring and evaluation of the actions implemented in each locality.

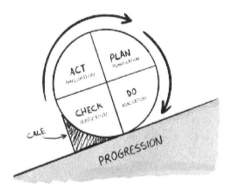

Figure 12.1. *The Deming wheel*

In 2020, the Ministry assigned IDF RHA the task of developing a method for improving the CHF pathway as part of the STSS "health system transformation strategy". In 2021, due to the evolution of the national strategy of the *Assurance maladie*, the latter contacted the IDF RHA CHF pathway team to consider the complementarity between the regional action plan and the national work plan.

Deployment of the pathway in the region is based on feedback from the fourteen 2018/2019 local events, to pass on this facilitation technique to local organizations with local event missions such as CPTSs (*Communautés professionnelles territoriales de santé* – "territorial health professional communities"), and DACs (*Dispositifs d'appui à la coordination* – "coordination support systems"), which will be able to benefit from support tools:

– local diagnosis produced by the *Assurance maladie* (local indicators and by health facilities);

– guide to self-assessment of the maturity of localities in order to identify actions to improve the healthcare pathway that are accessible to the locality and are to be implemented, produced by the IDF RHA;

– mapping of the healthcare offer, produced by the IDF RHA.

This deployment will be accompanied by monitoring indicators.

In addition, in 2022, the IDF RHA began developing the project "Generalizing the pathway for elderly CHF patients to avoid emergencies" as part of measure 5 of the *Pacte de refondation des urgences* ("pact to overhaul emergency services") making it possible to finance four actions (coordinating SRN between the GP and the health facility, two types of heart failure consultations in health facilities, training of an SRN in the CHF cooperation protocol), in 22 health facility-localities, a large proportion of which had carried out local events.

The project will be renewed in 2023, subject to a positive evaluation at the end of 2022. It is because of the collective intelligence generated by the local events (identification of actions to be implemented, co-construction of local organizations, knowledge of the localities, trust of partners, etc.) that this project was able to be set up quickly, as part of the regional strategy to improve the CHF pathway, and that the momentum can be collectively maintained.

Finally, a number of innovative CHF experiments are currently underway, within the framework of Article 51. These projects are experimenting with healthcare packages that incorporate the coordination, multi-disciplinary approach and new healthcare models needed to improve the CHF pathway.

In addition, from 2022, as part of the second *CAQES*, a result indicator "CHF patient (re)hospitalization rate" will be calculated every year for 3 years in localities of the IDF region, to be defined by the IDF RHA.

In this way, the local events on the CHF pathway have developed collective local intelligence and have been the first step in a regional improvement strategy for this pathway, which is taking other forms and involving other localities.

This method makes it possible to integrate the localities involved in this process into a common regional strategy for improving this pathway.

This simple, effective method is now being passed on, along with support tools (mapping of supply, self-assessment guide to regional maturity, description of CHF pathway indicators), to structures with local event missions, such as CPTSs and DACs.

12.3. Lessons learned

Several innovative experiments with new organizational and financing models, initiated by healthcare professionals, and supported by the supervisory authorities under Article 51, are underway and appear to be involved in the in-depth evolution of the healthcare system.

We are going to capitalize on the increased skills and conviction in the value of innovative working methods of institutional teams invested in supporting projects, in order to distribute methods more widely across institutions.

These new methods and transformations are complex, as paths and procedures must continue to evolve in line with the dual paradigm of agility and transformation of common law.

More broadly, the main challenge is to make mutual trust an objective but also to involve users at each and every stage of a project.

The strategy for improving the CHF pathway in the IDF region, based on local initiatives that are repeated, extended to other localities and passed on to other localities (CPTS and DAC), involves more and more healthcare professionals based in the IDF region and who, collectively, are committed to improving this chronic pathway.

The "local event" method is traditional, simple, human, accepted, even desired and appreciated by all (healthcare professionals, institutions and patients) and helps to generate collective local intelligence by enabling the sharing of experiences and the cross-fertilization of points of view on the CHF pathway, and making it possible to publicize the innovations currently being tested in this area to provide information on the local healthcare offer and to transmit local evaluation indicators. This method makes it possible to identify action plans for improving the CHF pathway that are tailored to each locality.

Improving the CHF healthcare pathway is a long-term project, which involves working with local authorities to create the conditions necessary for the adoption of the organizational innovations currently being tested on this pathway.

This collective intelligence approach is essential if we are to meet the needs arising from socio-demographic and epidemiological transformations (an aging population) and improve the management of increasingly prevalent chronic pathologies.

These two cases illustrate the evolution of the institutional position of the RHA and the *Assurance maladie*, which is moving from a vertical, top-down approach to a horizontal one in which the supervisory authorities become companions, co-constructors, local facilitators and partners in the development of collective intelligence.

Collective intelligence is based, on the one hand, on a simple, obvious, human method of meeting, direct exchange, sharing, expressing needs and listening, which had been collectively abandoned and must be rediscovered, and, on the other hand, on innovative support methods. In this sense, collective intelligence means continuing to drive change in our institutions toward a service-oriented perspective.

Appendix

Brief Descriptions of Organizations

ACCORD: assemble, coordinate, understand, research and debate (*assembler, coordonner, comprendre, rechercher, débattre*) within primary healthcare. The ACCORD research network aims to build a primary healthcare research ecosystem by bringing together healthcare professionals and researchers. It received funding for its creation in 2020, as part of a call for projects from IRESP (*Institut de recherche en santé publique* – "Institute for Public Health Research").

ACI: *Accord conventionnel interprofessionnel* is a national agreement negotiated and signed between the *Caisse Nationale d'Assurance Maladie* (France's national health insurance scheme), and representatives of various professionals, under which the latter undertake to perform certain tasks in return for which they receive specific remuneration.

ASALEE: *Action de santé libérale en équipe* (team-based healthcare action) is an experimental scheme set up in 2004 to improve primary healthcare management of chronic diseases. A cooperation protocol enables general practitioners to delegate actions or activities to nurses, including screening and monitoring of chronic pathologies.

CME: *Commission médicale d'établissement* is the representative body of the medical (doctors and midwives), pharmaceutical and odontological community in each French public health establishment. It is governed by Articles L.6144-1, L.6144-2 and R.6144-1 to R.6144-6 of the French Public Health Code. Until the ordinance of September 1, 2005, its missions were purely consultative. Subsequently, it was granted decision-making powers, which were later withdrawn by the HPST (*Hôpital, patients, santé et territoires* – "hospital, patients, health and localities") law of July 21, 2009.

Appendix written by Aline COURIE-LEMEUR.

Communautés 360: structuring a network of professionals in the disability sector to support people's life pathways.

Covid-19: Coronavirus 2019 is an infectious disease caused by the SARS-CoV-2 virus.

CPAM: *Caisse primaire d'assurance maladie*, France's primary health insurance fund, is a departmental body with a public health service mission. It is responsible for local relations with the beneficiaries of the *Caisse Nationale d'Assurance Maladie* (CNAM), France's national health insurance fund, created by the ordinances of October 4 and 19, 1945, which established the French social security system. Its missions are as follows: to register insured persons and manage their health insurance entitlements, process medical claims forms and provide health insurance and work accident/occupational disease benefits; to implement an annual risk management action plan in conjunction with health professionals; to develop a policy of prevention and health promotion; and to ensure a policy of health and social action through individual aid to insured persons and collective aid to associations.

CPOM: in French law, the *Contrat pluriannuel d'objectifs et de moyens* (CPOM – multi-year contract of objectives and means) is the contract by which an organization managing social or medico-social establishments or services, as defined in Article L.312-1 of the *Code de l'action sociale et des familles* (CASF), the French "social action and family code", makes a commitment to a pricing authority over a multi-year period, in order to receive corresponding budgetary allocations in line with the activity objectives pursued by its establishments. The legal status of the CPOM is defined in Article L.313-11 of the CASF.

CPTS: *Communautés professionnelles territoriales de santé* – "territorial health professional community" in France) brings together healthcare professionals from the same area who decide to collaborate, on their own initiative, around a healthcare project to meet the health needs of the population in their area. Although the scheme has been in existence since 2016, it has been made central by the 2019 healthcare law. An inter-professional conventional agreement between the *Caisse nationale d'assurance maladie* and the professionals concerned enables CPTSs to receive public funding. The French government aims to have 1,000 CPTSs covering the country by 2022. At present, just over 400 projects have been identified by the authorities.

DAC: *Dispositif d'appui à la coordination* is a coordination support organization in France and was created by the law relating to the *Organisation et à la transformation du système de santé* (OTSS – organization and transformation of the healthcare system) of July 24, 2019. It is a single, free point of entry for professionals and structures dealing with people in complex health and living situations, in particular to encourage them to stay at home. Each DAC is staffed by a multi-professional team, including doctors, nurses and social workers. It informs, guides and supports professionals, patients and their families in complex situations. It provides concrete solutions by assessing the person's situation and needs, and proposing a personalized, coordinated and supported healthcare pathway, in agreement with the attending physician and in liaison with professionals.

DD: *Agence régionale de santé d'Ile-de-France* is organized with a regional headquarters and departmental delegations in each *département* of Ile-de-France.

DLU: developed by the *Haute Autorité de santé* (HAS), the French national authority for health, and the *Agence nationale de l'évaluation de la qualité des établissements et services sociaux et médico-sociaux* (ANESM), French agency for the evaluation of the quality of social and medico-social establishments and services, the *Dossier de liaison d'urgence*, an emergency contact file, must be created for all EHPAD members, whether or not their medical records are accessible 24 hours a day. Created and updated regularly by the EHPADs coordinating doctor, it is designed to improve the transfer of useful information needed by the doctor intervening in an emergency to ensure optimum care for the resident in the EHPAD or in an emergency department. The aim is to reinforce the safety, continuity and quality of care in emergency situations, and avoid inappropriate hospitalization.

DREES: *Direction de la recherche, des études, de l'évaluation et des statistiques* is a department of the French central public administration that produces statistics and socio-economic studies. It reports to the Ministry of Health.

E-Parcours: a program that aims to roll out digital coordination tools to healthcare professionals in the regions, as part of a healthcare pathway.

EHPAD: *Établissement d'hébergement pour personnes âgées dépendantes* is a medico-social establishment. It is currently the most widespread institution catering for the elderly. It is a medicalized retirement home with all the associated services, such as catering, medical care and assistance subject to authorization, enabling it to operate.

HPST Law: a law of July 21, 2009 on hospital reform and patients, health and localities (*Hôpital et relative aux patients*).

MAIA: action method for the integration of assistance and care services in the field of autonomy. "This method brings together all the players involved in supporting people aged 60 and over who are losing their autonomy, and their caregivers" (*Caisse nationale de solidarité pour l'autonomie* – French "national solidarity fund for autonomy"), with a view to promoting the continuity of healthcare pathways and the management of complex situations.

MRA: "medical records assistant", commonly referred to as ARM (*Assistant de régulation médicale*) in French receives and directs telephone calls to *Samu-Centres*. The assistant coordinates medical emergency calls under the responsibility of the regulating doctor.

MSP: *maisons de santé pluriprofessionnelle* (multi-professional health centers) are a collective, coordinated approach to professional practice, created in 2007. MSPs are legal entities and offer local healthcare services without accommodation, as well as preventive initiatives. They are a response to the changing practice patterns sought by many healthcare professionals. Despite a number of recent developments, healthcare professionals working in MSPs are generally self-employed.

PRS: *Projet régional de santé* ("regional health project") is designed to steer, plan and program the resources of the State's health policy in the region. In line with the national health strategy, it defines the multi-year strategy and objectives of the Regional Health Agency, as well as the measures required to achieve them. It complies with the financial provisions set out in the finance and social security financing acts. It is drawn up for a period of 5 years by the CEO of the Regional Health Agency, after receiving the official opinion of the Prefect of the Region, the Regional Council, the Departmental Councils, the Municipal Councils and the Regional Conference on Health and Autonomy.

RHA: France's Regional Health Agency, or *Agence régionale de santé* (ARS), is a public administrative establishment created on April 1, 2010. It is responsible for implementing regional health policy and steering the health system at a regional level as closely as possible to the needs of the population. RHAs report directly to the French Ministry of Health.

Samu: *Service d'aide médicale urgente* ("emergency medical services") is a call center that responds to the health needs of the population 24 hours a day and provides pre-hospital care, particularly prior to referral to a health facility. The *Samu* performs medical regulation, the aim of which is to provide a medical response tailored to the patient's needs. It directs patients to the right medical service for their condition, with a range of responses corresponding to different levels of severity and urgency. The *Centre de réception et de régulation des appels* (CRRA15) ("call reception and regulation centre") is the service specifically in charge of telephone responses, with all the players involved in a single operation: emergency medicine regulation, general medicine regulation, specialized regulation (poison and toxicovigilance centers, etc.) and ambulance coordination.

SAS: *Service d'accès aux soins* ("access to healthcare service") aims to guarantee access to vital, urgent and unscheduled care for the population, anywhere and at any time, because of a clear and coordinated chain of care between hospitals and urban healthcare providers in the same area. It is being deployed as part of the *Pacte pour la refondation des urgences* ("pact to overhaul emergency services") and has been reaffirmed by the *Ségur de la santé* (Health Segur). It can trigger an unscheduled consultation in town, a remote consultation, recourse to an emergency service or urgent transport intervention. A pilot phase is underway, with the aim of making the system widely available by 2022.

Ségur de la santé: from May 25 to July 10, 2020, it brought together the French government and representatives of the healthcare system. Thirty-three measures were selected, leading to the signing of the Ségur healthcare agreements on July 13, 2020 and a Ségur law promulgated on April 26, 2021.

UCP: unscheduled or urgent care practitioner is commonly referred to as an OSNP (*Opérateur de soin non programmé*) in French. The practitioner provides "access to healthcare services", welcomes, guides, regulates and prioritizes cases over the telephone, in order to connect patients in need of care with the available supply in real time.

List of Authors

Annie BARTOLI
LAREQUOI
UVSQ
Guyancourt
France

Sophie BATAILLE
Agence Régionale de Santé
d'Ile-de-France
Paris
France

Élise BLÉRY
Agence Régionale de Santé
d'Ile-de-France
Paris
France

Laëtitia BOREL
LAREQUOI
UVSQ
Guyancourt
France

Emmanuelle CARGNELLO-CHARLES
LiREM
UPPA
Pau
France

Laurent CENARD
Fondation Santé Service
Villejuif
France

Yves CHARPAK
Fondation Charpak, l'esprit des sciences
Larchant
France

Olena Yuriivna CHYGRYN
Sumy State University
Ukraine

Aline COURIE-LEMEUR
LAREQUOI
ISM-IAE
Université de Versailles
France

Cécile DEZEST
LiREM
UPPA
Pau
France

Isabelle FRANCHISTEGUY-COULOUME
LiREM
UPPA
Pau
France

Sylvain GAUTIER
Inserm
UFR Simone Veil Santé
UVSQ
Versailles
France

Liliia Mykolaivna KHOMENKO
Sumy State University
Ukraine

Vincent MABILLARD
Université libre de Bruxelles
Belgium

Hélène MARIE
Agence Régionale de Santé
d'Ile-de-France
DD Seine-et-Marne
Paris
France

Michel MARTY
Assurance maladie
Paris
France

Jan MATTIJS
Université libre de Bruxelles
Belgium

Benoît NAUTRE
Université Clermont Auvergne
Clermont-Ferrand
France

Béatrice PIPITONE
Agence Régionale de Santé
d'Ile-de-France
Paris
France

Charlotte ROUDIER-DAVAL
Agence Régionale de Santé
d'Ile-de-France
Paris
France

Marianne SARAZIN
Groupe Mutualiste de Saint-Étienne
and
Inserm
École des Mines de Saint-Étienne
France

Jihane SEBAI
LAREQUOI
UVSQ
Guyancourt
France

Bérangère L. SZOSTAK
LAREQUOI
UVSQ
Guyancourt
France

Fatima YATIM
LIRSA
CNAM
Paris
France

Index

A

action, 32, 34, 35, 39, 40, 49, 57, 59,
61, 66, 67, 75, 95, 107, 111, 121,
125, 127, 134, 139, 145, 146, 166,
168, 170, 173, 174, 177, 181, 185,
193, 206, 219, 222, 223, 225,
227–229

adaptability, 28, 61, 165, 171,
175–177

adaptation, 18, 22, 30, 41, 49, 59,
122, 124, 135, 138, 153, 185, 212

aging, 58, 98, 181, 197, 211, 226

alliances, 75, 141, 143, 148, 149,
151, 152, 154, 155, 158, 215

ambidexterity, 74

approach, 7–9, 26–28, 30, 33, 41, 45,
48, 53, 57, 59, 62, 66, 68, 69, 83,
108, 110, 122, 124, 128, 138, 145,
148, 149, 151, 157, 173, 174, 177,
181, 182, 184, 186, 188, 190–192,
197, 202, 204, 207, 208, 212, 213,
216, 218, 224, 226, 230

appropriation, 48, 108, 129, 134, 138,
165, 168, 170–172, 176, 216

authorities, 26, 34, 51, 57, 59, 60,
64–66, 68, 69, 72, 75, 85, 106, 107,
115, 122, 142, 145, 147–151, 153,
154, 156, 157, 186, 211, 212,
215–218, 225, 226, 228

autonomy, 35, 65, 66, 68, 73, 74, 76,
99, 105, 134, 146, 154, 216, 229,
230

C

capital, 18, 20, 22, 29, 86

capitalization, 32, 129

catalyst, 122, 131, 132, 167, 187

challenge, 31, 34, 35, 58, 62, 72, 110,
112, 113, 115, 116, 123, 158, 169,
174, 176, 193, 204, 211, 219, 222,
223, 225

change(s), 14, 15, 20, 39, 41, 44, 46,
47, 49–51, 53, 54, 59, 62, 64, 65,
69, 72–76, 83, 84, 85, 87, 91, 93,
99–113, 116, 117, 119, 121, 122,
133, 144, 148, 150, 151, 158, 168,
172, 175, 186, 201, 202, 205–208,
211–214, 217–219, 222, 226

co-creation, 83, 85–87, 89–91,
    93–97, 177
co-design, 83, 87, 89, 169, 175, 177
co-development, 135, 213
co-production, 83, 85–87, 89, 90, 95
cohesion, 30, 61, 86
collaboration, 7–9, 18, 22, 26, 32, 33,
    60, 69, 86, 88, 109, 116, 123, 130,
    133, 136, 147, 153, 177, 183, 184
communication, 29, 42, 83, 89, 92,
    96, 97, 121, 124, 135, 151, 154,
    156, 158, 191, 195, 206
community, 18, 20, 22, 25, 27, 34,
    35, 39, 43, 47, 49, 54, 60, 63, 86,
    87, 121, 127, 128, 131, 132, 186,
    211, 215, 221, 222, 227, 228
compartmentalization, 58, 62, 63, 74,
    76, 111, 147, 185, 196
complementarity, 61, 73, 108, 109,
    113, 148, 157, 223
complex, 25, 32, 49, 58, 61, 64, 67,
    72, 75, 86, 90, 93, 98, 112, 141,
    145, 147, 150, 157, 166, 167, 169,
    219, 225, 229, 230
concept, 25, 26, 37, 38, 40, 41, 48,
    57, 58, 72, 87, 88, 138, 170, 183,
    185, 203, 204
constraints, 44, 45, 123, 125, 126,
    134, 138, 148, 165, 169, 192, 211,
    213, 220, 222
consultation, 121, 130, 137, 146, 148,
    165, 167, 169, 171, 175, 177,
    189–191, 207, 212, 218, 221, 231
convergence, 59, 62, 64, 68, 70, 125,
    131, 146–149, 217
cooperation, 8, 22, 32, 37, 57–60, 62,
    67, 68, 71, 75, 110, 121, 122, 136,
    147, 149, 153, 155, 157, 168, 182,
    185, 190, 221, 222, 224, 227

coordination, 25–28, 32, 38, 39, 57,
    59–71, 73, 75, 76, 84, 90, 92, 98,
    122, 124, 126–132, 134, 136, 137,
    141–157, 182, 188–190, 193,
    195–197, 214, 216, 217, 219, 221,
    222, 224, 228–230
creation, 31, 32, 39, 41, 47, 59, 60,
    63, 69, 76, 83, 84, 86, 87, 89, 90,
    92, 95, 97, 98, 134, 142, 143, 147,
    152, 157, 173, 182–184, 188, 189,
    195, 215, 227
creativity, 30, 40, 61, 165, 166, 169,
    170, 173, 174, 183, 203
crisis, 18, 22, 25, 28–32, 34, 37, 38,
    40–42, 44, 45, 47, 48, 50–55,
    65–67, 70–72, 76, 121–125, 129,
    132–136, 138, 143, 158, 166, 168,
    172, 175, 177, 191, 196, 205, 215,
    217, 218, 220, 223
culture, 8, 18, 22, 30, 34, 54, 75, 109,
    110, 135, 152, 156, 169, 185

D

decompartmentalized, 57, 58, 134,
    135
democracy, 73, 86, 106, 107, 111,
    114, 115, 118, 119, 133, 139, 140
design, 61, 84, 86–91, 94, 95, 100,
    153, 165–177, 183, 184, 195, 196,
    203–205, 212, 213, 215, 218
diagnosis, 66, 87, 100, 122, 125, 129,
    146, 190, 192, 205, 208, 220, 224
differences, 58, 74, 86, 110, 119, 175
differentiation, 71, 74
digitization, 83–86, 88–99
dimensions, 39, 40, 118, 171
directions, 7, 9, 11, 17, 20, 21, 214
diversity, 61, 74, 114, 116, 152, 157
durability, 75

E

e-health, 83, 89, 91, 95, 96, 98, 100
ecosystem, 31, 41, 63, 64, 74, 84, 99,
    173, 186, 219, 227
effectiveness, 87–90, 144, 169, 170,
    181, 211, 218
efficiency, 8, 35, 37, 39, 58, 84, 88,
    89, 92, 123, 136, 138, 145, 170,
    190, 219
elderly, 33, 37, 42, 43, 49, 63, 131,
    146, 204, 205, 215, 216, 224, 229
empowerment, 35, 71, 90, 106, 117,
    118, 177, 218
ethical, 83, 90, 94, 96, 207
evaluation, 8, 31, 86, 143, 165, 184,
    186, 187, 195, 214, 216, 223–225,
    229
exchange, 41, 50, 52, 54, 59, 93, 98,
    122, 124, 127, 132, 137, 184, 189,
    192–194, 196, 206, 207, 215, 216,
    222, 223, 226
experiments, 63, 110, 156, 170, 181,
    182, 186, 188, 193, 197, 198, 201,
    202, 205, 214–217, 223–225
expert, 106–109, 111, 129, 142, 187,
    209
exploitation, 47, 74

F, G, H

facilitators, 46, 50, 62–65, 67, 74,
    122, 226
finance, 21, 28, 51, 66, 68, 75, 84, 93,
    123, 126, 135, 139, 144, 150, 169,
    177, 186, 218, 224, 230
governance, 30, 37, 42, 52, 54, 57,
    59–61, 84–86, 88, 89, 94, 96, 99,
    133, 169, 176, 183, 185, 213, 214
holism, 85

I

identity, 105, 113, 114, 116–119
improvement, 88, 132, 139, 146, 223,
    224
incentives, 54, 60, 186, 190, 193
influence, 7, 9, 14–17, 27, 28, 45, 89,
    155, 171, 173, 185
informal, 29, 45, 156, 216, 222
information, 13, 29, 31, 32, 45, 53,
    59, 83, 90, 91, 93, 94, 96, 97, 99,
    100, 107, 108, 116, 122, 127–132,
    134, 146, 151, 171, 184, 187, 188,
    192, 201–203, 206, 214, 215, 217,
    225, 229
initiatives, 21, 33, 68, 71, 99, 109,
    110, 112, 122, 124, 126, 153, 212,
    213, 219, 225, 230
innovative, 8, 31, 37, 38, 46, 49, 50,
    59, 121, 123, 126, 131–133, 135,
    136, 138, 139, 141, 142, 144, 166,
    174, 177, 181, 186, 188, 192, 193,
    196, 211, 212, 216, 219, 221, 222,
    224–226
institutional, 76, 86, 88, 90, 114, 122,
    132, 134, 143–148, 150, 151, 153,
    169, 188, 216, 225, 226
institutionalization, 39, 46, 75, 114,
    117, 145
institutions, 29, 30, 32, 33, 37, 38, 42,
    43, 51, 54, 62, 66, 71, 97, 99, 107,
    111, 112, 114, 115, 122, 125, 132,
    134, 136, 144, 148, 204, 211, 214,
    215, 219, 220, 223, 225, 226
instrument, 69, 71, 75, 88, 97
integration, 27, 47, 52, 57, 63, 71, 74,
    92, 105, 108, 111–114, 116, 119,
    143, 151, 172, 193, 196, 229

intelligence, 7–9, 83, 85–88, 91, 93,
    97–100, 203, 212, 213, 218, 219,
    222, 224–226
intensity, 54
intrapreneurship, 172, 174

K, L

know-how, 39, 63, 141, 152, 153,
    155–158, 166, 193, 215
knowledge, 8, 28, 29, 33, 53, 54, 61,
    62, 65, 74, 85, 87, 88, 92, 95, 100,
    106, 108–114, 117, 118, 122, 125,
    128, 137, 142, 145, 155–157, 166,
    173, 175, 176, 182–184, 193–196,
    201, 208, 224
leadership, 18, 20–22, 29, 30, 45, 47,
    52, 54, 89, 137, 142, 156, 158
learning, 8, 18, 37, 38, 41, 45, 52, 54,
    61, 62, 75, 87, 93, 99, 100, 145,
    148, 157, 171, 175, 208, 219
legitimization, 111, 113, 165, 171,
    174, 177

M

mandate, 105, 111, 114, 115
mediating role, 18, 22
mediation, 21, 152, 154, 173
medical, 27, 29, 32, 33, 39, 58, 61,
    87, 90, 93–97, 99, 100, 105, 106,
    108, 110–114, 116, 118, 119, 121,
    122, 126–131, 133–139, 144, 167,
    169, 172, 173, 175, 187–189, 191,
    192, 196, 207, 208, 211, 214, 215,
    217–220, 227–230
medico-social, 34, 58, 59, 61, 110,
    123–125, 144, 146, 150, 186, 229
meeting, 53, 75, 169, 194, 212, 215,
    216, 226
method, 53, 60, 91, 146, 169, 177,
    188, 212–216, 218, 219, 222–226,
    229

mission, 20, 27, 31, 34, 39, 45, 47,
    49, 52, 123, 136, 137, 145, 149,
    150, 152, 153, 155, 175, 214, 215,
    228
model, 18, 21, 25, 30, 42, 47, 54, 57,
    59–61, 67, 75, 99, 109–112, 114,
    116, 143, 147, 149, 150, 176, 213,
    215
multiplicity, 58

N, O

network, 29–32, 35, 64, 67, 131, 132,
    137, 138, 145, 146, 151, 156, 186,
    193, 195, 205, 220, 227, 228
objectives, 59, 62, 68, 69, 71, 91,
    110, 123, 136, 138, 139, 141, 148,
    149, 152, 153, 155, 156, 158, 170,
    171, 173, 190, 216–218, 222, 228,
    230

P

pandemic, 25, 31, 33, 40, 67, 71, 84,
    98, 99, 121–123, 125, 127–129,
    132–135, 137, 138, 166, 181, 202,
    204–207
paradigm, 28, 52, 57–60, 63, 65, 67,
    72–74, 76, 108, 110, 188, 202, 225
partners, 8, 30, 31, 34, 57, 65, 70, 72,
    121, 124, 132, 137, 142, 149–151,
    154–156, 173, 188, 193, 213, 216,
    219, 224, 226
partnership, 8, 87, 108, 116, 122,
    124–126, 130, 135, 137, 138,
    141–145, 147, 148, 150, 152–157,
    189, 213

patient, 8, 26, 27, 37, 58, 59, 62, 71,
    83, 84, 90, 92, 94, 95, 97, 98,
    105–119, 123, 129–134, 136, 137,
    140, 143, 150, 157, 168, 169, 181,
    182, 184–198, 205–208, 211,
    217–219, 222, 224, 230
performance, 8, 18, 22, 39, 85, 87,
    88, 111, 118, 149, 157, 177, 181,
    182, 196, 197, 214, 215
pilot, 100, 125, 129, 130, 141, 152,
    153, 231
pooling, 28, 58, 147
power, 38, 39, 45, 53, 69, 70, 73,
    117, 124, 177, 203
prevention, 27, 39, 59, 143, 192, 217,
    219, 228
principles, 37, 49, 61, 62, 88, 92, 116,
    118, 123, 138, 156, 197, 202, 203,
    218
processes, 8, 30, 40, 84–89, 92, 95,
    108, 126, 183, 195, 196
progression, 75, 205
proximity, 39, 54, 66, 70, 115, 183,
    193, 197

Q, R

quality, 21, 27, 29, 32, 33, 39, 40, 51,
    58, 84, 92, 93, 98, 111, 116, 136,
    142, 144, 145, 151, 153, 155, 187,
    190, 211, 212, 217–219, 229
rebalance, 139
reciprocity, 21, 30
recognition, 30, 65, 67, 70–73, 76,
    88, 107–109, 118, 142, 144, 181,
    198, 205
reform, 37, 39, 59, 61, 64, 65, 88,
    105, 106, 109–112, 114, 119, 144,
    168, 229
regeneration, 85
regulation, 62, 68, 130, 133, 150, 230

regulatory, 68, 71, 72, 75, 91, 105,
    107, 117, 122, 125, 126, 129, 139,
    188, 212, 215
reorganization, 63, 147, 202
routine, 174, 205

S

sharing, 18, 28, 32, 53, 66, 84, 125,
    126, 128, 129, 131, 139, 145, 168,
    183, 186, 190, 193, 215, 216, 225,
    226
shock, 38, 41, 48, 51, 52, 166
skills, 30, 41, 47, 59, 61, 63, 70,
    72–76, 93, 105, 108, 109, 113, 124,
    125, 141, 142, 145, 147–149, 151,
    155–158, 166, 171, 173, 174, 177,
    183, 187, 198, 201, 204, 208, 217,
    222, 225
space, 27, 48, 59, 125, 127, 174, 175,
    177, 181–186, 193–198, 216
standardization, 76, 168
strategic, 41, 66, 87, 96, 98, 121, 133,
    141, 143, 145, 147–152, 155, 156,
    167, 186, 187, 197, 214
stress, 18, 22, 95
structural, 25, 26, 28, 58, 122, 123,
    133, 139, 201, 207
structures, 8, 21, 31, 33, 39–41, 54,
    59, 67, 69, 75, 90, 133, 141–145,
    147–149, 153, 154, 166, 182, 183,
    185, 203, 204, 225, 229
structuring, 25, 26, 29, 33, 34, 49, 57,
    62, 63, 127, 144, 146, 152, 204,
    228
systemic, 27, 31, 67, 84, 122, 151,
    169

T

teams, 26, 29, 31–33, 44, 47, 52, 53,
    67, 70, 124, 132, 136, 145, 158,
    175, 186, 193, 214, 221, 225

technological, 28, 83–85, 88–95, 98, 182, 197, 204, 208, 209
technologies, 8, 83, 84, 88, 89, 92–94, 96–100, 118, 201, 202, 204
telemedicine, 94, 196, 203, 206, 208, 215, 221
tensions, 84–86, 94, 122, 194, 196, 197
training, 34, 43, 57, 105, 106, 109–114, 116, 118, 119, 129, 140, 142, 157, 172, 174, 177, 187, 201, 224
transformation, 39, 41, 44, 49, 54, 55, 58–62, 74, 76, 83, 84, 89, 94, 118, 136, 142, 166, 173, 208, 217, 218, 223, 225, 228

transparency, 21, 91, 92, 95–98, 156
trust, 18, 22, 30, 70, 84, 85, 96, 97, 116, 122, 125, 126, 130, 137, 139, 149, 154, 156, 194, 208, 224, 225

U, W

uncertainty, 29, 74, 148, 154, 166
unexpected, 38, 40
user-citizens, 106, 107, 114, 116, 118, 119
weaknesses, 123

Other titles from

in

Innovation, Entrepreneurship and Management

2023

BOUVIER-PATRON Paul
Frugal Innovation and Innovative Creation
(Smart Innovation Set – Volume 40)

CASADELLA Vanessa, UZUNIDIS Dimitri
Agri-Innovations and Development Challenges: Engineering, Value Chains
and Socio-economic Models
(Innovation in Engineering and Technology Set – Volume 8)

DARTIGUEPEYROU Carine, SALOFF-COSTE Michel
Futures: The Great Turn
(Innovation and Technology Set – Volume 18)

PEYROUX Élisabeth, RAIMOND Christine, VIEL Vincent, VALIE Émilie
Development and Territorial Restructuring in an Era of Global Change:
Theories, Approaches and Future Research Perspectives

SAULAIS Pierre
Knowledge and Ideation: Inventive Knowledge Analysis for Ideation
Stimulation
(Innovation and Technology Set – Volume 17)

2022

AOUINAÏT Camille
Open Innovation Strategies
(Smart Innovation Set – Volume 39)

BOUCHÉ Geneviève
Productive Economy, Contributory Economy: Governance Tools for the Third Millennium
(Innovation and Technology Set – Volume 15)

BRUYÈRE Christelle
Caring Management in Health Organizations: A Lever for Crisis Management
(Health and Innovation Set – Volume 3)

HELLER David
Valuation of the Liability Structure by Real Options
(Modern Finance, Management Innovation and Economic Growth Set – Volume 5)

MATHIEU Valérie
A Customer-oriented Manager for B2B Services: Principles and Implementation

MORALES Lucía, DZEVER Sam, TAYLOR Robert
Asia-Europe Industrial Connectivity in Times of Crisis
(Innovation and Technology Set – Volume 16)

NOËL Florent, SCHMIDT Géraldine
Employability and Industrial Mutations: Between Individual Trajectories and Organizational Strategic Planning
(Technological Changes and Human Resources Set – Volume 4)

DE SAINT JULIEN Odile
The Innovation Ecosystem as a Source of Value Creation: A Value Creation Lever for Open Innovation
(Diverse and Global Perspectives on Value Creation Set – Volume 4)

SALOFF-COSTE Michel
Innovation Ecosystems: The Future of Civilizations and the Civilization of the Future
(Innovation and Technology Set – Volume 14)

VAYRE Emilie
Digitalization of Work: New Spaces and New Working Times
(Technological Changes and Human Resources Set – Volume 5)

ZAFEIRIS Konstantinos N, SKIADIS Christos H, DIMOTIKALIS Yannis, KARAGRIGORIOU Alex, KARAGRIGORIOU-VONTA Christina
Data Analysis and Related Applications 1: Computational, Algorithmic and Applied Economic Data Analysis
(Big Data, Artificial Intelligence and Data Analysis Set – Volume 9)
Data Analysis and Related Applications 2: Multivariate, Health and Demographic Data Analysis
(Big Data, Artificial Intelligence and Data Analysis Set – Volume 10)

2021

ARCADE Jacques
Strategic Engineering
(Innovation and Technology Set – Volume 11)

BÉRANGER Jérôme, RIZOULIÈRES Roland
The Digital Revolution in Health
(Health and Innovation Set – Volume 2)

BOBILLIER CHAUMON Marc-Eric
Digital Transformations in the Challenge of Activity and Work: Understanding and Supporting Technological Changes
(Technological Changes and Human Resources Set – Volume 3)

BUCLET Nicolas
Territorial Ecology and Socio-ecological Transition
(Smart Innovation Set – Volume 34)

DIMOTIKALIS Yannis, KARAGRIGORIOU Alex, PARPOULA Christina, SKIADIS Christos H
Applied Modeling Techniques and Data Analysis 1: Computational Data Analysis Methods and Tools
(Big Data, Artificial Intelligence and Data Analysis Set - Volume 7)
Applied Modeling Techniques and Data Analysis 2: Financial, Demographic, Stochastic and Statistical Models and Methods
(Big Data, Artificial Intelligence and Data Analysis Set – Volume 8)

DISPAS Christophe, KAYANAKIS Georges, SERVEL Nicolas, STRIUKOVA Ludmila
Innovation and Financial Markets
(Innovation between Risk and Reward Set – Volume 7)

ENJOLRAS Manon
Innovation and Export: The Joint Challenge of the Small Company
(Smart Innovation Set – Volume 37)

FLEURY Sylvain, RICHIR Simon
Immersive Technologies to Accelerate Innovation: How Virtual and Augmented Reality Enables the Co-Creation of Concepts
(Smart Innovation Set – Volume 38)

GIORGINI Pierre
The Contributory Revolution
(Innovation and Technology Set – Volume 13)

GOGLIN Christian
Emotions and Values in Equity Crowdfunding Investment Choices 2: Modeling and Empirical Study

GRENIER Corinne, OIRY Ewan
Altering Frontiers: Organizational Innovations in Healthcare
(Health and Innovation Set – Volume 1)

GUERRIER Claudine
Security and Its Challenges in the 21st Century
(Innovation and Technology Set – Volume 12)

HELLER David
Performance of Valuation Methods in Financial Transactions
(Modern Finance, Management Innovation and Economic Growth Set –
Volume 4)

LEHMANN Paul-Jacques
Liberalism and Capitalism Today

SOULÉ Bastien, HALLÉ Julie, VIGNAL Bénédicte, BOUTROY Éric,
NIER Olivier
Innovation in Sport: Innovation Trajectories and Process Optimization
(Smart Innovation Set – Volume 35)

UZUNIDIS Dimitri, KASMI Fedoua, ADATTO Laurent
Innovation Economics, Engineering and Management Handbook 1:
Main Themes
Innovation Economics, Engineering and Management Handbook 2:
Special Themes

VALLIER Estelle
Innovation in Clusters: Science–Industry Relationships in the Face of
Forced Advancement
(Smart Innovation Set – Volume 36)

2020

ACH Yves-Alain, RMADI-SAÏD Sandra
Financial Information and Brand Value: Reflections, Challenges and
Limitations

ANDREOSSO-O'CALLAGHAN Bernadette, DZEVER Sam, JAUSSAUD Jacques,
TAYLOR Robert
Sustainable Development and Energy Transition in Europe and Asia
(Innovation and Technology Set – Volume 9)

BEN SLIMANE Sonia, M'HENNI Hatem
Entrepreneurship and Development: Realities and Future Prospects
(Smart Innovation Set – Volume 30)

CHOUTEAU Marianne, FOREST Joëlle, NGUYEN Céline
Innovation for Society: The P.S.I. Approach
(Smart Innovation Set – Volume 28)

CORON Clotilde
Quantifying Human Resources: Uses and Analysis
(Technological Changes and Human Resources Set – Volume 2)

CORON Clotilde, GILBERT Patrick
Technological Change
(Technological Changes and Human Resources Set – Volume 1)

CERDIN Jean-Luc, PERETTI Jean-Marie
The Success of Apprenticeships: Views of Stakeholders on Training and Learning (Human Resources Management Set – Volume 3)

DELCHET-COCHET Karen
Circular Economy: From Waste Reduction to Value Creation
(Economic Growth Set – Volume 2)

DIDAY Edwin, GUAN Rong, SAPORTA Gilbert, WANG Huiwen
Advances in Data Science
(Big Data, Artificial Intelligence and Data Analysis Set – Volume 4)

DOS SANTOS PAULINO Victor
Innovation Trends in the Space Industry
(Smart Innovation Set – Volume 25)

GASMI Nacer
Corporate Innovation Strategies: Corporate Social Responsibility and Shared Value Creation
(Smart Innovation Set – Volume 33)

GOGLIN Christian
Emotions and Values in Equity Crowdfunding Investment Choices 1: Transdisciplinary Theoretical Approach

GUILHON Bernard
Venture Capital and the Financing of Innovation
(Innovation Between Risk and Reward Set – Volume 6)

LATOUCHE Pascal
Open Innovation: Human Set-up
(Innovation and Technology Set – Volume 10)

LIMA Marcos
Entrepreneurship and Innovation Education: Frameworks and Tools
(Smart Innovation Set – Volume 32)

MACHADO Carolina, DAVIM J. Paulo
Sustainable Management for Managers and Engineers

MAKRIDES Andreas, KARAGRIGORIOU Alex, SKIADAS Christos H.
Data Analysis and Applications 3: Computational, Classification, Financial,
Statistical and Stochastic Methods
(Big Data, Artificial Intelligence and Data Analysis Set – Volume 5)
Data Analysis and Applications 4: Financial Data Analysis and Methods
(Big Data, Artificial Intelligence and Data Analysis Set – Volume 6)

MASSOTTE Pierre, CORSI Patrick
Complex Decision-Making in Economy and Finance

MEUNIER François-Xavier
Dual Innovation Systems: Concepts, Tools and Methods
(Smart Innovation Set – Volume 31)

MICHAUD Thomas
Science Fiction and Innovation Design
(Innovation in Engineering and Technology Set – Volume 6)

MONINO Jean-Louis
Data Control: Major Challenge for the Digital Society
(Smart Innovation Set – Volume 29)

MORLAT Clément
Sustainable Productive System: Eco-development versus Sustainable
Development (Smart Innovation Set – Volume 26)

SAULAIS Pierre, ERMINE Jean-Louis
Knowledge Management in Innovative Companies 2: Understanding and
Deploying a KM Plan within a Learning Organization
(Smart Innovation Set – Volume 27)

2019

AMENDOLA Mario, GAFFARD Jean-Luc
Disorder and Public Concern Around Globalization

BARBAROUX Pierre
Disruptive Technology and Defence Innovation Ecosystems
(Innovation in Engineering and Technology Set – Volume 5)

DOU Henri, JUILLET Alain, CLERC Philippe
Strategic Intelligence for the Future 1: A New Strategic and Operational
Approach
Strategic Intelligence for the Future 2: A New Information Function
Approach

FRIKHA Azza
Measurement in Marketing: Operationalization of Latent Constructs

FRIMOUSSE Soufyane
Innovation and Agility in the Digital Age
(Human Resources Management Set – Volume 2)

GAY Claudine, SZOSTAK Bérangère L.
Innovation and Creativity in SMEs: Challenges, Evolutions and Prospects
(Smart Innovation Set – Volume 21)

GORIA Stéphane, HUMBERT Pierre, ROUSSEL Benoît
Information, Knowledge and Agile Creativity
(Smart Innovation Set – Volume 22)

HELLER David
Investment Decision-making Using Optional Models
(Economic Growth Set – Volume 2)

HELLER David, DE CHADIRAC Sylvain, HALAOUI Lana, JOUVET Camille
The Emergence of Start-ups
(Economic Growth Set – Volume 1)

HÉRAUD Jean-Alain, KERR Fiona, BURGER-HELMCHEN Thierry
Creative Management of Complex Systems
(Smart Innovation Set – Volume 19)

LATOUCHE Pascal
Open Innovation: Corporate Incubator
(Innovation and Technology Set – Volume 7)

LEHMANN Paul-Jacques
The Future of the Euro Currency

LEIGNEL Jean-Louis, MÉNAGER Emmanuel, YABLONSKY Serge
Sustainable Enterprise Performance: A Comprehensive Evaluation Method

LIÈVRE Pascal, AUBRY Monique, GAREL Gilles
Management of Extreme Situations: From Polar Expeditions to Exploration-Oriented Organizations

MILLOT Michel
Embarrassment of Product Choices 2: Towards a Society of Well-being

N'GOALA Gilles, PEZ-PÉRARD Virginie, PRIM-ALLAZ Isabelle
Augmented Customer Strategy: CRM in the Digital Age

NIKOLOVA Blagovesta
The RRI Challenge: Responsibilization in a State of Tension with Market Regulation
(Innovation and Responsibility Set – Volume 3)

PELLEGRIN-BOUCHER Estelle, ROY Pierre
Innovation in the Cultural and Creative Industries
(Innovation and Technology Set – Volume 8)

PRIOLON Joël
Financial Markets for Commodities

QUINIOU Matthieu
Blockchain: The Advent of Disintermediation

RAVIX Joël-Thomas, DESCHAMPS Marc
Innovation and Industrial Policies
(Innovation between Risk and Reward Set – Volume 5)

ROGER Alain, VINOT Didier
Skills Management: New Applications, New Questions
(Human Resources Management Set – Volume 1)

SAULAIS Pierre, ERMINE Jean-Louis
Knowledge Management in Innovative Companies 1: Understanding and Deploying a KM Plan within a Learning Organization
(Smart Innovation Set – Volume 23)

SERVAJEAN-HILST Romaric
Co-innovation Dynamics: The Management of Client-Supplier Interactions for Open Innovation
(Smart Innovation Set – Volume 20)

SKIADAS Christos H., BOZEMAN James R.
Data Analysis and Applications 1: Clustering and Regression, Modeling-estimating, Forecasting and Data Mining
(Big Data, Artificial Intelligence and Data Analysis Set – Volume 2)
Data Analysis and Applications 2: Utilization of Results in Europe and Other Topics
(Big Data, Artificial Intelligence and Data Analysis Set – Volume 3)

UZUNIDIS Dimitri
Systemic Innovation: Entrepreneurial Strategies and Market Dynamics

VIGEZZI Michel
World Industrialization: Shared Inventions, Competitive Innovations and Social Dynamics
(Smart Innovation Set – Volume 24)

2018

BURKHARDT Kirsten
Private Equity Firms: Their Role in the Formation of Strategic Alliances

CALLENS Stéphane
Creative Globalization
(Smart Innovation Set – Volume 16)

CASADELLA Vanessa
Innovation Systems in Emerging Economies: MINT – Mexico, Indonesia, Nigeria, Turkey
(Smart Innovation Set – Volume 18)

CHOUTEAU Marianne, FOREST Joëlle, NGUYEN Céline
Science, Technology and Innovation Culture
(Innovation in Engineering and Technology Set – Volume 3)

CORLOSQUET-HABART Marine, JANSSEN Jacques
Big Data for Insurance Companies
(Big Data, Artificial Intelligence and Data Analysis Set – Volume 1)

CROS Françoise
Innovation and Society
(Smart Innovation Set – Volume 15)

DEBREF Romain
Environmental Innovation and Ecodesign: Certainties and Controversies
(Smart Innovation Set – Volume 17)

DOMINGUEZ Noémie
SME Internationalization Strategies: Innovation to Conquer New Markets

ERMINE Jean-Louis
Knowledge Management: The Creative Loop
(Innovation and Technology Set – Volume 5)

GILBERT Patrick, BOBADILLA Natalia, GASTALDI Lise,
LE BOULAIRE Martine, LELEBINA Olga
Innovation, Research and Development Management

IBRAHIMI Mohammed
Mergers & Acquisitions: Theory, Strategy, Finance

LEMAÎTRE Denis
Training Engineers for Innovation

LÉVY Aldo, BEN BOUHENI Faten, AMMI Chantal
Financial Management: USGAAP and IFRS Standards
(Innovation and Technology Set – Volume 6)

MILLOT Michel
Embarrassment of Product Choices 1: How to Consume Differently

PANSERA Mario, OWEN Richard
Innovation and Development: The Politics at the Bottom of the Pyramid
(Innovation and Responsibility Set – Volume 2)

RICHEZ Yves
Corporate Talent Detection and Development

SACHETTI Philippe, ZUPPINGER Thibaud
New Technologies and Branding
(Innovation and Technology Set – Volume 4)

SAMIER Henri
Intuition, Creativity, Innovation

TEMPLE Ludovic, COMPAORÉ SAWADOGO Eveline M.F.W.
Innovation Processes in Agro-Ecological Transitions in Developing Countries
(Innovation in Engineering and Technology Set – Volume 2)

UZUNIDIS Dimitri
Collective Innovation Processes: Principles and Practices
(Innovation in Engineering and Technology Set – Volume 4)

VAN HOOREBEKE Delphine
The Management of Living Beings or Emo-management

2017

AÏT-EL-HADJ Smaïl
The Ongoing Technological System
(Smart Innovation Set – Volume 11)

BAUDRY Marc, DUMONT Béatrice
Patents: Prompting or Restricting Innovation?
(Smart Innovation Set – Volume 12)

BÉRARD Céline, TEYSSIER Christine
Risk Management: Lever for SME Development and Stakeholder Value Creation

CHALENÇON Ludivine
Location Strategies and Value Creation of International
Mergers and Acquisitions

CHAUVEL Danièle, BORZILLO Stefano
The Innovative Company: An Ill-defined Object
(Innovation between Risk and Reward Set – Volume 1)

CORSI Patrick
Going Past Limits To Growth

D'ANDRIA Aude, GABARRET Inés
Building 21st Century Entrepreneurship
(Innovation and Technology Set – Volume 2)

DAIDJ Nabyla
Cooperation, Coopetition and Innovation
(Innovation and Technology Set – Volume 3)

FERNEZ-WALCH Sandrine
The Multiple Facets of Innovation Project Management
(Innovation between Risk and Reward Set – Volume 4)

FOREST Joëlle
Creative Rationality and Innovation
(Smart Innovation Set – Volume 14)

GUILHON Bernard
Innovation and Production Ecosystems
(Innovation between Risk and Reward Set – Volume 2)

HAMMOUDI Abdelhakim, DAIDJ Nabyla
Game Theory Approach to Managerial Strategies and Value Creation
(Diverse and Global Perspectives on Value Creation Set – Volume 3)

LALLEMENT Rémi
Intellectual Property and Innovation Protection: New Practices
and New Policy Issues
(Innovation between Risk and Reward Set – Volume 3)

LAPERCHE Blandine
Enterprise Knowledge Capital
(Smart Innovation Set – Volume 13)

LEBERT Didier, EL YOUNSI Hafida
International Specialization Dynamics
(Smart Innovation Set – Volume 9)

MAESSCHALCK Marc
Reflexive Governance for Research and Innovative Knowledge
(Responsible Research and Innovation Set – Volume 6)

MASSOTTE Pierre
Ethics in Social Networking and Business 1: Theory, Practice and Current Recommendations
Ethics in Social Networking and Business 2: The Future and Changing Paradigms

MASSOTTE Pierre, CORSI Patrick
Smart Decisions in Complex Systems

MEDINA Mercedes, HERRERO Mónica, URGELLÉS Alicia
Current and Emerging Issues in the Audiovisual Industry
(Diverse and Global Perspectives on Value Creation Set – Volume 1)

MICHAUD Thomas
Innovation, Between Science and Science Fiction
(Smart Innovation Set – Volume 10)

PELLÉ Sophie
Business, Innovation and Responsibility
(Responsible Research and Innovation Set – Volume 7)

SAVIGNAC Emmanuelle
The Gamification of Work: The Use of Games in the Workplace

SUGAHARA Satoshi, DAIDJ Nabyla, USHIO Sumitaka
Value Creation in Management Accounting and Strategic Management: An Integrated Approach
(Diverse and Global Perspectives on Value Creation Set –Volume 2)

UZUNIDIS Dimitri, SAULAIS Pierre
Innovation Engines: Entrepreneurs and Enterprises in a Turbulent World
(Innovation in Engineering and Technology Set – Volume 1)

2016

BARBAROUX Pierre, ATTOUR Amel, SCHENK Eric
Knowledge Management and Innovation
(Smart Innovation Set – Volume 6)

BEN BOUHENI Faten, AMMI Chantal, LEVY Aldo
Banking Governance, Performance And Risk-Taking: Conventional Banks
Vs Islamic Banks

BOUTILLIER Sophie, CARRÉ Denis, LEVRATTO Nadine
Entrepreneurial Ecosystems
(Smart Innovation Set – Volume 2)

BOUTILLIER Sophie, UZUNIDIS Dimitri
The Entrepreneur
(Smart Innovation Set – Volume 8)

BOUVARD Patricia, SUZANNE Hervé
Collective Intelligence Development in Business

GALLAUD Delphine, LAPERCHE Blandine
Circular Economy, Industrial Ecology and Short Supply Chains
(Smart Innovation Set – Volume 4)

GUERRIER Claudine
Security and Privacy in the Digital Era
(Innovation and Technology Set – Volume 1)

MEGHOUAR Hicham
Corporate Takeover Targets

MONINO Jean-Louis, SEDKAOUI Soraya
Big Data, Open Data and Data Development
(Smart Innovation Set – Volume 3)

MOREL Laure, LE ROUX Serge
Fab Labs: Innovative User
(Smart Innovation Set – Volume 5)

PICARD Fabienne, TANGUY Corinne
Innovations and Techno-ecological Transition
(Smart Innovation Set – Volume 7)

2015

CASADELLA Vanessa, LIU Zeting, DIMITRI Uzunidis
Innovation Capabilities and Economic Development in Open Economies
(Smart Innovation Set – Volume 1)

CORSI Patrick, MORIN Dominique
Sequencing Apple's DNA

CORSI Patrick, NEAU Erwan
Innovation Capability Maturity Model

FAIVRE-TAVIGNOT Bénédicte
Social Business and Base of the Pyramid

GODÉ Cécile
Team Coordination in Extreme Environments

MAILLARD Pierre
Competitive Quality and Innovation

MASSOTTE Pierre, CORSI Patrick
Operationalizing Sustainability

MASSOTTE Pierre, CORSI Patrick
Sustainability Calling

2014

DUBÉ Jean, LEGROS Diègo
Spatial Econometrics Using Microdata

LESCA Humbert, LESCA Nicolas
Strategic Decisions and Weak Signals

2013

HABART-CORLOSQUET Marine, JANSSEN Jacques, MANCA Raimondo
VaR Methodology for Non-Gaussian Finance

2012

DAL PONT Jean-Pierre
Process Engineering and Industrial Management

MAILLARD Pierre
Competitive Quality Strategies

POMEROL Jean-Charles
Decision-Making and Action

SZYLAR Christian
UCITS Handbook

2011

LESCA Nicolas
Environmental Scanning and Sustainable Development

LESCA Nicolas, LESCA Humbert
Weak Signals for Strategic Intelligence: Anticipation Tool for Managers

MERCIER-LAURENT Eunika
Innovation Ecosystems

2010

SZYLAR Christian
Risk Management under UCITS III/IV

2009

COHEN Corine
Business Intelligence

ZANINETTI Jean-Marc
Sustainable Development in the USA

2008

CORSI Patrick, DULIEU Mike
The Marketing of Technology Intensive Products and Services

DZEVER Sam, JAUSSAUD Jacques, ANDREOSSO Bernadette
Evolving Corporate Structures and Cultures in Asia: Impact of Globalization

2007

AMMI Chantal
Global Consumer Behavior

2006

BOUGHZALA Imed, ERMINE Jean-Louis
Trends in Enterprise Knowledge Management

CORSI Patrick, CHRISTOFOL Hervé, RICHIR Simon, SAMIER Henri
Innovation Engineering: the power of intangible networks

Printed and bound by CPI Group (UK) Ltd, Croydon, CR0 4YY

24/03/2024

14475064-0001